Understanding
Augmented Reality

Understanding Augmented Reality

Concepts and Applications

Alan B. Craig

AMSTERDAM • BOSTON • HEIDELBERG • LONDON • NEW YORK • OXFORD
PARIS • SAN DIEGO • SAN FRANCISCO • SINGAPORE • SYDNEY • TOKYO

Morgan Kaufmann is an imprint of Elsevier

Acquiring Editor: Steve Elliot
Development Editor: Benjamin Rearick
Project Manager: Anitha Kittusamy Ramasamy
Designer: Russell Purdy

Morgan Kaufmann is an imprint of Elsevier
225 Wyman Street, Waltham, MA 02451, USA

Library of Congress Cataloging-in-Publication Data
Application submitted

British Library Cataloguing-in-Publication Data
A catalogue record for this book is available from the British Library

ISBN: 978-0-240-82408-6

Printed and bound by CPI Group (UK) Ltd, Croydon, CR0 4YY

Transferred to digital print 2012

For information on all MK publications visit our website at *www.mkp.com*

To Cara and Colleen

Short Contents

Table of Contents

Foreword to Alan B. Craig's *Understanding Augmented Reality*

Time and again an idea conceived by science fiction is later realized by scientific innovators, from Jules Verne's detailed descriptions of spacecraft to H.G. Wells' concept of the laser. Thanks to its obvious utility and incredible capacity for instantaneous, clear communication, augmented reality is no exception. AR has been imagined a thousand times in fiction because of its unparalleled potential in applications ranging from industrial and commercial projects, to education, to creative storytelling, to countless other uses in everyday life. *Understanding Augmented Reality* is a valuable and welcome primer for anyone wishing to more deeply comprehend the mechanics and implications of this new media.

So why does augmented reality matter, and why now? To begin with, AR matters because it will almost certainly turn out to be as powerful and broadly applicable an innovation as was the Internet itself. This is the eventual, self-evident conclusion reached when anyone, upon achieving a basic level of comprehension, spends a few moments considering the limitless potential that augmented reality promises. Spatial and interactive in nature, AR builds on what has come before and takes connectedness to new places. It is a medium that allows you to interact with digital data in a visual and spatial manner that is utterly seamless with your environment and everyday life. For these reasons and more, augmented reality is extremely powerful and undoubtedly deserves the grand claims, excited entrepreneurs, and media attention that surround it.

By now you're probably thinking, "But how can this be? Why haven't I heard of augmented reality before if it's so world-changing?" Fair questions. Perhaps by examining the question 'Why now?' or phrased differently, 'Why not until now?' the answers will become clear.

Given the enormous scope of possibilities, why has it taken so long for augmented reality to find its legs and become utilized by the mainstream? How has a technology that appears to be the furthest fantasy of science fiction come into being? What's possible today, and what will be possible tomorrow? These are interesting questions, with even more interesting answers, because everything in the world of augmented reality is about to change.

In *Understanding Augmented Reality*, Alan B. Craig expertly and clearly explains its various modalities with the patience, candor and wit of your favorite professor, and the technical precision of a scientist. Through thoughtful argumentation and carefully selected examples, Craig will attempt to convince you of an idea that we fully believe and support: that AR cannot be categorized as a simple "technology," but is rather a full-scale medium comprised of a set of technological innovations combined with an expanding set of content conventions. The way people experience augmented reality is unlike anything that has come before and thus requires new thought models and production processes. Thanks to his nuanced understanding of the history and myriad applications of the medium, there's no one better to write this book than Craig.

Just as the innovation of video technology enabled the medium of film and television, a breakthrough in computer vision in the last decade has enabled what we now consider to be the fundamentals of AR. In AR, the extent to which we as developers can understand the space around the mobile device visually dictates the parameters within which we can express contextual 4D content and interactivity (we like to give interactive, spatial augmented reality the simple moniker "4D"). Vision science is the technical discipline that deals with and expands this understanding.

The technology that enabled film emerged at the turn of the last century. People watched "movies" and were astounded at what they had previously thought impossible. Simple actions like a train pulling into a station were enough to keep people spellbound. But the history of film is the history of special effects – camera techniques and editing began to allow for more magic. Then physical humor à la Charlie Chaplin came around, and basic plots evolved. Once those possibilities were exhausted, editing and special effects took center stage.

Our own "special effects" are now being created in augmented reality. Mathematically dexterous algorithms that can calculate the geometry of three-dimensional spaces and recognize specific objects are being developed and used now. Soon augmented reality's abilities will move beyond the planar, expanding the "storytelling canvas" to the complexities of any given room, location, or environment. As this patchwork of visual puzzle pieces continues to coalesce, it won't be long before our rudimentary programmed "eyes" – in mobile devices and eventually AR-enabled glasses – will be able to see and understand the world at large. But even these futuristic techniques will soon evolve to modalities that will empower even greater flexibility.

As augmented reality takes its place as a mass medium, it's so important for people to be educated about what it can do. Access, education, and insight will keep augmented reality open for all to experience, create, and tell stories with. *Understanding Augmented Reality* is the perfect place to start.

Brian Mullins
Founder, CEO, daqri

Gaia Dempsey
Co-Founder, Director of Marketing & PR, daqri

Preface

ABOUT THIS BOOK

This book takes the position that augmented reality is a medium. Although technology is critical in carrying out the implementation of augmented reality, the book focuses more on the information, experience, and interaction that is involved with augmented reality. This book is not a "how-to" guide for programming augmented reality applications, nor is it a tutorial on assembling an augmented reality system. Nonetheless, there is plenty of useful information in this book that will help guide developers and those who study augmented reality and its applications.

In much the same way that a book about making movies must address the technology involved, such as cameras and projectors, this book does address the core technological ingredients for augmented reality. However, in the same way that a book about making movies must address ideas of storytelling, editing, and how to make best use of the affordances of the medium, so too this book addresses content, interaction, and the core affordances of the medium. It is only by exploring augmented reality as a medium that we will be able to reach beyond the capabilities of the current technology and be able to envision the bigger picture of the capabilities and potential of augmented reality. Indeed, my hope is that readers of this book will come away thinking "wow, if only we had a technology that could fulfill this requirement, then we could do …." rather than "well the technology that is available can only do this, so that means we can only think about things that fit within those limitations." When we see the possibilities and dream big, then the technology required to enable it will follow. If not, we will invent it.

Although the goal of the book is to foster a broader look at augmented reality and its applications, it is also important to come away with a strong feel for where we are currently both with the medium and the technology that is involved. Therefore, throughout the book there are photos and brief descriptions of current and historic AR applications. Additionally, Chapter 8, "Augmented Reality Applications," provides a look at several more applications.

I tried to select applications for inclusion that range across a variety of application areas and that utilize different technologies and different styles of interaction.

Finally, Chapter 9 takes a look at some of the likely directions AR might head in the not so distant future.

HOW THIS BOOK CAME TO BE

In order to address how this book came to be requires that two factors be addressed. The first is how I came to be involved with augmented reality and the second is how I came to write this book.

I came to be involved with augmented reality as an outgrowth of my interest in virtual reality through the 1990s and 2000s, which was a result of my interest in information representation. I had seen a demonstration of augmented reality in the 1990s that was given at the SIGGRAPH Computer Graphics conference by the HITLab at the University of Washington and I was very intrigued. However, at the time I was consumed with other efforts in virtual reality, visualization, data mining, and web development so AR stayed relegated to the back of my mind with the exception of some off-and-on experiments I was doing with ARToolKit.

A few years later I had the opportunity to spend a significant amount of time with Mark Billinghurst when we both spoke at the same conference in Brazil. I saw his newer demonstrations and learned more about what he was doing, as well as some AR demonstrations on smartphones. It became totally clear that the time had come to turn more attention to AR. I had been trying to find ways that we could migrate some of the ideas we were pursuing in the CAVE and other VR environments out into the real world and, at the same time, make these ideas available to the public in general. CAVEs and other VR environments are costly and you must go to the devices to use them. Smartphones and tablets, however, were becoming ubiquitous and are highly portable/mobile. At this point some of my early experiments led to funding from the National Science Foundation and credibility within my own institution, so I began pursuing AR in earnest.

The book came about as a result of people asking me if there was a book that was similar to *Understanding Virtual Reality* that focused on augmented reality instead of virtual reality. As I surveyed the landscape of books about augmented reality I didn't find anything of that nature. About that time, representatives from Morgan Kaufmann Publishing were asking William Sherman and I about writing further books on virtual reality and I brought up the idea of doing an AR book. As we discussed the idea further and continued to survey the marketplace it seemed like doing a project such as *Understanding Augmented Reality* would be a good idea. However, *Understanding Virtual Reality* already existed, and we saw that there would be a lot of overlap in content between the two books. Consequently we decided that *Understanding Augmented Reality* would be a shorter, lighter book that would be an easier, quicker read than UVR. We also decided to do UAR as a paperback book to make it more widely accessible. People interested in further depth on the topics that overlap could refer to UVR and other resources that were available. While writing *Understanding Augmented Reality* it became apparent that there must be some overlap, but in most cases, the reader can refer to UVR for further depth on many of the topics addressed here.

INTENDED AUDIENCE

In much the same way that movies have become ubiquitous, I believe that the medium of augmented reality will be ubiquitous in the near future. As such, it is paramount that everyone who partakes of the medium, particularly scholars, developers, and critics of the medium, become literate in the medium. This book is a first step toward achieving that literacy. Consequently, the intended audience for this book is indeed anyone who participates or plans to participate with the emerging medium of augmented reality. In other words, this book is for everyone. AR developers will find the book particularly useful as they explore the affordances of the medium that exist beyond the technology of today. Scholars and critics of the medium will find this book to be a starting framework in which to situate studies and criticism of the medium. Augmented reality content developers will find the book useful in helping establish a point of beginning for their journey. This book asks the question of what content is and how content in augmented reality is similar and different to content in other media. Finally, the generation of the 21st century will find their world to operate at the juncture between physical and digital reality, and this book provides some guidance on how to think about that juncture and how to live in the augmented world.

RELATIONSHIP OF THIS BOOK WITH UNDERSTANDING VIRTUAL REALITY AND DEVELOPING VIRTUAL REALITY APPLICATIONS

As stated previously, this book came to be largely by the request of people who asked for a book that was similar in nature to *Understanding Virtual Reality*, but focused on augmented reality instead. From the very beginning, the goal was for this book to be smaller, lighter, and an easier read than *Understanding Virtual Reality*. This is in large part in response to the existence of UVR. *Understanding Augmented Reality* provides the foundational ideas and concepts necessary to understand augmented reality, but for readers who desire more depth in the areas that overlap with virtual reality, they are directed to UVR.

Developing Virtual Reality Applications was written to fulfill a desire on the part of application developers to see a wide variety of VR applications and to learn from them what works, what doesn't work, and why. I believe it is currently too early in the field of augmented reality to have a strong corpus of applications to draw on for such a work. I believe that in the future there is room for a book *Developing Augmented Reality Applications* that is the analog of *Developing Virtual Reality Applications* whether someone else writes it or I do.

Finally, *Understanding Augmented Reality* is not a book to teach how to program augmented reality applications. In the same way that UVR and DVRA were not programming manuals, UAR does not purport to be such a resource. UAR focuses at a higher level. UAR addresses concepts and applications of augmented reality and how they relate to the medium of augmented reality.

SPECIAL FEATURES OF THIS BOOK

Certain examples in this book are "active" in that they can be experienced in augmented reality. The way to engage with these experiences, as well as to view additional examples, videos, and other content, is to go to the companion website for this book. It contains information and instructions for how to try the AR examples as well as links and other useful information.

SUPPLEMENTAL MATERIALS

Supplemental materials for instructors or students can be downloaded from Elsevier: http://booksite.elsevier.com/Craig-UAR/

About the Author

Alan B. Craig, PhD, has been with the National Center for Supercomputing Applications (NCSA) for over 25 years. Additionally, he is the Associate Director for Human–Computer Interaction at the Institute for Computing in Humanities, Arts, and Social Science (I-CHASS). He is also the Humanities, Arts, and Social Science liaison for the Extreme Science and Engineering Discovery Environment (XSEDE).

Dr. Craig is no stranger to writing. He has also written *Understanding Virtual Reality* by William R. Sherman and Alan B. Craig and *Developing Virtual Reality Applications* by Alan B. Craig, William R. Sherman, and Jeffrey D. Will, all for Morgan Kaufmann Publishing. Additionally, he has written numerous book chapters, journal articles, and popular articles. He speaks nationally and internationally on a variety of topics to audiences ranging from academia to government to industry.

Over the course of his career, he has been involved both in the study of, and development of, many technologies and concepts, including virtual reality, augmented reality, scientific visualization, high-performance computing, collaborative systems, data mining, and web systems. He has received three U.S. patents for his innovations. In addition to his work in the visual representation of information, Dr. Craig has been deeply involved in the use of sound to represent data, as well as multimodal systems. His work has ranged over the entire reality continuum from the real, to the digital, and back to the real via personal fabrication, as well as at the edges between worlds. In all his endeavors he has focused primarily on applications related to education.

Outside of his professional life, Dr. Craig is involved in numerous other creative endeavors, focusing primarily on the writing, recording, and performance of music.

Acknowledgments

A multitude of people contributed to both my journey in exploring the medium of augmented reality and the writing of this book. The danger of listing individuals is that it is very easy to overlook someone who should be included. To anyone who I miss, I apologize and I appreciate your contribution greatly.

Within each of the different groups of people that I list here, I have no real ordering of the individuals. Consequently, I am referring to each person listed as a key person who assisted in some way, especially as related to the category they are in.

My first acknowledgment is to Mike Morgan (formerly of Morgan Kaufmann Publishing) for giving me my start as a book author. Along with that I acknowledge the contributions of the coauthors of my previous books, William R. Sherman and Jeffrey D. Will. Both of them contributed more than they realize to this book.

The National Science Foundation has supported my work over the years, both related to augmented reality and to other endeavors that led to my work in AR. In particular, Anna Kerttula enthusiastically encouraged and supported me in my efforts in AR. She saw the big picture and introduced me to countless researchers who have contributed in numerous ways.

Thom Dunning and Danny Powell of the National Center for Supercomputing Applications and Marshall Scott Poole and Kevin Franklin of the Institute for Computing in Humanities, Arts, and Social Science have provided me with the freedom to pursue interesting research directions and to write this book. All of my colleagues at each of these institutions have contributed to this book in one way or another.

Mark Billinghurst was my first hero when it comes to augmented reality. For years I watched the work he was doing knowing that one day I would begin my own journey with AR. When Morgan Kaufmann Publishing asked me who would be the best person to serve as a technical editor, I, without hesitating, suggested Mark Billinghurst. I thought his more technical approach to AR would complement my perspective especially well. I was thrilled when he accepted the role. Robert E. McGrath of NCSA was involved in my augmented reality quest from the beginning and also read the entire manuscript and offered many useful suggestions and improvements, as well as great discussions along the way. The book is much better due to each of their contributions. At this point, however, I take full responsibility for the contents of the book. Each of them provided great ideas, corrections, and suggestions. I incorporated many of them, though I was not able to implement all of them. Hence, if there is any incorrect information, anything missing, or anything that could have been organized or stated better, it is my responsibility, and chances are that one or both pointed it out but it didn't make it to the book for one reason or another. Thanks, guys! It was great having your input all along the way.

Brian Mullins and Gaia Dempsey from daqri are the real deal when it comes to augmented reality. Thanks for the great discussions and all the support on the AR projects. Likewise, Michael Simeone from I-CHASS provided lots of great discussions as well as numerous photos for the book. Stephen Guerin provided an interesting perspective on AR, especially on structured light, in addition to the photos he provided.

I have had the privilege of working with many talented students along the way. Students who contributed directly to my AR projects include Margarita Mouschovious, Lauren Semeraro, Sarah Butler, Joe Noonan, Nick Zukoski, Alejandro Gutierrez, Jack Snyder, and Edgar Kautzner. Ryan Rocha was a former student of a colleague of mine who I hired to create some stunning models.

Beverly Carver was exceptionally patient and contributed in countless ways to this book, ranging from providing photographs, designing diagrams, discussions, and helping me establish an organization to the process.

Paul Magelli has been supportive of my efforts from the beginning.

Each of the following contributed above and beyond in some way, ranging from providing photographs, to technical expertise, to ideas: Dave Bock, Mark VanMoer, Bill Christison, Kalev Leetaru, Liz Wuerfel, Michael Vila, Martin Dean, Shaowen Wang, Janet Sinn-Hanlon, Travis Ross, Nick Clement, Tom McGovern, Owen Berbaum, Titus Berbaum, Holly McClain, Connor McClain, Maurice Godfrey, Alex Poulson, Adam Trost, Juli Borzsei, Tim Hudson, Ping Fu, Kerry Helms, Trish Barker, Barb Jewett, Paula Popowski, and Carla Scaletti.

A special thanks to everyone who provided photographs, and also to everyone who provided example applications for the book, as well as those who provided examples that didn't get included in the book. I learned from each one. Thank you to the folks at Morgan Kaufmann Publishing, as well as all the reviewers who were involved with the book.

Finally, thank you to my family and friends. Each one contributed to this book in one way or another.

CHAPTER 1

What Is Augmented Reality?

INTRODUCTION

This chapter introduces the idea of augmented reality (AR) and defines what is meant by the term *augmented reality* in the context of this book. It also distinguishes augmented reality from other related media and technologies, as well as introduces some terms that will aid in understanding the chapters that follow.

Throughout the entirety of this book, I consider augmented reality to be a medium, as opposed to a technology. By medium, I mean that it mediates ideas between humans and computers, humans and humans, and computers and humans. Of course, implementing augmented reality as a medium requires technology and a clear understanding of that technology. Numerous technologies can be used to implement augmented reality, and this book addresses a variety of different methods and types of technology that can be used. These technologies and the ideas behind them are covered in later chapters in the book. There are advantages and disadvantages with different technologies for different types of applications. The chapters that follow address the characteristics of the technologies and show the advantages and disadvantages of using them in different types of applications. By taking the stance that augmented reality is a medium, it will become much clearer how the technologies involved can be used to create compelling applications for a variety of purposes instead of as a mere technological novelty. In much the same manner as a book about making movies needs to treat not only the technologies involved, such as cameras, lights, and projectors, but also how to use the medium to tell a story, to evoke emotion, or to document an event, it is important to consider more than just technology to create compelling augmented reality applications.

Humans interact with different media in different ways. Typically, people *read* a book. They *watch* a movie. They *listen* to music. This book considers that the way people engage with augmented reality is to *experience* it. Augmented reality can appeal to many of our senses (although currently it is primarily a visual medium). Augmented reality is interactive, so it doesn't make sense to watch it or listen to it. We must *engage* with it in order to gain the experience that it provides. Augmented reality can support many different application areas. It can be applied in education, entertainment, medicine, and many more areas discussed in this book. Each of these different application areas and specific applications constitute an *experience*.

So what *is* this augmented reality experience? In brief, the core essence of an augmented reality experience is that you, the participant, engage in an activity in the same physical world that you engage with whether augmented reality is involved or not, but augmented reality adds digital information to the world that you can interact with in the same manner that you interact with the physical world. I'll define augmented reality more precisely later in this chapter, but for now, consider it that you are engaged in the regular normal world, but there are additions to that world that consist of digital information that is placed in the world to augment the world with things you would not normally see, hear, feel, touch, etc. What's an example of an augmented reality experience? Imagine for a moment that you go to visit a vacant lot where you intend to build your dream home. Now let's consider an augmented reality experience in which you go to that (vacant) lot, but through the use of technology you are able to see your dream home in place on that lot. You can walk around the house and see it from all different viewpoints just like you could if the house was actually completed on the lot. You can interact with the house, open the door, and so on just like you could in the real world. However, AR can also offer the potential to do things that are not possible in a normal interaction in the real world. Perhaps you want to see the house in a different color, move the house on the lot, or see the house take off like a rocket ship. These are all possible with augmented reality.

Let's start by looking to the past to see where some of the ideas behind augmented reality came from. Then, we will be able to define augmented reality more precisely and explore how it works and what it is good for.

WHERE DID AUGMENTED REALITY COME FROM?

Since the beginning of time, humankind has sought to alter and improve their environment. Early attempts to modify and enhance their world involved manipulating physical objects in the physical world. For example, early humans cut clearings in jungles, gathered rocks to sit on, and sharpened branches into spears. Later, they learned to represent information symbolically and learned to create imagery, such as paintings on cave walls for functional purposes—to indicate a map to a favorite location, to tell a story, or purely as an aesthetic adornment (Figure 1.1).

As humankind progressed, they began to discover and make tools to aid them in altering their environment. However, most changes they made were rather permanent and required a lot of effort to make and alter. At this point, the world was purely in the physical realm (Figure 1.2).

As humankind and technology progressed, ideas became much more important, and those ideas were represented symbolically, whether realistically (such as a literal drawing) or symbolically (such as a map). At this point, the world consisted of physical entities, but also ideas and representation of those ideas in physical media. Ideas were expressed as paintings, sculpture, music, dance, and

FIGURE 1.1

In ancient times, people adorned their dwellings with drawings regarding their life experiences. Note that these drawings remain today, long after they were created. *Photo courtesy of Kevin Connors.*

FIGURE 1.2

Ancient humans used primitive tools to manipulate their environment. Here, the results of altering and augmenting the natural environment are shown. This is the sphinx and the pyramid of Khafre at Giza. The sphinx was carved from a single piece of limestone. *Photo courtesy of the Central Intelligence Agency.*

FIGURE 1.3
Even children desire to alter their physical world—even if it is just for fun. *Photo courtesy of Alan B. Craig.*

FIGURE 1.4
A speed limit sign conveys specific information for a specific place. *Photo courtesy of Alan B. Craig.*

more. Mapping technology improved, and the field of semiotics matured (Figure 1.3).

It wasn't until the 20th century that it became feasible to create, store, and retrieve information rapidly. The "industrial age" saw rapid improvements in the ability to construct, deconstruct, and modify physical structures with relative ease. However, the rate at which they could be constructed and dismantled still remained rather long, measured in years, in months, or, at the best, in days. Adornments to the physical world remained in the physical realm, that is, any modification to the environment was manifested with other physical entities that had weight and occupied space. Thus, if it was desired to make a piece of information available in a specific physical space, the only real way to do it was to create a physical artifact that either was or contained a representation of that piece of information. For example, if it was desired to indicate the maximum rate of speed at a certain place on a specific road, a physical sign would be erected that was constructed to convey the desired information (Figure 1.4).

If it was desired to change the information regarding that place, it was necessary to construct a new sign, or at least to repaint the sign. Advances in technology made it possible to construct more generic signs with information that could be changed at will. Thus, if there was a need to change the speed limit, whether permanently or temporarily, the sign could be updated with the flick of a few switches (Figure 1.5).

Additional technology allows the addition of still more information based on what is happening at that place and time. This additional technology allows the physical sign to indicate the maximum speed allowed at that place and time, but also indicates a driver's current rate of speed (Figure 1.6).

FIGURE 1.5
A speed limit sign conveys specific information for a specific place. The speed limit shown on this sign can be changed at will by an appropriate official. The sign does not need to be repainted to indicate the new speed limit. *Photo courtesy of U.S. Department of Transportation.*

FIGURE 1.6
A sign can also convey information about what is happening at that place in real time. In this case, a sign indicates the speed of a car at that point in time and space. *Photo courtesy of Alan B. Craig.*

Finally, a modern sign can not only convey the speed limit and your current rate of speed, but it can also determine whether or not you are abiding by the law and inform you of your status (Figure 1.7).

The important thing to note about this series of speed limit signs is that in all cases they are conveying information specific to a particular place at a particular point in time. In each case just described, there is a physical component to the sign and an information component. The physical component has weight and takes up space. The information component is much less physical in nature. It can take the form of paint, which can be repainted, or the configuration of lightbulbs (physical) that can be switched on or off to communicate information relevant to that location and time (information). It is easier and quicker to change the information on the electrical sign than

FIGURE 1.7
This sign compares your speed with the speed limit at this place and indicates when you are exceeding the speed limit. *Photo courtesy of U.S. Department of Transportation.*

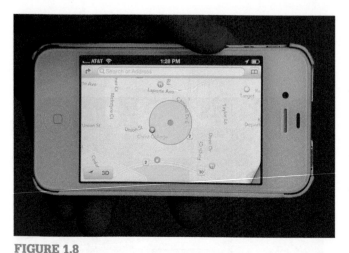

FIGURE 1.8

A smartphone allows you to store, manipulate, and retrieve information very rapidly. In this case, the information helps you find your way. *Photo courtesy of Liz Wuerffel.*

to repaint one of the older style signs. As technology has progressed, it has become easier and faster to store, retrieve, and display information.

The advent of the information age and the digital computer allowed information to be represented digitally. With the computer, huge amounts of information can be stored, manipulated, and retrieved very rapidly in a very small amount of space. With this ability to modify and retrieve information instantaneously comes a more powerful way of modifying and augmenting our environment (Figure 1.8).

The ability to store, manipulate, and retrieve information very rapidly with ubiquitously available devices such as home computers, laptop computers, tablet computers, and smartphones, combined with a pervasive network interconnecting these devices, has led to the ability to do astounding things that are beneficial in everyday living.

Along with an increase in power, and a decrease in cost and size of computing devices, the ability to compute simulations of natural and/or fantastic events makes the line between what is "real" and what is simulated, or "virtual" become increasingly. With the capability of computing very complex simulations, it becomes possible to replace some physical objects and devices with simulations that behave in the same way as the device that is being emulated. For example, it is now possible to simulate most musical instruments to the point that a simulation of an instrumental performance can be indistinguishable from a performance using an actual, physical instrument to all but the most discerning listeners.

The ability to generate and render three-dimensional (3D) computer graphics in real time led to the ability to create scenes that were not possible to create in a purely physical world. While trick photography and artistry gave a glimpse into impossible worlds, or visions of worlds that appear to be real, computer graphics enabled anything that could be imagined to be rendered and displayed to our senses, to the point of fooling our senses. Not only full-blown virtual reality systems, 3D movies, and supercomputer simulations are fooling our senses. Image editing programs such as Photoshop® and others allow anyone to create imagery that appears to capture something real, but truly only represents an idea in the mind of its creator. On a daily basis, we all encounter things that, if we stop and think about it, push the issue of whether it is something real (physical) or something that only appears to be, or acts as though it is real.

Three-dimensional movies and 3D television sets (with 3D content) have exposed many people to stereoscopic imagery and whetted the appetite among the general consumer for 3D graphical content and an experience with entities that seem real, yet are actually either photographed or synthesized imagery. Even with 3D movies, the imagery is created for a specific, predefined point of view, and the story is predetermined by the movie creator. Changing the position of your head does not result in the ability to change the perspective that you are seeing the movie from. Computer games and gaming systems offer interactivity and the ability to change the perspective from which you are viewing the scene, but these actions are detached from your own body and are mediated through devices such as joysticks, mice, and buttons. Newer gaming systems such as the Kinect (Figure 1.9) and Wii (Figure 1.10) engage the participant in a more physical, bodily interaction.

FIGURE 1.9
The Kinect system is an add on to the Xbox gaming system and allows participants to interact with the game or program by moving their bodies. Note that the participant does not need to hold or wear any special devices. In this photo, the participant "chops" fruit that is flying through the air with a sword that is controlled by "karate chop"-type motions. *Photo courtesy of Alan B. Craig.*

FIGURE 1.10
The Wii gaming system supports physical interaction with a computer game. Note the wireless physical controllers that the participants hold. Here the participants play a game of baseball where one participant "pitches" the ball through physical interaction and the other participant "swings" the bat using a swinging motion. *Photo courtesy of Emma Barclay.*

With each of the systems described here (3D movies, gaming systems, etc.), the imagery is situated with the display wherever the display is in the real world. For example, the imagery for a movie is on the movie screen. If you move the movie screen and projector, the imagery moves with it. Likewise, computer gaming systems behave the same way. Wherever the display is, the imagery is as well. There is no sense of the objects or characters in the display being in a specific place in the real world. If a movie is playing in Los Angeles, the objects and characters are on a screen in a theater in Los Angeles. That same movie might be playing in Chicago, and the objects and characters in the movie are on a screen in a theater in Chicago. A person playing a Wii in their living room in Nashville sees the characters and objects in the game on their television in their living room in Nashville. The scenes may be *set* in different locations, but those settings are not tied geographically to those locations in the real world. The settings can be made to *appear* to be in a specific place, but there is no relationship geographically between the place the setting appears to be and the corresponding *actual* location in the real world (Figure 1.11).

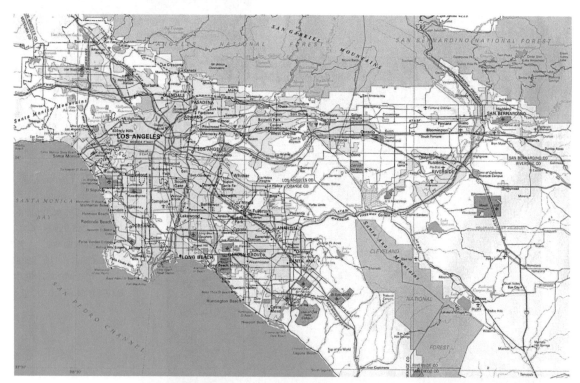

FIGURE 1.11

A typical map appears the same regardless of where you view it. This map of Los Angeles looks the same whether you are looking at it in Los Angeles, California, or Austin, Texas. *Used by permission of the University of Texas Libraries, The University of Texas at Austin.*

FIGURE 1.12
This GPS unit mounted in the dashboard of a car helps the driver find their way.
Photo courtesy of Chrissie Klinger.

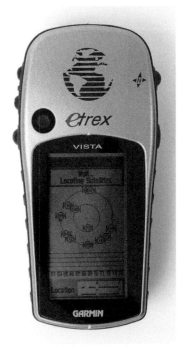

The Global Positioning System (GPS) now makes it possible to determine your location wherever you are. Some GPS applications allow you to seek information that is specific to where you are at the moment. For example, you might use a GPS equipped smartphone to look for coffee shops near where you are. The results you obtain are for shops within a certain distance from where you are at that moment in time. Likewise, you can use a GPS mapping system in your car and see where you are at the moment on a map on a small display on your dashboard (Figures 1.12–1.15).

Each of these technologies takes a step toward, but does not in itself allow for the user to be engaged interactively in, the real world, with digital enhancements that are spatially registered with the real world. In order for humankind to alter and improve their world digitally, without altering it physically, requires a constellation of ideas and technologies in order to achieve the effect of digital enhancement of the real world in a significant way.

FIGURE 1.13
GPS units are also available as small, handheld devices. *Photo courtesy of Liz Wuerffel.*

(a)

(b)

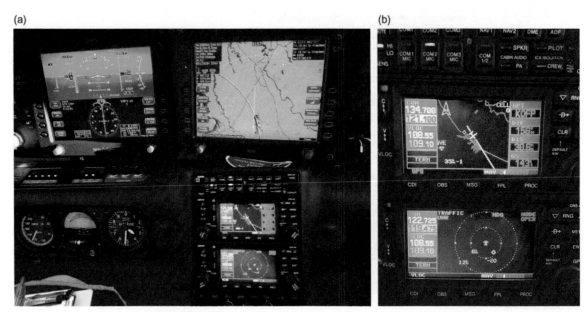

FIGURE 1.14
In this display in a "Technically Advanced Aircraft," GPS and advanced transponder capabilities provide the pilot with situation awareness of his or her location, as well as that of other aircraft. Photo (a) shows the plethora of instruments and displays that the pilot sees and photo (b) shows a more detailed view of two of the displays. *Photos courtesy of Martin Dean.*

FIGURE 1.15
The Nokia City Lens smartphone application allows users to see what restaurants are available near where they are and in the direction that they are pointing the phone. *Photo courtesy of Michael Simeone.*

Other Enhancements

In addition to visual elements, humankind has enhanced and adorned their world with other types of enhancements. For example, in addition to the natural sound elements in the world (leaves rustling, ocean waves crashing, etc.), humans have learned to create their own sounds whether for utilitarian or aesthetic reasons. In the beginning, augmentations to the sounds of the real world occurred in real time, in a location near the place where the sound originated. When the sound was over, the sound was gone. The sound traveled a certain amount of distance, but then faded away such that only those in proximity of the sound were able to hear it (Figure 1.16).

Later technology allowed sounds to be recorded for play at a later date. This enabled sound enhancement to the real world to be played at will rather than only when and where the performer(s) is. Additionally, the recordings could be played back at any location that had the technology to use the recordings to make sound (Figure 1.17).

FIGURE 1.16
A didgeridoo player adds sounds to his environment. However, when he stops playing, the sound stops. Only people in the proximity of the didgeridoo are able to hear the sound. *Photo courtesy of Kevin Mills, Reston, Virginia.*

FIGURE 1.17
The invention of the phonograph allowed for audio performances to be recorded and distributed to be played back later in different places. *Photo courtesy of Leonardo Novaes.*

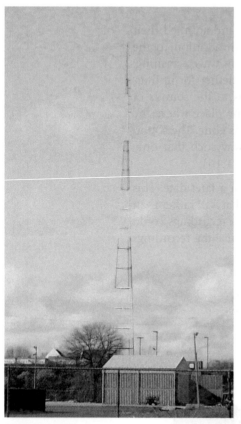

Other technologies allowed performances and other sounds to be added to the real world in real time, in more than one location simultaneously. Radio, followed later by television, allowed sound and (with television) visual imagery to be experienced in any location that had the proper technology within the proximity of the original location that the technology supported (Figure 1.18).

Not only are sound and visual enhancements and augmentations possible—smell is another potential augmentation to the real world. Just as there are natural smells in the real world, such as the smell of the ocean, the smell of animals, and the smell of food cooking, smells can be introduced artificially into the real world. A whole industry has been made that delivers room fresheners and incense. Likewise, the perfume industry has made a business of adding smells that move in the real world in close proximity to the person who is wearing the perfume (Figure 1.19).

Why Digital Enhancement of the Real World Rather Than Physical Enhancement?

The advent of the digital computer allowed information to be gathered, generated, manipulated, stored, and displayed in many new ways (Figures 1.20 and 1.21).

FIGURE 1.18
Radio and television stations enabled many people at different places to experience a performance at the same time as long as they had the correct technology (radio or television set) to pick up the broadcast. *Photo courtesy of Alan B. Craig.*

FIGURE 1.19
The perfume industry provides a plethora of scents that can be applied, primarily, to the human body.
Photo courtesy of Kevin Fedde.

FIGURE 1.20
Digital computers allowed information to be manipulated in new ways. Early computers, though, took up a lot of space and energy and were not very fast. *Photo courtesy of NASA.*

FIGURE 1.21
Modern computers range from large supercomputers that take specialized facilities to house them and much floor space to handheld smartphones and other special purpose devices, such as the gaming system shown here. *Photo courtesy of Alan B. Craig.*

When artifacts are made of physical materials, it requires significant effort and time to make alterations, especially when those alterations are significant. Consider a physical painting. The painting exists throughout time as it was created originally by the artist. The colors may fade over time, and the painting may become coated with dust, but the core essence of the painting remains the same, that is, a painting of a barn remains a painting of a barn. It doesn't transform into a painting of a fish instantaneously (Figures 1.22 and 1.23).

The two different paintings are actually renderings of an idea (information) that is manifested (represented) in paint and canvas. If someone desires to have a painting of a fish instead of a painting of a barn, he or she must either remove the painting of the barn and replace it with a painting of a fish or must paint a new painting on top of the painting of the barn. Either of these actions takes considerable effort and time.

FIGURE 1.23
An artist created this painting of a fish. It took time to paint. It was not displayed instantaneously. A digital version of this painting, however, could be displayed in a fraction of a second. If desired, the electronic display could display the painting of the barn in the same location. *Photo and painting courtesy of Beverly Carver.*

FIGURE 1.22
A painting of a barn remains a painting of a barn unless someone actively paints over the painting of the barn. *Photo and painting courtesy of Beverly Carver.*

In the digital realm, the idea of a barn can be represented as digital information displayed on some sort of electrically driven display. The result is something that looks more or less like a painting of a barn. However, the major gain by representing the painting digitally is that in a fraction of a second, a new idea (such as a painting of a fish) can be rendered and displayed on that same device almost instantaneously. To go even further, the images that are being rendered can be altered programmatically and can be changed based on any number of circumstances, such as sensors in the environment, the time of day, or even the whim of the creator or the owner of the display. Taking this idea to the extreme, if one has a digital computer with a display system, one can achieve the effect of having infinite paintings that they can display instantaneously.

AUGMENTED REALITY

What, then, is augmented reality? Augmented reality is a medium in which information is added to the physical world in registration with the world. However, as shown previously, there are many different ways that information can be added, changed, or modified in the physical world. If we take that definition at face value, virtually anything can be considered augmented reality. Indeed, the term *augmented reality* is being bandied about very widely, and it is not clear just exactly what people mean by the term. Some sources use a very broad meaning for the term, whereas others mean something very specific and narrow by it. In time, it will become apparent what is generally meant by the term, but at the moment it is being applied to a lot of different things, ranging from GPS mapping systems, to anything with a bar code on it, to mobile phone applications that overlay text on a scene, or anything that uses a pair of display glasses or goggles to view. It is not my intent to say what the "true" definition of augmented reality is, but because the term will be used throughout this book, it is important to nail down a definition of what I am and am not referring to when I use the term. It is also important to distinguish how augmented reality is, and is not, related to other media and technologies.

Ronald T. Azuma, in his 1997 paper *A Survey of Augmented Reality* (*Presence: Teleoperators and Virtual Environments* 6(4), pp. 355–385), asserts that there are three characteristics that define augmented reality:

1. Combines real and virtual
2. Interactive in real time
3. Registered in 3D

In determining what constitutes "augmented reality" for the purposes of this book, I look at those characteristics and further refine and clarify.

First, I provide a brief list of those features, followed by an explanation of each, and then a summary definition.

Key aspects (ingredients) of augmented reality:

- The physical world is augmented by *digital* information superimposed on a view of the physical world.
- The information is displayed in registration with the physical world.
- The information displayed is dependent on the location of the real world and the physical perspective of the person in the physical world.
- The augmented reality experience is interactive, that is, a person can sense the information and make changes to that information if desired. The level of interactivity can range from simply changing the physical perspective (e.g., seeing it from a different point of view) to manipulating and even creating new information.

The Physical World Is Augmented by Digital Information That Is Superimposed on a View of the Physical World

A key aspect of augmented reality as discussed in this book is that AR allows the overlay of digital information on the physical world. That is, there is a digital computer or processor involved. The digital information can be purely synthetic, such as from a computer simulation, or can be copies of real-world information represented digitally. There is no restriction on what sense the information pertains to, that is, it may be visual information, auditory information, or information regarding smell, taste, or touch. The information can be static, such as a digital photograph or 3D digital graphic model or a digital recording of a sound, or it can be based dynamically on a time evolving computer simulation, from real-time sensor data, or other dynamic sources of information.

An important aspect of augmented reality is that you "remain" in the physical world, that is, there is not an attempt to make you believe you are not in the real world at the position you are standing or sitting. In other media, such as virtual reality, and even cinema, the most common scenario is to place you in a scenario where the physical world is not visible or audible. In virtual reality systems, head-mounted displays preclude you from seeing the physical world. In a movie theater, the ambient lights are dimmed and people are told to remain quiet so that the only signals impinging on your visual and auditory senses are those from the virtual world or movie, respectively.

In augmented reality, you see, hear, smell, touch, and taste the physical world in exactly the same way that you would if there was no augmented reality involved. The digital information is added to, or *superimposed on* the physical world. Different technologies can be used to display the digital information, but a key aspect is that they don't fully occlude the physical world. For example, if augmented reality is experienced with a display headset, the physical world can be seen either because the display is made in such a way that you can see through the display (optical see-through) or because a video camera captures the real world from your point of view and displays that view onto your headset (video see-through). In the case of audio information, headphones or earpieces can be utilized that don't block out physical world sounds.

Note that there are two basic modes in which the digital world and the physical world can be merged. The first mode is to gather information from the physical world, generate the digital information in the computer, and meld those two worlds together in a computer to be displayed. The other mode is to simply project the augmentations onto the physical world by means of projection devices. This is addressed further in Chapter 3 in the section on projection displays (both stationary and mobile projection displays).

The Information Is Displayed in Registration with the Physical World

A key element to augmented reality rests with the idea of spatial registration. That is, the information has a physical space or location in the real world just like a physical counterpart to the digital information would have. For example, if the digital information being displayed as part of an augmented reality experience is a vase, then that vase sits in a location that is independent of where the viewer happens to be (Figures 1.24 and 1.25).

In the physical world, if there is a vase on a table, the vase stays in the same place regardless of the person viewing its location. If the person viewing the vase walks to the other side of the table, they see the other side of the vase, but the vase does not move based on the viewer's movement. Of course, if the person chooses to move the vase, they may do so, but the vase has a specific location in the physical world that doesn't change unless the person actively chooses to change the location of the vase by picking it up and moving it, by poking it with a stick, or by lifting one side of the table so the vase slides, or by interacting with it in some other way. The same holds true in augmented reality. The digital vase would stay in the same physical location unless the viewer chooses to explicitly move the vase. Of course, in augmented reality there can be more options of how to interact with the vase than in the real world (e.g., in AR you could have "magical" powers that allow you to levitate the vase by gazing at it or by chanting an incantation), but in general the digital vase behaves like a real-world equivalent.

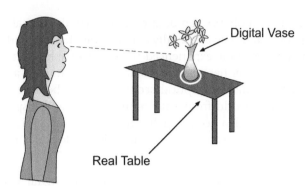

FIGURE 1.24
In this diagram, a digital vase sits on a real table. The vase has a location in the world. If the person moves or turns away from the table, the vase remains on the table. It is in registration with the real world. *Diagram courtesy of Beverly Carver.*

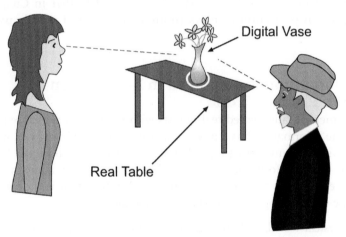

FIGURE 1.25
In this diagram, two people are looking at a digital representation of a vase on a real table. Each person sees the vase from his or her own perspective. Of course, in augmented reality anything is possible, so it could be made such that each person sees entirely different things. In the conventional mode, however, where two people are interacting in the same world, each person sees the vase on the table from his or her own point of view, just like they would see a physical vase on a table from their own point of view. *Diagram courtesy of Beverly Carver.*

The digital objects in augmented reality may or may not have a physical counterpart. In the example just given, there is a real-world equivalent of the digital vase. However, there is no requirement mandating a physical equivalent of an object in AR. Indeed, one of the more interesting aspects of AR is that anything that can be created digitally (and that is a lot of things!) can be rendered in an AR experience, whether permutations of physical objects or objects that could not exist in the physical world.

Registration with the real world must be both spatial in nature and temporal in nature. One of the technological hurdles in an AR system is to achieve very close registration with the real world. By close registration, I mean that the digital object should be placed in the physical world to very close tolerances. The tightness of the tolerances depends on the application. For example, with the vase example, it might be okay if the registration is off by 1/8 of an inch. However, for a surgeon using augmented reality to aid in performing surgery, an error of 1/8 of an inch could be deadly (Figure 1.26).

Temporal registration is even more difficult to achieve due to the inherent time lags involved with processing the information. Because the view of an object depends on the participant's physical point of view, the object must be re-rendered every time the viewer changes position even a tiny bit. If there is a lag in the system, and the viewer changes his or her perspective very rapidly, the lag in the computing might provide a noticeable lag in the scene where the participant sees the scene "catch up" with his or her change in point of view. Such lags can be somewhat overcome in systems that provide a video feed of the physical world by delaying the view of the physical world by the same amount as the lag in the digital representation, but latency will still be involved. This is discussed more thoroughly later in this book (Figure 1.27).

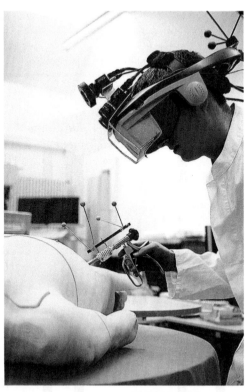

FIGURE 1.26
A surgeon tests a new augmented reality surgery application. *Photo courtesy of Tobias Blum.*

The Information Displayed Is Dependent on the Geographic Location of the Real World and the Physical Perspective of the Person in the Physical World

A key aspect to augmented reality is that the participant's physical point of view is taken into account just like it is in the real world. Going back to the vase example, in the physical world when you look at a vase on a table, you see it from a specific physical perspective. In fact, each of your eyes gets its own perspective of the vase, and because there is a separation between your eyes, this difference in perspective aids you in understanding the three dimensionality of the object you are looking at (more detail on this later in this book). Every time you move your head even slightly you see a slightly different view of the vase. Likewise if the vase moves for some reason, you also see it from a different point of view. The physical point of view must be integrated in augmented reality applications as described in this book.

FIGURE 1.27
This diagram illustrates the results of poor spatial registration. If the vase is supposed to be in the center of the circle, but instead appears to be anywhere except the center of the circle, such as it is in the second drawing, then there is a problem with spatial registration. An example of poor temporal registration would be if someone sets the vase on the table, but it doesn't appear at its resting point until sometime after it should have. *Diagram courtesy of Beverly Carver.*

Summarizing these key points leads to a definition of augmented reality as discussed in this book to be:

> Augmented reality: A medium in which digital information is overlaid on the physical world that is in both spatial and temporal registration with the physical world and that is interactive in real time.

This definition is both broad enough to include a wide variety of application areas and narrow enough to not include every application that merely includes location information or superimposes text on a map.

Note that in other works augmented reality is sometimes defined as a special case of virtual reality. For example, in *Understanding Virtual Reality*, Sherman and Craig define augmented reality as

> *A type of virtual reality in which additional information, otherwise imperceptible to the human system, is made perceptible and registered with the display of the physical world.*

If one takes the stance that augmented reality is a subset of virtual reality, this would be a reasonable definition. However, one could also take the stance that virtual reality is a subset of augmented reality in which the physical world is hidden and the only stimulus on the participant's senses is digital information.

Wikipedia offers a definition of augmented reality as:

> Augmented reality (AR) is a term for a live direct or indirect view of a physical, real-world environment whose elements are augmented by computer-generated sensory input such as sound, video, graphics or GPS data.

And distinguishes it from virtual reality:

> By contrast, virtual reality replaces the real world with a simulated one.

The Wikipedia definition of AR is a reasonable definition, but it doesn't address the necessity of spatial and temporal resolution with the physical world. I include it as an example of a broader definition of augmented reality that is in fairly common use. However, for the purpose of this book, I will restrict AR to mean those applications that rely on spatial, and when appropriate, temporal registration with the physical world. The spatial registration can be either *absolute* (a very specific place on the globe) or *relative* (with respect to some entity). An example of an application that uses absolute spatial registration would be an application that allows you to see an as of yet not constructed building in place at the actual address in a specific city. An example of an application with relative spatial registration would be an application that lets you see the internals of some object. For example, an application that lets you hold a calculator in your hand but lets you see the circuit board and components inside it would use relative spatial registration. The registration is done with respect to that object rather than an absolute place on earth, that is, no matter where you take the object, the internals are in registration with that object correctly, but it is not tied to any specific place on the planet.

The relationship between virtual reality and augmented reality is discussed in more detail later in this chapter.

Note that with augmented reality applications, augmentations and enhancements do not always need to be *added* to the world, but in some cases, the point of an augmented reality application is to hide unnecessary information from view. Thus, the augmentation is the augmentation of *simplicity*. AR can help cut through the clutter and enable the participant to see the important features of the environment more clearly.

Also note that augmented reality can be manifested with many different technologies. However, the same definition applies regardless of the tools and techniques used to implement it. The technology used to implement augmented reality is discussed in detail in subsequent chapters in this book.

Augmented reality applications that fall within this book's definition of augmented reality are plentiful and span application areas, including education, manufacturing, medicine, military, entertainment, advertising, as well as many others.

THE RELATIONSHIP BETWEEN AUGMENTED REALITY AND OTHER TECHNOLOGIES

Although augmented reality isn't a technology per se, but rather a medium that utilizes numerous other technologies, since it is new, people tend to try to understand it in terms of something they already understand, or at least think they understand. On first description or experience of AR I have heard people say things like "Oh, so it's just like bar codes" or "So this is the same thing as GPS?" and numerous other generalizations that range from reasonable to completely comical. This section addresses some of the other media, technologies, and topics that people seem to try to conceptualize AR within.

First I address different media, then different technologies, and finally other ideas related to the spectrum between real and virtual worlds.

Media
Virtual Reality

One of the most obvious media that people think of when they first see or hear about augmented reality is virtual reality (VR). As stated earlier, virtual reality can be regarded as a special case of augmented reality, or augmented reality can be considered a special case of virtual reality. According to Sherman and Craig in *Understanding Virtual Reality*, virtual reality is:

> A medium composed of interactive computer simulations that sense the participant's position and replace or augment the feedback to one or more senses—giving the feeling of being immersed or being present in the simulation.

Note that in general, virtual reality is a fully synthetic environment. That is, the only thing impinging on your senses is synthetic imagery, whether that imagery is visual, auditory, or otherwise. Note also that while VR systems do track your location and orientation in order to create the point of view of the display appropriately, it is not always grounded to a specific location. Likewise note that a key ingredient for many virtual reality applications is a sense of immersion and presence. That is, VR systems typically attempt to *fool* the participant into believing that what she is interacting with is in some way real. Some AR systems and applications do this, but a sense of presence is usually already there within AR applications because the participant is *actually present* in the physical world in which she is interacting (Figures 1.28–1.31).

Telepresence

Telepresence allows you to be in one place, yet be able to perceive and act like you are present in a different place. This differs from *remote control* by how you interface with the remote environment. With remote control, you use some type of controller and perhaps communication system to control something at a distance, but your actions and perception are that you are controlling something at a distance. For example, if you press a button that causes a light to turn on 1000 miles away, that would be remote control of that light. Telepresence, however, simulates that you are in the remote location. With this example, you would see the environment that is 1000 miles away from your actual location and you would interact with that environment as though you were actually there. Then, to turn on that light you would turn it on just as you would if you were right there. Or, if you are sitting in a flight simulator cockpit but are actually flying an airplane (that actually exists) in a remote location, and when you look out the window you see that remote location in

FIGURE 1.28

This virtual reality application fully immerses the participant in a synthetic environment that is computed in real time and reacts to the participant's movements and actions. Here, the author is experiencing the CAVE QUAKE II first-person shooter game in a CAVE. A CAVE is a display device that fully surrounds the participant in 3D stereographic computer-generated imagery displayed from the participant's point of view. *Photo courtesy of Kalev H. Leetaru. CAVE QUAKE II VR application courtesy of Paul Rajlich, Visbox Inc.*

FIGURE 1.29

Virtual reality applications don't necessarily require that participants believe they are in the world that is presented. However, the participant can manipulate objects as though they are real, physical entities. In this application, a CAVE device is used to allow a researcher to view and interact with a molecule as though it was in the space with him. This image is taken from the VMD application developed at the University of Illinois. *Photo courtesy of Kalev H. Leetaru. VMD application courtesy of John Stone.*

FIGURE 1.30
Many virtual reality experiences use a head-mounted display to ensure that the participant does not see the physical world. *Photo courtesy of William R. Sherman.*

FIGURE 1.31
An alternative way to interact with a VR application is with a BOOM-style device. Note that the participant is unable to see the physical world, and the BOOM determines the appropriate point of view by integrating values provided by the joints in the articulated arm structure. The participant may interact with the VR application via buttons on the BOOM device or by using a tracked data glove. *Photo courtesy of William R. Sherman.*

the same way that you would if you were actually flying the airplane that is in that location, then you are experiencing telepresence (Figure 1.32).

The relationship of augmented reality with telepresence is exactly the same as it is with the nonaugmented world. If you are using an augmented reality application as though you are in a remote location and the augmented reality application affects that remote location, it would be considered augmented reality in telepresence. An example of an augmented reality telepresence application would be to have a telepresence situation where people at a distance can see me (and I can see them) giving a demonstration of augmented reality as though I was in the room with them, yet I am actually doing the demonstration in my own office.

Telepresence is included as a case of "augmented virtuality" on Milgram's virtuality continuum. (See later.)

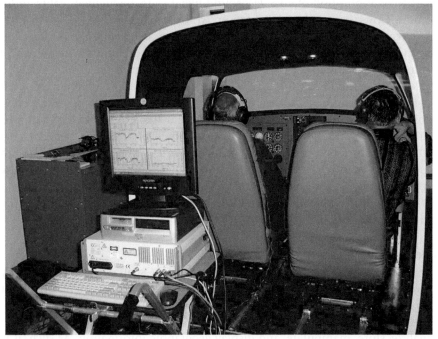

FIGURE 1.32
If these pilots, who are sitting in a stationary location in a flight simulator, were coupled to an actual airplane that they were flying by their actions in this stationary cockpit, and the views they saw in the windows were provided by live video feeds from that remote airplane, and their gauges reflected actual measurements from the remote airplane, they would be experiencing telepresence. *Image courtesy of NASA.*

Technologies
Global Positioning System (GPS)

Often, when I describe augmented reality to people or show them an example of an augmented reality application, people respond with "Oh, so it is like GPS!" This response always puzzles me, but because people tend to respond this way, it is important to address what GPS is and how it is similar and different from augmented reality.

GPS, or the *Global Positioning System*, is a technology that is used for tracking location. In this sense, there *is* a relationship with augmented reality. GPS can, in fact, be used with augmented reality, but in actuality, it is a support technology for augmented reality. However, because the role that GPS plays in AR can be provided by numerous different technologies, AR does not *depend* on GPS in general. Most people are familiar with GPS as a portable device that they carry, an application on their smartphone, or a unit that they have in their car that shows their position on a map and gives them directions of how to get to places from their current location. At first blush, this particular application of GPS *does* sound like it is an augmented reality application. However, on closer inspection, we realize that while the application is *in* registration with the physical world, it is not overlaying the information *on* the physical world—the application overlays your location in the world onto an abstract map on the display. The display is updated continuously to reflect your current location on the map, and your current direction. In order to fulfill the definition of AR used in this book, the indicator of your current position would have to be displayed on the actual world. So, for example, an application that shows the direction you should go as a computer-generated arrow that appears to be on the ground in front of you would qualify as an augmented reality application. Of course, there are many other ways the application could be manifested as AR, such as indicating footsteps in front of you to follow or the representation of a person in front of you indicating which way you should go (Figures 1.33 and 1.34).

Geographic Information Systems (GIS)

Because augmented reality depends so much on spatial registration, many people equate it with anything having to do with maps. One of the most pervasive technologies that people equate with maps is geographic information systems, commonly referred to as GIS. GIS provides the capability to analyze, store, manipulate, and display geographic information. As such, it is based locationally and is often seen displaying maps and map information. However, because the display is not typically registered with the real world or real-world objects, GIS is not typically used in a manner that is augmented reality.

FIGURE 1.33
The Global Positioning System, or GPS, uses a constellation of satellites to aid in locating and tracking objects on earth. *Image courtesy of NASA.*

FIGURE 1.34
This GPS device uses information from GPS satellites to indicate your location and direction on a map. Although this is a very useful tool and is spatially registered, it is not an augmented reality application. *Photo courtesy of Alvaro Daniel Gonzalez Lamarque on morguefile.com.*

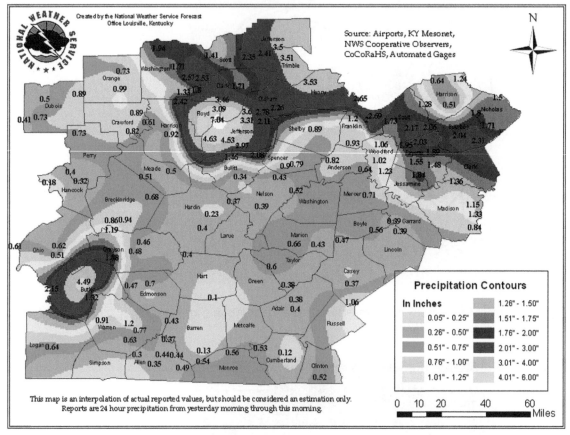

FIGURE 1.35

This map in a GIS used by NOAA depicts a 24-hour precipitation total on the morning after a flood. Note the legend and scale indicators. *Image courtesy of NOAA Research.*

One technique that is used commonly in GIS is the layering of information, often on a map. The technique of layering information can be used in AR, but most geographic information systems are not AR applications (Figures 1.35 and 1.36).

Other Ideas Related to the Spectrum Between Real and Virtual Worlds

Cyberspace

Because augmented reality is new and has to do with virtual objects and mixing the digital world with the real world, there is a tendency to want to couple the idea with the idea of cyberspace. William Gibson coined the term *cyberspace* in his book *Neuromancer*, in 1984. He refers to a "consensual

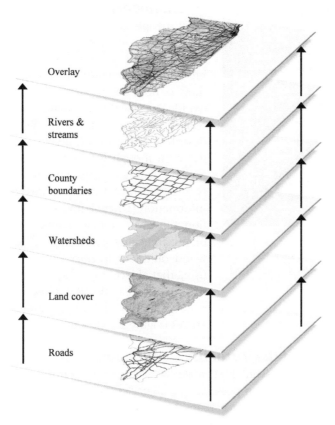

Overlay

Rivers & streams

County boundaries

Watersheds

Land cover

Roads

FIGURE 1.36

Many GIS applications provide an interactive interface that allows the user to turn on and off different layers of information. This image depicts some of the different layers available in this particular system. The idea of layering information is useful in augmented reality. In the case of a typical GIS, the layering is often on a map. In the case of AR, the information is layered onto the physical world. *Image courtesy of Dan Dong and Shaowen Wang, CyberInfrastructure and Geospatial Information Laboratory, University of Illinois.*

hallucination" of data and interactions in a technological space. So, some may say that the world that exists on a computer network is cyberspace. The important things that happen in cyberspace are the social interactions between people with other people and with data. Cyberspace can be supported in numerous different technologies. For example, some people consider the "space" that you are in when you are on a telephone conversation to be cyberspace. The "space" created by the Internet can be considered cyberspace in that there is some sort of presence that supports communication and interaction between people and data. In this sense, augmented reality is, indeed, related to cyberspace, but it is not the same thing as cyberspace.

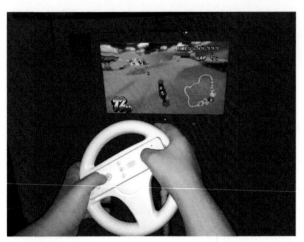

FIGURE 1.37
This image depicts a mixed reality application. A real-world (toy) steering wheel is used to interact with the digital world of a Wii-based racing game. *Photo courtesy of Holly McClain.*

Mixed Reality

Many people use the term *mixed reality* interchangeably with augmented reality. However, in this book I consider mixed reality to be a broader interpretation that consists of anything of both the physical world and the digital world. The specific constraint of registration is relaxed. Thus, an example of the GPS mapping described earlier would qualify as "mixed reality" even though it is not considered an "augmented reality" application in this book. It is mixed reality in that it is mixing real-world information (where I am) with digital information (an abstract map display). Another type of mixed reality application is to use a real-world object to interact with a digital world, using that object in the way it is used in the real world. Note that all AR applications are mixed reality, but not all mixed reality applications are AR (Figure 1.37).

Virtuality and the Virtuality Continuum

The term *virtuality* essentially separates what something is from what the essence of that thing is, that is, it possesses the characteristics of something but lacks its physical embodiment. Hence, many of the digital objects and creations in augmented reality are examples of virtuality. This term is often heard in the context of the "virtuality continuum," which is an idea described by Paul Milgram [Milgram, P., Takemura, H., Utsumi, A., and Kishino, F. (1994). "Augmented reality: A class of displays on the reality-virtuality continuum" (pdf). In *Proceedings of the SPIE Conference on Telemanipulator and Telepresence Technologies*, Vol. 2351 (November 1995), pp. 282–292]. The idea of a virtuality continuum is that there is a complete range of realness between the fully real and the fully virtual. Milgram expresses that everything between the fully real and the fully virtual is mixed reality and that mixed reality is made up of augmented reality and augmented virtuality. In his definition, augmented reality is the case where the real world is augmented by virtual entities, and augmented virtuality is where the virtual world is augmented by real-world entities (Figure 1.38).

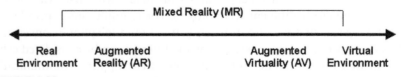

FIGURE 1.38
The virtuality continuum expresses the range of realness from fully real to fully virtual.

The Reality Continuum

In much the same way that the virtuality continuum expresses a range of real-ness between the virtual and the real, the reality continuum also expresses that range but is more concerned about the transformation between real (physical) and virtual realms. The reality continuum asserts that real (physical) entities can become virtual, virtual entities can become physical, and there are mixed states along the continuum. One of the simplest examples of how a physical object can become virtual is by scanning. The idea of document scanning is ubiquitous. One can scan a physical document and have a digital copy of that document that emulates many but not all of the characteristics of the original physical document. For example, it conveys the same message as the physical document, but you can't really fold the digital document into a paper airplane like you can the original. Likewise, 3D scanners exist that allow you to scan 3D physical objects to create virtual 3D objects. The virtual objects are digital representations of many of the aspects of the original object and can be manipulated in many new ways but don't have mass or take up space in the same manner as the original physical object (Figure 1.39).

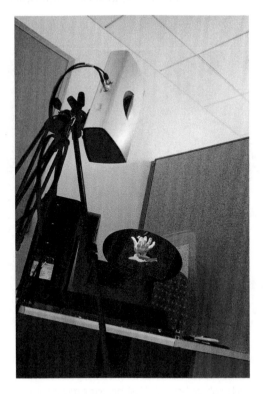

FIGURE 1.39
This 3D scanner enables you to create a 3D digital model of a 3D physical object. In this case, the object is a 3D casting of a hand. *Photo courtesy of Travis Ross, Visualization Laboratory, Imaging Technology Group, Beckman Institute, University of Illinois.*

Some physical entities can be emulated as digital artifacts or systems. For example, for many years, musicians have used physical devices for signal processing. They connected a physical device between their instrument and their amplifier or tape recorder. The net result was that the signal their instrument produced was altered in some manner that they desired. Now, however, many of these same signal processing activities can be performed entirely in software. Thus, there is no need for the original physical device. Of course, there needs to be a conversion of the signal into the digital realm, but once there, there is no need for the specialized hardware processors. So is this software emulation of the device real? It achieves the same end effect as the real physical device but has no physical body or container. So it is real in that it performs the desired task, but it is not real if the desire is to throw the device and break a window. The emulation falls somewhere on the reality continuum (Figure 1.40).

Likewise, other real-world characteristics can be brought into the virtual realm. For example, a plethora of different devices can bring real (physical)-world information into the virtual world, including sensors (such as sensors that measure temperature, light level, and wind speed) and other transducers such

FIGURE 1.40
In the past, electric guitar players used a variety of physical devices to alter the sound of their instruments. Today, many of those effects can be achieved in software, lessening the need for the "real" devices like those shown here. Is the end result any less real? Musicians argue over the quality of the results, but no one can deny that there is a very real transformation of their sound. Over time these systems will improve and become indistinguishable from their physical counterparts. *Photo courtesy of Bill Christison.*

as microphones in tandem with analog-to-digital converters. Thus, real-world sounds can be imported into the virtual world, and digital cameras and video recorders can bring other aspects of the physical world into the digital realm.

In a manner similar to scanning objects to make digital representations of physical objects, it is possible to make physical objects from digital representations of them. These digital representations can originate by scanning or otherwise importing them into the computer, or they can be "born digital." By "born digital," I mean that the digital representations were created directly in the computer. By using software that allows you to create models of objects and processes, you can create the virtual representation of something that may or may not already exist in the real world. Indeed, it is possible to create objects that would be *impossible* in the real world. So, however the digital entity came to be, it is possible to manifest that creation in the physical world unless it has characteristics that are impossible to implement in the physical world (such as it breaks the laws of nature, e.g., it defies the laws of gravity). Technologies related to *rapid prototyping* such as 3D printers, computer numerically controlled (CNC) laser cutters, and CNC milling machines allow digital creations to be manufactured in the physical world. In some cases, the objects are complete and ready to use in the physical world. In other cases, the systems can generate parts that must be assembled and/or make up a part of the end product. The basic path that information undergoes before being "printed" as a physical object is that it must exist as a digital entity first. How does that digital entity come to be? It can be born digital and designed in the computer by an artist or a draftsman, it can be captured from the real world via a 3D scanner, or it can be created by a computer algorithm or any number of other ways. The point is, in order to fabricate an object with these types of fabrication devices, the object must be a virtual object first. Only then can these CNC devices do their part in creating the physical object. Different devices serve different functions. For example, a CNC laser cutter does as its name implies. It cuts shapes from a two-dimensional material such as wood or plastic. The resulting piece that is cut out, or (depending on the object being made) the piece that has had something cut out of it, is used either as the final object or as a component in the final object. A CNC milling machine begins with a 3D piece of material and removes all the material that doesn't contribute to the final object. A 3D printer actually creates a 3D object from some raw material such as plastic, metal, or fiber. Many different technologies are available to create the 3D printout, but the end result is that a 3D digital object becomes a 3D physical object (Figures 1.41 and 1.42).

The Metaverse and the Metaverse Roadmap

The term *metaverse* found its origin in *Snow Crash*, a novel by Neal Stephenson published in 1992. The idea of the metaverse is a cyberspace

FIGURE 1.41

This is an assortment of objects "printed" on a 3D printer. Thus, these objects were brought from the digital world into the physical world. *Photo courtesy of Alan B. Craig.*

FIGURE 1.42

A small, low-cost, homemade (from a kit) 3D printer. This example shows that these types of devices are coming down in price and that 3D printing will become much more accessible by the general public. *Photo by Alan B. Craig.*

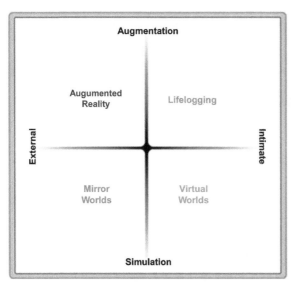

FIGURE 1.43

This chart shows where the Acceleration Studies Foundation (ASF) situates augmented reality on their roadmap to the metaverse. *Image courtesy of the Acceleration Studies Foundation.*

that everyone is interconnected in. It is somewhat like our current Internet accessed through the medium of virtual reality. The metaverse, though, encompasses all of those things we think of when we think about the digital age, including simulation, the World Wide Web, different types of interfaces, collaborative environments, and numerous different types of worlds, all digitally based.

A group called the Acceleration Studies Foundation (ASF) is creating a "roadmap" to the metaverse and has created a pair of orthogonal axes on which different related media can be placed. As can be seen from Figure 1.43, the ASF has situated augmented reality to be nearer the "augmentation" end of the spectrum that runs between full simulation (digitally created worlds) to augmentation (of the physical world) and the "external" end of their spectrum that scales between the very intimate, personal, inward end of the scale to those things more external to the individual and more focused in the world.

SUMMARY OF RELATED TECHNOLOGIES

The technologies listed earlier that are either related to augmented reality directly or perceived by some as related to augmented reality are summed up in Table 1.1. This helps in seeing what differentiates augmented reality from these related technologies.

Table 1.1 The Relationship between Augmented Reality and Other Media, Technologies, and Ideas

	Classification	Fully Synthetic Virtual World	Fully Real Virtual World	Absolute Spatial Registration Critical	Relative Spatial Registration Critical	Real-Time Interactivity Critical
Augmented reality	Medium (supported by technology)	No	No	Maybe	Yes	Yes
Virtual reality	Medium (supported by technology)	Yes	No	No	Yes	Yes
Telepresence	Medium (supported by technology)	No	Yes	Maybe	Yes	Yes
Global positioning system	Technology	N/A	N/A	Yes	Yes	No
Geographic information system	Technology	N/A	N/A	No	Yes	No
Fabrication	Technology	No	Yes	No	No	No
Cyberspace	Descriptive idea	No	Maybe	No	No	Maybe
Mixed reality	Descriptive idea	Maybe	Maybe	Maybe	Maybe	Maybe
Virtuality	Descriptive idea	Maybe	Maybe	Maybe	Maybe	Maybe
Metaverse	Descriptive idea	Maybe	Maybe	Maybe	Maybe	Maybe

SUMMARY

This chapter has set the stage for the chapters that follow by defining what augmented reality is (and isn't), addressed the notion that augmented reality is actually a medium, and asserted that augmented reality can be realized with a variety of different technologies and that there is a continuum of reality wherein things can be more or less real and that entities can move from the real to the virtual and back again (more or less).

As you move forward in the book, it is important to remember the definition of augmented reality as it is used in this book. As a refresher, here is the definition stated earlier in this chapter: *Augmented reality is a medium in which digital information is overlaid on the physical world that is in both spatial and temporal registration with the physical world and that is interactive in real time.*

The next chapter looks specifically at how augmented reality is achieved and some of the different approaches that can be taken to implement different types of augmented reality systems. Following that are chapters devoted more specifically to the different technologies used in AR systems (both hardware and software) and then a look at content for augmented reality systems. Regarding the issue of content we will address questions including what *is* the content? how *is* it created? What constraints are there on content, and what makes for compelling content? After that, the issue of interactivity and interaction is addressed, followed by the special issues of mobile-augmented reality applications. Then we'll take a look at issues surrounding AR applications, including some example applications, and then, finally, a look at the future of augmented reality and how it all ties together. Let's have some fun!

CHAPTER 2

Augmented Reality Concepts

INTRODUCTION

This chapter looks at the ingredients of augmented reality (AR) and the broad categories of technologies required to implement augmented reality and shows how augmented reality systems work.

HOW DOES AUGMENTED REALITY WORK?

This section briefly addresses how augmented reality works at a very high level. I will begin by stating how augmented reality applications can be described as a two-step process and then fill in more detail of what is involved in each of those two steps and the different types of technology that can be used to carry out those steps.

The Two-Step Process of Augmented Reality Applications

In general, two primary things need to happen for every time step of an augmented reality application. The two steps are:

1. The application needs to determine the current state of the physical world and determine the current state of the virtual world.
2. The application needs to display the virtual world in registration with the real world in a manner that will cause the participant(s) to sense the virtual world elements as part of his or her physical world and then return to step 1 to move on to the next time step.

Obviously there are a number of substeps in each of those two steps, but at the core of what is happening, these are the two key overarching steps. When you consider those two steps, you can see readily that many different methods could be used to achieve them and many different technologies could be used to implement those methods.

39

There are three major components to an augmented reality system to support the steps just listed. Chapter 3 of this book addresses the hardware components in much greater detail, but here it is important to have an understanding of the structural components and their roles in implementing an AR application. The three core components include:

1. *Sensor(s)* to determine the state of the physical world where the application is deployed
2. A *processor* to evaluate the sensor data, to implement the "laws of nature" and other rules of the virtual world, and to generate the signals required to drive the display
3. A *display* suitable for creating the impression that the virtual world and the real world are coexistent and to impinge on the participant's senses such that he or she senses the combination physical world and virtual world

FIGURE 2.1
The six degrees of freedom include X, Y, and Z locations and yaw, pitch, and roll, which are the rotations about the axis they are on. Note that in an AR system there are various different coordinate systems at play at any given moment. There is a coordinate system associated with the world at large, with the participant, and with each entity in the world. In general, the X, Y, and Z values are related to location, and yaw, pitch, and roll are related to orientation. *Diagram courtesy of Beverly Carver.*

Some might say that there is a fourth category, which would be "input devices" such as buttons, keyboards, and other actuators. However, these are actually sensors in which the participant takes an active role in setting their values. Other sensors are more passive in nature, in that the participant doesn't take an active role in determining their values.

Taking these in order, we will see more on the role that each of these components plays in the overall system.

Sensor(s)

In order to be able to respond correctly to the physical world, an augmented reality application must have information about the real world in real time.

Three primary categories of sensors are used in AR systems:

1. Sensors used for tracking
2. Sensors for gathering environmental information
3. Sensors for gathering user input

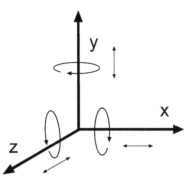

Sensors Used for Tracking

Because AR depends on being spatially registered, there must be some mechanism to determine information about the position of the participant, the real world, and any AR devices. Note that *position* includes both *location* and *orientation*. In order to fully determine position requires information about six degrees of freedom of the entity being tracked. The six degrees of freedom in this case include X location, Y location, Z location, yaw, pitch, and roll (Figure 2.1).

At a minimum, this information must include the participant's location and orientation in the real world (or the participant's surrogate, such as a smartphone or other interaction device).

Camera (Computer Vision)

Many current augmented reality applications use techniques from *computer vision* to determine the participant's location and perspective with respect to the real world. Note that the location and orientation may be *absolute* in nature (the location and orientation are very specific places regardless of the location and orientation of anything else (in other words, a specific place in the world)), or the location and orientation may be *relative* (they are determined with respect to the location and orientation of something else). An example of relative location is if the location is determined with respect to a table in the environment. If there is a virtual representation of a vase on the (real) table and if someone moves the table, the vase would move with it. If the location were absolute, such as a latitude and longitude, the vase would remain in place even if the table were moved (Figure 2.2).

In order to enable computer vision, the sensor required is a camera. The camera "sees" the real world and, based on what it "sees," can determine where it (the camera) is located and how it is oriented with respect to the scene. In order to carry out computer vision, software is needed to analyze the images collected by the camera in order to determine what the camera "sees." Based on that information the software calculates where the camera *must* be in order to see that view. Thus, there must be cues in the environment that the camera can use as landmarks to aid in determining location and orientation with respect to those landmarks. The landmarks can be natural features in the environment or can be placed artificially into the environment.

In order to make the computer vision problem simpler, many AR applications utilize landmarks that are placed artificially into the environment that are images that the application can easily recognize. Images used specifically for this purpose are called *fiducial markers*, and sometimes *fiducial symbols*.

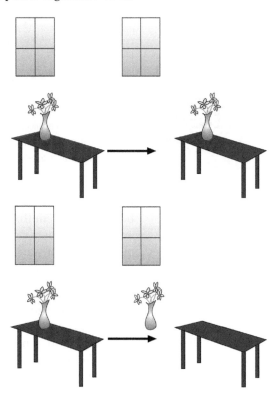

FIGURE 2.2

An object can be registered in an absolute position in the real world or registered relatively. If it is registered relatively, it is registered with respect to some other object. In this diagram, the top view shows the vase registered with respect to the table. Consequently, if the table moves, the vase moves with the table. The bottom view shows the vase registered absolutely in the real world. It has a specific place in X, Y, and Z locations that is independent of the location of anything else. Hence, even if the table moves, the vase stays in its own location in the world. *Diagram courtesy of Beverly Carver.*

FIGURE 2.3
A very typical fiducial symbol. *Image courtesy of Robert McGrath.*

FIGURE 2.4
Some AR applications use "quick response" (QR) codes as fiducial markers. The three boxes in the corners provide information about the orientation of the code and other information, such as a URL, where the object the fiducial marker represents is located is contained in the rest of the marker. *QR code courtesy of daqri.*

FIGURE 2.5
This photo shows a sheet of paper with several fiducial symbols on it. When you view it with a tablet device using an AR application, you can see several virtual objects in registration with the fiducial symbols. In this case, you can see three different species of plants, each species in registration with the marker that it is associated with. *Photo courtesy of Alan B. Craig.*

When the system "sees" a fiducial marker it can determine where the camera is with respect to that symbol and how it is oriented with respect to the symbol. It is apparent that either the symbol can move with respect to the camera and/or the camera can move with respect to the symbol. Regardless, the computer vision software must determine the relative location and orientation of the camera compared to the symbol (Figures 2.3 and 2.4).

In addition to providing information about the relative position of the camera with respect to the marker, markers can also provide additional information to the AR application. For example, a certain graphical object can be associated with a particular symbol. When this is done, that object is displayed from the point of view that it should be displayed from based on the relative position of the camera to the marker (Figure 2.5).

In general, it is beneficial for a fiducial marker to be a unique pattern that is very easy for the computer vision software to recognize as a fiducial marker, but it is also beneficial for the marker to be asymmetrical. It is much easier to determine the relative positioning of the camera and the marker if some aspect of the marker is asymmetrical. It is not necessary that the overall marker be asymmetrical, but it is important that there is some aspect of the marker that makes it possible for the vision software to determine which way the marker is oriented.

Historically, a fiducial marker typically conveyed two pieces of information to the AR system. The first was to designate what computer graphics object to display, and the second was what point of view should be displayed. The information to be conveyed does not need to be limited to those two items. For example, one could encode further information in the fiducial marker such as the URL of an object to be displayed. This way, the object would not be required to be loaded onto the AR system a priori and could be fetched from a network-based server when needed. Likewise, the same marker could be used to represent numerous different objects depending on the state of rest of the system. That is, the AR system could "see" the marker, execute a query to the server system, and the server could deliver whatever object was correct for the current state of the system at that point in time and space and associate it with that particular marker (Figure 2.6).

In order to embed more information into the marker, people have utilized QR codes as fiducial markers. These codes can represent a great deal of information, are easy to recognize as markers, and are asymmetrical in nature. The three larger boxes on a QR code represent an asymmetry in the overall marker and make it possible for the computer vision system to determine the relative orientation of the camera and the marker.

As the complexity of an AR application grows, it may be necessary to have more fiducial markers in the scene at any one place and time. This provides a solution if many different virtual entities need to be present simultaneously in a small amount of physical space that need to be able to be manipulated independently from each other (Figures 2.7 and 2.8).

In general, fiducial markers are physical entities that are placed in a scene. They may be static or mobile. For example, fiducial markers can be attached to physical objects—if the physical object moves, the marker moves with it in tandem. An example of this might be to have a fiducial marker on an object such as a generic paddle, which could then be represented in the AR scene as whatever the application designer desires, or it might be attached to a physical prop such as a

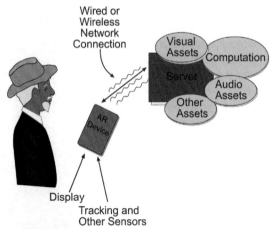

FIGURE 2.6

A server-based AR system offloads some of the burden of an AR system to a server that may be located remotely from the participant and connected via a wired or wireless network. In this example, in the interest of portability, the participant is using a handheld device to interact with the system, but is taking advantage of the greater computational power and storage of a remote server. There are other potential advantages of a server-based system noted in the text. The disadvantage is that the participant must be able to connect to a network to use the system. *Diagram courtesy of Beverly Carver.*

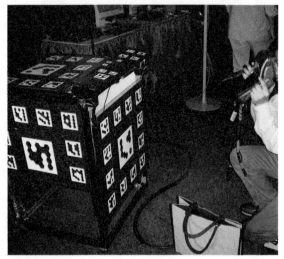

FIGURE 2.7

Multiple fiducial markers can be present in a single view of the vision system. Each marker must be unique from the others and be able to be discerned from each other by the computer vision software. *Photo courtesy of Alan B. Craig.*

FIGURE 2.8
Fiducial markers can be placed in an environment where they are stand alone or in conjunction with other types of real-world entities. In this scene, the markers are placed on a white cube as well as on a colorful background scene that contributes to the AR application. There is also a physical model of a dinosaur skeleton that is part of the content of this AR application. *Photo by Alan B. Craig.*

FIGURE 2.9
Fiducial markers can be added to common everyday items such as this spatula and trowel or to very generic items such as a simple paddle. *Photo courtesy of Alan B. Craig.*

hand trowel. In this way, the participant could engage with the empty trowel, but via augmented reality he could see dirt, a plant, or whatever the application designer wishes in the trowel (Figures 2.9 and 2.10).

Fiducial markers are usually physical objects, such as pieces of paper with ink printed on them, but there is nothing to prevent them from being displayed electronically, such as on a laptop screen, an iPad, or a smartphone. On these types of devices the markers can be created dynamically such that the marker itself can change based on the situation, or change over time, etc. This is different from the idea of changing what objects are associated with the marker, but both of these methods can achieve a similar result (Figure 2.11).

It is entirely possible to use real-world objects as fiducials in augmented reality applications. Some natural and man-made objects provide the same types of traits as specifically made abstract markers. For example, the human face can be recognized and because it is also asymmetrical, it is possible to use a person's face in the role of a fiducial marker. This has been done to great effect by using a face as a marker in an

FIGURE 2.10
When an object with a fiducial marker is viewed through a smart tablet, one can see a representation of an object registered with that fiducial marker—in this case, a three-dimensional (3D) representation of a flower.

AR application that superimposes a virtual mask, a hat, or sunglasses onto a participant. This has been done for the marketing of products to allow guests to try on costumes (virtually) in museums and just for fun (Figure 2.12).

City skylines are readily recognizable and are asymmetrical. Consequently, they can be used to help an augmented reality application that uses computer vision as its primary sensor. An example of an application that might use a skyline would be one that allows an architect to walk around the downtown area of a city and see how his planned (not built) skyscraper will look from different perspectives in the skyline (Figure 2.13).

The idea of using natural features to aid in visual tracking for augmented reality is developing rapidly. Indeed, there is a great deal of research and application in an area known as natural feature tracking (NFT). NFT can be applied in many ways beyond the types of natural features (face, skyline) described earlier. NFT is being used successfully to utilize many surfaces, such as patterned cloth, posters, and real-world objects such as computer keyboards or

FIGURE 2.11
Fiducial markers can even be displayed on electronic devices. In this case, the marker is displayed on an iPad. *Photo courtesy of Alan B. Craig.*

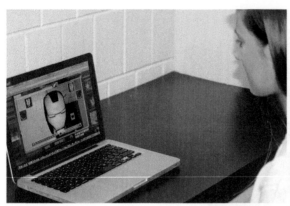
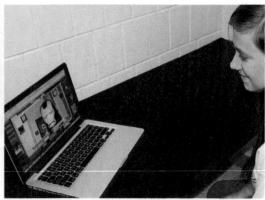

FIGURE 2.12

This pair of photos shows the web-based Iron Man 2 Augmented Reality Experience (http://www.iamironman2.com/). This augmented reality experience makes use of the human face as the fiducial marker for the computer vision to see. The generic human face (two eyes, nose, mouth) provides natural features that can be tracked. This particular application makes use of the web camera on the laptop that the participant is using. In the application, the participant sees herself as though she is looking in a magic mirror and rather than seeing her face and head as she would expect, she sees her head covered with the helmet from the Iron Man 2 movie. The helmet tracks with her head so it moves appropriately as she turns her head or moves it from side to side. *Photos courtesy of Olivia Neff.*

brick walls, as "markers" in AR systems that exploit computer vision as their tracking mechanism (Figure 2.14).

As NFT systems improve and become ubiquitous, it is highly likely that the blatant fiducial markers of early AR systems will become but an interesting historical blip on the timeline of the evolution of AR.

Global Positioning System (GPS)

GPS is a navigation system that utilizes a network of 24 satellites in outer space. The receiver can determine its location in X and Y if it can receive 3 satellites by measuring the amount of time it takes for the GPS signal to travel from the satellite to the receiver. By comparing the amount of time the signal takes from several different satellites, the location of the receiver can be computed to within several meters. If there are 4 or more satellite signals available, the altitude of the receiver can also be computed. AR systems can take advantage of the location information provided by a GPS receiver to gain information about its location in X, Y, and potentially Z. However, in general, a GPS is not that helpful in determining the orientation of the receiver in yaw, pitch, and roll. This limits the role of a GPS in AR systems in general, but the GPS information can still be used to great advantage—if it is available. One example of how GPS information can be useful in AR applications is to enable the system to know roughly where it is, and thus what natural

FIGURE 2.13
Skylines are very recognizable and seldom change. Hence, they can potentially be used as fiducial markers. *Photo courtesy of Kevin Connors (http://www.morguefile .com/).*

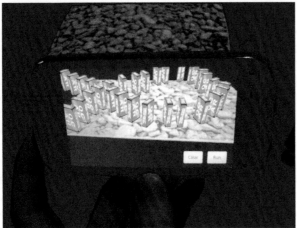

FIGURE 2.14
Some AR applications, such as this application from Qualcomm, can track natural features, such as the image of gravel seen in this example. In this application, the participant can place (virtual) dominos on the gravel by using the touchscreen on a smartphone. They can then knock the dominos over by intersecting their (real) hand with a (virtual) domino and see the chain reaction of the dominos falling. *Photo courtesy of Bev Carver.*

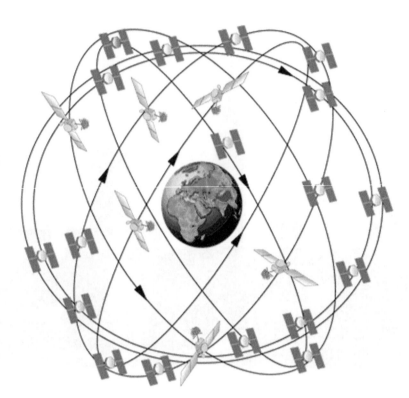

FIGURE 2.15
A constellation of 24 satellites makes it possible for a GPS receiver to determine its location on earth. In order to calculate a two-dimensional (2D) location (latitude and longitude), the receiver must be within view of at least three satellites. If the receiver is within view of 4 or more satellites the system can determine not only latitude and longitude, but also altitude. *Image courtesy of gps.gov.*

landmarks to look for if it is using a computer vision-based system. For example, in the earlier example regarding using a city skyline as a fiducial symbol, a GPS can provide information regarding what city the system is near. This can radically reduce the amount of searching that the system must do to utilize the correct skyline information. GPS is not suitable as the only sensing mechanism for AR applications that require information about point of view and/or very high-resolution information about the location of the device (Figures 2.15 and 2.16).

Gyroscopes, Accelerometers, and Other Types of Sensors
A multitude of other sensor types can be useful in augmented reality applications. The goal is to get information about the physical world and to use that information to inform the application. Some of the more common sensors that are used, particularly in mobile AR applications (more detail in Chapter 7) because many handheld devices are equipped with them, include accelerometers, compasses, and gyroscopes.

Gyroscopes report values related to orientation, that is, they can provide information including yaw, pitch, and roll. Gyroscopes don't provide location

FIGURE 2.16
A GPS satellite that plays a part in enabling terrestrial navigation and location determination via a GPS receiver. *Image courtesy of gps.gov.*

information. They can be useful in measuring the orientation of a handheld computer or interaction device.

Compasses provide information regarding what direction they are pointing. Just like an old-fashioned compass, an electronic compass can report whether you are pointed north, south, east, west, or anywhere in between.

Accelerometers do exactly what their name implies. They report acceleration. They can be used to determine the direction something is moving and changes in movement, and they do not depend on the presence of GPS signals. However, using accelerometers for a navigation system is hazardous because each number from the accelerometer is dependent on the number that came before it. Hence, any errors are amplified over time. Thus it is important to have some type of error correction or another sensor that can provide a reality check for the accelerometers. On the positive side, accelerometers are inexpensive and can provide data useful in AR systems (Figure 2.17).

Sensors for Gathering Environmental Information

There are a number of other sensors that are used less commonly in AR systems but can provide information about the physical world at the time and place that the AR application is being used. For example, temperature sensors, humidity

FIGURE 2.17

This pair of photos shows a circuit board from an Apple iPhone. The close-up shows an accelerometer that is a part of the device. As can be seen, accelerometers are small and can be mounted to circuit boards. The accelerometer is the square that is about ¼ inch on each side. *Photos courtesy of Liz Wuerffel.*

sensors, and other sensors can be used to overlay atmospheric information on a scene in an AR application. An AR application that uses these types of sensors could be used to make a handheld "magic lens" from a smartphone that makes it possible to "see" where the hot spots are on a surface that you are looking at.

Other sensors can measure most any environmental condition, such as pH (how acidic or basic something is), voltage, radio frequency information, and many more specific aspects of the physical world (Figure 2.18).

Sensors for Gathering User Input

The sensors discussed previously are primarily passive sensors from the perspective of the participant in the AR experience. That is, those sensors do their job without the participant consciously taking action with them. Certainly as the participant moves, the sensors report that move and update the display appropriately, but it is not a conscious action on the part of the participant to engage with a sensor actively.

Some of the most common sensors that gather user input would include buttons, touchscreens, keyboards, and other typical user interface devices. Most portable devices such as smartphones and tablets have a set of sensors in the form of buttons and keyboards (whether real or virtual) that an AR application designer can make use of to provide the participant with a way to directly interact with and control an application. These sensors are useful when a participant is initiating the experience and at any point where the participant is allowed to make a conscious decision about how to proceed with the experience. They are also useful in other ways that the participant might use—for tasks such as pointing to a place on a map on a touchscreen or enlarging the view on their tablet (Figure 2.19).

Note that cameras can be used as a sensor to gather user input if a gesture recognition system is provided. In this case, the camera tracks the participant's hands or fingers and interprets their movements as a direct input from the user.

Of course, in AR, the entire world can be a user interface. Another example of using a camera as a sensor to detect use input is to create "virtual buttons" in the environment. In this way, anything can be used as a "device" to provide input from the participant. For example, you could paint buttons on the real world that are used by the AR application in exactly the same way they would be used if they were physical buttons. In this case, the camera and computer vision would be used to gather user input. There is no need to limit this idea to buttons, either. One could create virtual buttons, sliders, dials, or anything you can dream up (Figure 2.20).

FIGURE 2.18
Many sensors are available in very small sizes. This chemical sensor from NASA was designed for cell phones. *Image courtesy of NASA.*

Processor

At the heart of any augmented reality system is a processor that coordinates and analyzes sensor inputs, stores and retrieves data, carries out the tasks of the AR application program, and generates the appropriate signals to display. In other words, every augmented reality system includes a computer of some sort. Computing systems for augmented reality can range in complexity from simple handheld devices such as smartphones and tablets to laptops, desktop computers, and workstation class machines all the way through powerful distributed systems. In some cases, a handheld computer is in communication with a powerful server that might be located at a distance.

In all cases, the computer must have enough computational ability to do the tasks it needs to do in *real time*. By real time I mean that every time any action is made, such as a button press or a change in orientation of a handheld device or change in point of view, the system must respond with an updated

FIGURE 2.19
This photo shows a person pressing a virtual "button" on a smart tablet. *Photo courtesy of Alan B. Craig.*

FIGURE 2.20
This is an example of using "virtual" buttons. In this application from Qualcomm, the application participant can change the color of an object by "pressing" the button of the color that she would like the object to be. The camera and vision system determine what color is not visible on the marker and make the object (the teapot) that color. In the first image the participant is covering the yellow "button" (in the world), and in the next image she is covering the red "button." *Photos courtesy of Michael Simeone.*

display of the combination of the physical world and the virtual world with no apparent lags or hesitation. In other words, the scene must be updated smoothly and at a rate that the participant in the experience perceives as a constant stream of information. To draw an analogy, a typical movie in the cinema is played at a rate of 24 frames per second, which is a sufficient frame rate for the viewer to perceive as smooth motion. If the frame rate were reduced to about 10 frames per second, the viewer would perceive the movie as a series of individual pictures rather than as a single motion picture. AR applications must sustain a frame rate of at least 15—preferably more— frames per second for the participant to perceive the display as continuous. Displays that are simulating the feel of a solid object must be updated about 1000 times per second or else the object will feel "mushy." In augmented reality it is particularly important that the rate of display of the virtual enti- ties matches or is close to the rate that the physical world is displayed or the participant will perceive the virtual world lagging the physical world. In cases where the physical world is mediated by the computer, the displays can be synchronized, but in cases where the physical world is perceived directly, any lag in the creation and display of the virtual components becomes obvious.

Display

A display is the component that causes an appropriate signal to impinge on a participant's senses. For example, a visual display shows visual imagery to the participant. One example of a visual display is a computer monitor. An

audio display causes the sounds made by the system to be audible to the participant. An example of an audio display would be headphones or a loudspeaker. A wide variety of displays are available for presenting signals to the participant, and numerous different technologies can be used to implement those displays. Just a note about the terminology of the word *display*—the term can mean the device that actually presents the signals to the participant, but it can also refer to the signals that are being displayed. For example, a computer monitor can be referred to as a display, but if that display is showing a scene of a tree and a house, the tree and house can also be referred to as a display. So, in this case, the scene is a display and that scene is presented by a display. In general, in this book the term refers to the device that is presenting the signals, but, in other cases, can refer to the information that is being displayed. I will be careful to point out if I am using the term to refer to the display of information.

Categories of Displays

Displays can be categorized in numerous ways. Displays are covered in detail in Chapter 3. Broadly, displays can be categorized as to what sense they provide stimulation. The most common displays are for visual signals and audio signals, but there are also displays for olfactory signals (smell), gustation (taste), and haptics (touch).

Another way displays can be categorized is by whether they are attached to the participant in some way or are not attached in any way to the participant. For example, in the realm of visual displays, a computer monitor is not connected directly to the participant. However, a head-mounted display is worn on the head in the form of a helmet or glasses. The smartphone and smart tablet each provide a visual display that is held in the hand.

CONCEPTS RELATED TO AUGMENTED REALITY

A number of concepts are important to study in order to understand augmented reality. There are books and other publications that focus on each of these topics specifically in great depth and detail. I provide a very basic overview of each of these concepts in this book and encourage the reader to study any of these topics that are of interest for their particular applications of augmented reality in greater detail.

Computer Graphics

In short, computer graphics are visual images created by a computer. Because many augmented reality applications make use of visual imagery overlaid on the real world, it is important to understand where this imagery comes from. This book is not intended to be a primer on computer graphics, but rather to

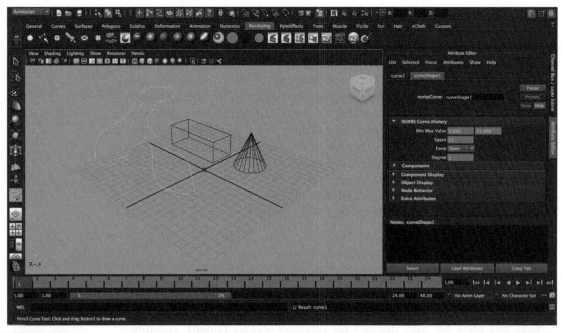

FIGURE 2.21

Computer graphics programs such as Maya from Autodesk can be used to create three-dimensional computer graphics objects. It is easy to make simple shapes and free-form drawings. You can attach material properties, control lighting, and then render an image. These computer graphics objects are suitable for many augmented reality applications. *Screenshot courtesy of Alan B. Craig.*

provide a brief overview of some of the main concepts as they pertain directly to augmented reality.

In general, graphical objects are described mathematically. That is, there is some set of numbers or mathematical expressions that describe the visual graphical element that will be displayed. Most commonly in augmented reality, the objects are described as 3D objects that are then rendered with respect to the chosen point of view, lighting, material properties, and so on to generate a 2D image that will drive the visual display. It is important to understand exactly what is meant by "three dimensional" and "two dimensional." That concept is covered later in this chapter.

There are many different approaches, methods, and techniques in the field of computer graphics, and many of them can be applied in augmented reality systems. At the current time, the most prevalent method is to describe the object as a mesh of polygons in a three-dimensional coordinate system. The polygonal mesh can be created in a number of different ways. One method is for a computer graphics artist to create the mesh by hand by plotting points as an artist. Instead of specifying every vertex and polygon, there are computer graphics modeling programs that support the artist with powerful tools (Figure 2.21).

One example tool that can be used is revolving a profile curve around an axis to create a surface of revolution (Figure 2.22).

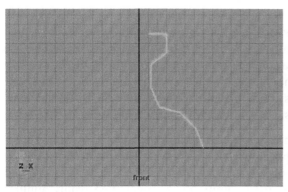 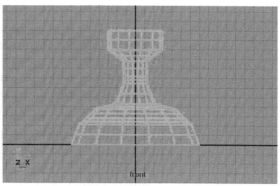

FIGURE 2.22

In the first of this pair of images, the computer graphics artist has drawn a curve that will be rotated about the *Y* axis. The second picture shows the mesh resulting from that rotation. This surface is referred to as a surface of rotation. *Images courtesy of David Bock.*

FIGURE 2.23

This example of a desktop 3D scanner (the Cyberware M-15) shows the actual 3D object in place on the scanner and the resultant 3D computer graphics model on the screen on the right. *Photo courtesy of Nicholas Homer, Idaho Museum of Natural History.*

Another method for creating a polygonal mesh is by scanning the physical world object that you want to represent with a three-dimensional scanner (Figure 2.23). The other common method is to have a computer program generate the mesh automatically, according to some criteria. By generating the mesh programmatically, the object can vary its form according to different parameters. This is not to say that objects created by an artist or from a 3D scan cannot be altered by different parameters, but the method does offer the ability to create objects that are purely algorithmically derived. An example of an object that could be created programmatically based on parameters in the environment is an *isosurface*. An isosurface is a representation of a surface that depicts a surface of constant value within a three-dimensional set of data. So if one wanted to represent a surface of constant temperature, one could create an isosurface with that temperature specified as a threshold value. Then, one would know that all values inside that surface are below the threshold value and all values outside that surface are above that threshold value, or vice versa.

In addition to the mesh, the computer graphics object also has surface properties that describe the appearance of the object. The properties describe numerous attributes of the object, such as color, reflection characteristics, and surface texture. A technique used commonly in augmented reality applications is *texture mapping*. With texture mapping, a two-dimensional graphical image (that can be created programmatically or even as an image taken by a digital camera) can be applied to the mesh and mapped to surface properties. This technique can be used to make photorealistic objects and can also be used to reduce the polygonal complexity of objects in certain cases. For an extreme example, consider modeling a house as a simple cube with photographs of the view of that house from different perspectives pasted on the cube. This is an extreme example that would not likely be satisfactory in practice, but it conveys the idea of using images on polygons as a way of communicating more information than is carried directly in the geometry of the polygonal mesh.

In addition to computer graphics objects, there are a couple more important parts of a computer graphics scene. One is the concept of lights. One can place virtual "lights" in the scene that will be incorporated into the rendering of the final image. The lighting can affect the colors, shadows, and other aspects in the computer graphics scene in the same manner as they do in the physical world with physical objects or can be used in very unnatural ways to create "impossible," although compelling, visuals not present in the natural world. Another concept within the area of computer graphics is the computer graphics "camera." This virtual camera is used to determine the point of view used to create the final image. In much the same way as photographers in the physical world can choose their point of view by how they place their camera, in the computer graphics world, the placement and characteristics of the "camera" determine the final image that will be created. Once the camera is placed, information about the scene, including objects, lighting, and materials, is passed to a program to render the scene into a 2D image that is then displayed. This process is repeated over time with changes in perspective by moving the camera, or changes in the objects that occur over time, and new images are created and displayed in succession leading to an animation of the computer graphics scene. In AR systems, the computer graphics camera is usually placed in exact registration with the camera that is being used as a sensor in the augmented reality application. In this way, the image that is rendered will correspond to the image that should be seen by the AR system.

If you desire to create stereoscopic imagery (more on this later in this chapter and in Chapter 3), the rendering system computes a different image for each of the participant's eyes. The image computed for each eye is created specifically for the perspective that should be displayed based on the location of that eye. When the image pair is displayed—with the left eye image being shown to the participant's left eye and the right eye image shown to the participant's right eye—the participant will perceive a stereoscopic image that appears three dimensional.

Although geometric, polygonal-based computer graphics are by far the most commonly used in AR systems, other methods and techniques can be used. For example, some of these include nonuniform rational B splines (NURBS), constructive solid geometry (CSG), volume rendering (ray casting and ray tracing), and particle rendering. There are a plethora of texts and web materials that discuss computer graphics in far more detail than can be done in this book.

Dimensionality

In the world of computer graphics and augmented reality, the idea of dimensionality is not as clear-cut as one might expect. The physical world is three dimensional. Virtual worlds can exist in one, two, three, or more dimensions. However, that world can also be displayed in different dimensions. Stepping back from augmented reality for a moment, consider a movie. The world that the movie is created in is the physical world (I will ignore computer graphics special effects in the movies for now), which is three dimensional. However, movies are typically displayed on a two-dimensional movie screen. Thus, the virtual world of the movie is three dimensional, but the display of that world is two dimensional. How then do we perceive the world of the movie as being somewhat three dimensional? There are a variety of *depth cues* that we as humans use to discern the three dimensionality of the physical (and also virtual) world. Indeed, each of our eyes has a two-dimensional retina on which images of the three-dimensional world are sensed. Depth cues are discussed later in this chapter. What, though, about movies that are billed as being "3D"? What is different about them? Why do we perceive them as more three dimensional than regular movies? The answer to that is that they exploit a depth cue that is not used in traditional movies. *Stereopsis* is one of the depth cues that takes into account that we have two eyes that can be used to discern the three-dimensional nature of the world. Stereopsis is covered in depth in the section on depth cues. Don't forget, however, that even 3D movies are displayed on a two-dimensional screen surface (Figures 2.24 and 2.25).

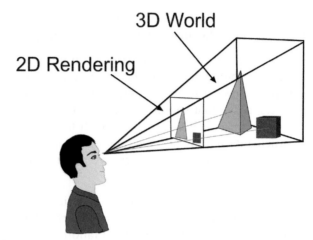

FIGURE 2.24

This diagram illustrates very simply how the computer renders the image that will be displayed to a participant's eye. The 2D rendering plate in the diagram represents the matrix of pixels that will be displayed. Note that the image is created based on the point of view that the participant has with respect to the 3D world. If the participant moves, a new rendering must be made in real time to incorporate that change in view. If the display is stereoscopic, an image must be made for the point of view of each of the participant's eyes. *Diagram courtesy of Beverly Carver.*

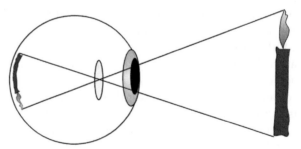

FIGURE 2.25

In this very simple diagram of the eye, light rays enter through the pupil, pass through the lens, and are then sensed on the retina (rear) of the eyeball. Note that the image on the retina is two dimensional, although curved. Each of our eyes actually senses only a two-dimensional image. Consequently, the brain must interpret depth cues from one or both of the eyes' two-dimensional images. *Diagram courtesy of Beverly Carver.*

Returning to the discussion of augmented reality, the real world and the computer graphics are combined and displayed on a two-dimensional display. The physical world is three dimensional. The virtual world can be any dimensionality. Objects in the virtual world can be any number of dimensions. The augmented reality scene is rendered on a two-dimensional display using a variety of depth cues to help the participant understand the world as it is presented via an augmented reality interface.

Recall that augmented reality is not limited to visual elements. The second most common sense used in augmented reality applications is hearing. Sounds can exist in one, two, three, or more dimensions and can be displayed in one, two, or three dimensions. Sounds also have depth cues that help us in discerning where a sound is emanating from. They are covered in the section on depth cues.

Depth Cues

Depth cues are information used to determine how far away things are from us and how we understand the three-dimensional world we live in. Our perceptual systems are tuned to take cues from the environment and make sense of those cues to determine the relative locations of objects in the world. Depth cues are naturally available and interpreted in our interactions with the physical world, but can also be used to advantage in augmented reality applications. Artists, moviemakers, and others have introduced depth cues into their work (whether intentionally or as a side effect from observing the physical world) to help their audience understand the three dimensionality of the world they are representing with their artwork. AR application developers can do the same thing.

The following categorization of depth cues is taken from the book *Understanding Virtual Reality*. Additional detail on depth cuing is available there and in other works on computer graphics, art, perception, and other topics.

Visual Depth Cues

The first broad category of depth cues is the collection of cues used to understand the visual world in 3D. Artists have used these "tricks" for hundreds of years to help us understand the images they have drawn or painted. Photography automatically captures depth cues from the physical world. Computer graphics programs have built many depth cues into software so that the artist doesn't have to explicitly think about them. All they need to do is place their objects in a 3D digital world and certain depth cues are provided automatically because the software uses the laws of physics and the behavior of light when it is rendering an image from a 3D digital world into a 2D image for display.

Monoscopic Image Depth

Human beings typically have two eyes. The fact that each eye sees the world from a different perspective gives information about the three dimensionality of the world. Many depth cues, however, don't rely on having two eyes available and work as depth cues with even one eye. We refer to these kinds of depth cues as monoscopic depth cues.

Interposition. Interposition means that if something is in front of something else, the object in front occludes the object behind. So if one object blocks all or part of another object from view, our brain understands that the object that does the blocking from view is in front of the object that is blocked. Note that this cue is especially important, and especially difficult to implement in augmented reality, because it can be difficult for an augmentation to occlude a physical object from view, although it can be done. It can be easier in the other direction. If a real-world object should occlude a virtual object, the computer can draw only the part of the virtual object that is not occluded by the real-world object. However, in order for virtual objects to occlude real-world objects the system needs to determine which objects are in front of which other objects. This means the system needs to determine the depth that real-world objects are in the scene and then determine which way to do the occlusion.

Shading. Shadows that are cast as light is blocked by objects give us clues as to where those objects are in a three-dimensional world. Consequently, computing shadows can give participants valuable information about the scene they are viewing.

Size. The size that objects appear to be gives us clues as to their distance. If we see two objects that we know are the same size, we know that the one that appears smaller is farther in the background than the larger one. Likewise, we do carry a memory of the size of many objects and use that memory to aid us in determining the distance of an object compared to others based on that memory.

Linear perspective. Linear perspective operates on the basis that parallel lines converge to a vanishing point. For example, it becomes apparent that a road into the image looks like the edges of the road are getting closer together. Thus, if there is something along the side of the road where the road is narrower, you perceive that that object is farther back in the scene than something along the road where the road is (apparently) wider.

Surface texture gradient. Your vision is less able to discern detail farther away than it is up close—something that has a lot of detail will appear to have less detail the farther it is from you. For example, if you are looking at a field of pebbles, you can see the pebbles that are near to you whereas the pebbles in a distance tend to blur into each other. This gives you a clue of relative distance.

Height in the visual field. Something that appears higher in your visual field is farther from you than something lower in your visual field. In the real world, the horizon appears higher in your visual field than other objects unless those objects are in the air.

Atmospheric effects. If there are any impurities in the air, such as haze or fog, things in the distance will be less visible than things that are close to you. This helps discern the relative distance between an object and yourself.

Brightness. All other things being equal, something that is brighter will appear to be closer than something that is less bright.

Stereoscopic Image Depth (Stereopsis)

Stereopsis is the depth cue we get from seeing the same scene from two slightly different physical perspectives. Each eye sees a slightly different image than the other. Our mind analyzes those differences and uses them (in conjunction with other depth cues) to figure out the relative locations of different elements of the scene. The stereopsis cue is much stronger for objects that are close to the observer and relatively nonexistent for very distant objects. In order to exploit stereopsis in augmented reality systems you need the ability to deliver the two images to their respective eye. That is, you need to ensure that the image that is computed based on the perspective of the left eye is displayed to the left eye and the image that is computed based on the perspective of the right eye is displayed to the right eye. This can be accomplished numerous different ways and these ways are discussed in Chapter 3.

Motion

Motion cues. There is a very powerful depth cue that results from the relative motion of objects and the participant's body motion. Every time a person moves his or her head even slightly he or she sees the world from a slightly different perspective. This provides a strong cue of the relative distance to objects. The way this works is that there is a parallax that leads to closer objects appearing to move faster than more distant objects in the view. The altered perspective also changes many other depth cues in a way that supports the motion cue. These cues are all integrated with the participant body's own sense of proprioception to understand the relationship between his or her body and the objects. In order to exploit the motion cue from the participant moving their head, the system needs a way to determine the head's location and orientation continuously. This is accomplished most frequently in augmented reality with computer vision techniques, but there are many ways to achieve this. Alternative methods are discussed in Chapter 3.

Motion cues can also exist even when the participant is not moving. For example, if you are looking at two roads that cross your field of vision, cars will appear to be moving faster on the road that is closer to you than the road that is farther away.

Physiological

There are two primary physiological depth cues based on the changes a body undergoes when observing objects at different distances.

Accommodation. When you look at an object at a specific distance, your eyes focus on that object. It requires a muscular change to focus on objects at different distances. This is not unlike the fact that you need to adjust the focus on a camera lens for objects at different distances. Your body senses these changes and helps you determine the relative distance you are from different objects by these tiny muscular changes.

Convergence. When you look at objects at different distances, your two eyes alter their angle relative to each other. That is, they rotate inward for closer objects. For example, when you look at something very close, your eyes are aimed more toward each other than when you are looking at objects farther away. This provides information to your brain regarding the distance of the object you are looking at.

Auditory Depth Cues

Auditory depth cues are somewhat analogous to visual depth cues in that there are characteristics of sounds that give us hints as to where the sounds are coming from. A more general term for auditory depth cues is *sound localization*. Sound localization is what we do to determine where the source of a sound is compared to where our body is. Some auditory depth cues work with only one ear engaged (monaural), and others work with both ears engaged (binaural).

Interaurel delay. Our two ears are located in different places. Thus it takes sound a different amount of time to reach each of our ears. This timing difference gives us clues as to the direction and depth that a sound is coming from.

Amplitude. Typically, if all other factors are the same, a louder signal will be perceived as being closer than a softer signal. Additionally, the difference in loudness of a sound in each of our ears gives information about the direction of a sound.

Echoes and reverberation. Echoes and reverberation give us information about the environment that a sound is in. A sound that is very close to us has a less pronounced reverberation associated with it because we primarily hear the direct sound. A more distant sound has the opportunity to be reflected off of many surfaces. The combination of those reflected sounds provides information about the distance of the sound, and also information about the environment. For example, a small room sounds different than a large hall, which sounds different than wide-open spaces. We can simulate echoes and reverberation with signal processing. We can also simulate the sonic environment of different types of spaces.

Filtering. Another clue about the distance of a sound is that as sound travels over surfaces such as the ground or grass, the high-frequency components of the sound are diminished more than the low-frequency components of the sound. Thus, as you get closer to a sound source it generally sounds brighter.

An example of this differential filtering is that you can hear the drums and lower-frequency components of a marching band as it approaches you before you begin to hear the higher-frequency instruments.

Our own bodies filter sounds and partially occlude sounds from different directions. This provides additional information to our perception of location and distance of sounds.

Our outer ear, or *pinnae*, has numerous folds in it. Sounds entering the outer ear from different directions pass through different places in the folds and are thus filtered differently from each other. This information provides a great deal of information about the location of a sound in three dimensions. Additionally, moving our head slightly changes which folds the sounds pass through. The effects of sounds coming from different directions through the pinnae can be simulated by using *head-related transfer functions* (HRTFs). HRTFs can be measured for a specific pair of ears by inserting a microphone inside each ear. Then, sounds of different frequencies can be played from multiple locations and the resultant recordings can be analyzed to determine the filtering that took place for each frequency from each direction. Then, using the correct HRTF for the desired scenario of sound and direction, one can use the derived functions to filter other sounds to make them appear to come from the direction specified by the HRTF.

The act of causing a sound to seem to come from a specific location is called *spatialization*. The process by which a listener figures out the direction the sound is coming from is called *localization*. Note that in some scenarios it is necessary to track the listener's head position in order to process sounds so that they appear to come from a specific place no matter how the listener moves about or turns his head.

Registration and Latency

Registration and latency both refer to proper alignment of the virtual world with the physical world. Although registration can refer to temporal registration, it is used primarily in reference to the geographic (spatial) registration of the system. Latency is directly related to temporal registration.

Registration

Recall that registration is a part of the definition of augmented reality as addressed in this book. Registration is one of the critical, yet challenging aspects of augmented reality currently. In brief, registration refers to how accurately the virtual world aligns spatially with the physical world. For example, if a goal in an augmented reality application is to display a pair of (virtual) sunglasses on my (real) face, are the sunglasses placed correctly on my face, resting on the bridge of my nose, or do the sunglasses appear to be off to one side, too high, too low, or perhaps floating in front of my face or even appear to be inside my head? Improper registration can ruin the effect of augmented reality if the goal of the AR application is a seamless melding of the real world and the virtual world.

Correct registration depends on a number of different variables. One is the accuracy of your tracking system. Registration can only be as accurate as the system is able to determine the positions of all the different aspects of the system at any moment in time, including the physical world, the virtual world, and the participant(s), as well as any technology involved in the application. Another thing that leads to accurate registration is the successful resolution of all the coordinate systems that are in play at any given moment. For example, each object has its own coordinate system. There is a real-world coordinate system, a virtual world coordinate system, and a coordinate system for any interaction devices and participants.

The symptoms of improper registration include virtual objects not being in proper alignment with the real world, perhaps mislocated or floating above or below where they should be. Additionally, sometimes it can appear as though the objects are "swimming" or not affixed solidly where they belong.

Latency

Latency is the amount of time some aspect of the virtual world lags behind when it should occur ideally. As such, it can be thought of as one aspect of temporal registration. Latency can occur from a variety of sources. Every action pertaining to the virtual world requires some amount of time to occur. For example, it takes time to compute what should be displayed. It takes time for those images to make it to the display and actually appear. It takes time for the system to ascertain its position in the world. The combination of all these delays contributes to the overall lag, or latency, in the system.

In some applications, latency may not matter greatly to the overall goal of the augmented reality system, but latency is a critical issue in others. Latency is always present in any system that does any processing or communication. Virtual reality systems also suffer from latency, but it is less critical in many VR systems than it is in AR systems. This is because in VR systems, all information is mediated such that all activities can be synchronized together. That is, there is an overall latency, but all activities take place simultaneously. In AR systems, however, there is not the option of synchronizing latency with the real world because there is no latency in the real world. For example, if I am looking at a visual scene that integrates virtual objects with real-world objects and I turn my head, there is no lag or latency in my view of the real world, but there is latency in the virtual world, so if latency is sufficient I see the virtual world "catch up" with the real world. By using technology such as video see-through head-mounted displays, the view of the real world is mediated, making it possible to introduce latency in the display of the real world to match that of the virtual world. This technique allows the virtual world and real world to appear in synchrony, albeit with an overall delay compared to the unmediated real world. Of course, as a participant in the experience, my own body's sense of proprioception informs me that there is an overall delay. That is, if I turn my head and see the virtual world and real world update together, I can still sense that the whole display lagged behind my bodily motion.

There is no way to eliminate latency in AR systems. The critical question is whether the lag in the system is sufficient to render the AR system useless for your particular application. In many cases, a reasonable amount of latency is perfectly acceptable. If not, I would direct the reader to other resources that focus specifically on tuning applications for maximum performance and for using predictive techniques that allow the system to anticipate what you are *likely* to do next so it can begin responding before the action has even been taken.

INGREDIENTS OF AN AUGMENTED REALITY EXPERIENCE

Putting everything together it becomes clear that there are several ingredients to any AR experience. These ingredients are explored throughout the book, but it is prudent to identify the key ingredients right up front. In a high-level view, every augmented reality application consists of at least the following ingredients:

1. Augmented reality application
2. Content
3. Interaction
4. Technology
5. The physical world
6. Participant(s)

Let us take a brief look at these ingredients one at a time.

Augmented Reality Application

The AR application is the computer program that orchestrates and controls different aspects of the augmented reality experience. An example of a very simple AR application is a simple AR browser. An AR browser might do something as simple as making it appear that a specific 3D object is placed on a specific fiducial marker placed in the real world.

It is important to draw a distinction between the AR application and the *content* (see later) used within the application. When this distinction is executed skillfully, the same AR application can be used in many different contexts. For example, an AR application that places simulated sculptures in a real-world space for the purpose of teaching an art appreciation course could be repurposed by using different content and using it to train soldiers regarding the kinds of landmarks they need to locate when they are deployed to a place they have not yet experienced in the real world.

The AR application also interacts with the various sensors, devices, and displays used in the experience. In actual practice, many of these lower level tasks are handled in AR libraries that are used by many different AR applications.

Content
Content is key to any AR application. Chapter 5 is dedicated to content, which consists of all aspects of an augmented reality application that do not fall into any of the other ingredient categories. Content includes all objects, ideas, stories, sensory stimuli, and "laws of nature" for the experience. The laws of nature govern what actions take place during the experience. This may include computational simulations, game rules, or any other aspects of the content that are under computer control.

Interaction
By definition, every augmented reality experience must be interactive in one way or another. One of the most typical ways the world is interactive is that it allows the participant to view/perceive the world from different physical points of view. Beyond this basic interaction, participants may interact with the experience by pressing buttons, by making physical gestures, by speaking commands, or by any number of different actions. Interaction in AR is covered in Chapter 6.

Technology
Every AR experience does involve technology. Some require much more sophisticated technology than others, but all have a base level of technology. At a minimum, an AR experience requires some sort of sensor to gather information about the real world, some form of computation to integrate the virtual elements of the experience with the real world, and some mechanism to display the virtual elements of the experience.

The Physical World
Every AR experience takes place in the physical world. By definition, the physical world is a key part of the AR experience. The physical world may or may not be an exact place (although it can be), but in some cases a generic space is used to represent the physical world at large. That is, in some cases the experience must take place where the experience indicates. For example, if an AR experience is to decorate the (real) Eiffel Tower like a Christmas tree, then you must be near the Eiffel Tower. In other cases, the experience

can take place virtually anywhere. One could conceive of an application in which one decorates a (virtual) Eiffel Tower where the (virtual) Eiffel Tower is in a football field in the United States instead of in France. In still others the experience takes place someplace other than the place represented by the experience. For example, a school classroom could be used as the site of an AR experience that emulates an archeological dig at a specific and/or nonexistent archeological site.

Participant(s)

All of the magic of an AR experience takes place in the mind of one or more participants. Indeed, the role of AR technology is to provide artificial stimuli to cause the participant(s) to believe that something is occurring that really is not. Things that don't really exist in the physical realm have characteristics that cause them to be perceived as though they do. The participant(s) has an active role in what takes place in the AR experience. All of their motions, actions, and activities affect how the system responds. When there are multiple human participants, the stakes are even higher in terms of complexity of interaction. Of course, there might be participants that other participants believe are real but are actually digital creatures—mere augmentations to the physical world. They're not real. Or are they?

AUGMENTED REALITY EXPERIENCE

This book shows a number of examples of AR applications throughout its pages. Some of the applications are available so that you can try them yourself. This book has a companion website, which contains information and instructions about which examples you can try and how to do them. In some cases, there will be software for you to download from the companion site, whereas in others there will be pointers to where you can obtain software and examples. In still others, it might be a video example rather than an application for you to try yourself.

For further instructions regarding the examples in this book and others, see http://booksite.elsevier.com/Craig-UAR/.

SUMMARY

This chapter took a look at how augmented reality systems work to create an augmented reality experience for participants. It addressed the ideas of different sensors to gather input from the physical world, basic processing of information, and how to display information to the participant(s) in the real world.

The next chapter looks at the hardware aspects of these issues in much more depth.

CHAPTER 3

Augmented Reality Hardware

INTRODUCTION

As much as we would like for augmented reality (AR) systems to be "fully virtual," such a hope is not a reality *yet*. Augmented reality systems currently require both hardware and software to implement a compelling AR experience. The software tells the system what to do, and the hardware is the equipment that does it. Software is covered in Chapter 4. This chapter addresses the different hardware components required to support an AR application, as well as different technologies that can be used to provide those functions. In many cases, several different types of technologies can be used to implement those functions. AR systems are truly not "one size fits all." In many cases, an AR developer has a choice between technologies. This chapter explores the advantages and disadvantages of different implementation schemes, especially as they vary for different types of applications. Multiple trade-offs can be made between many different aspects of different types of hardware. For example, cost is often a trade-off for fidelity. That is, the better you need the final results to be in terms of specifications, the more that solution is likely to cost. In general, other aspects of hardware choices are subject to trade-offs. Different types of applications need to optimize for different capabilities and thus the trade-off choices a designer makes will likely be different from developer to developer and application to application. For some augmented reality applications, generality is the most important characteristic. This chapter addresses many aspects of hardware, as well as the trade-offs and decisions that must be made.

It is important to note that the capabilities of these types of hardware are changing rapidly. The concepts in this chapter will remain reasonably constant, but the good news is that there is a constant progression toward better, faster, and less expensive hardware that works to the AR application developer's advantage. For example, if a developer wishes to do something that requires a somewhat faster processor than is currently available, it is reasonable to assume that faster processors will be available in the future.

69

MAJOR HARDWARE COMPONENTS FOR AUGMENTED REALITY SYSTEMS

As Chapter 2 explained, all AR systems have at least three basic hardware components. In review, these three components include:

1. Sensors
2. Processors
3. Displays

There are many different forms that each of those three elements can take. Each of these elements also carries out different roles within different applications. In each section that follows, the different roles that the element carries, and the different means for implementing those roles, are examined.

Finally, these elements must be combined to form a cohesive AR *system*.

Sensors

As discussed in Chapter 2, sensors acquire information about the real world and communicate that information to the AR application.

Roles of Sensors

Sensors provide information about the real world to the AR application for a variety of purposes. One of the main purposes is to provide information about the location and orientation of the participant (or a surrogate for the participant, such as a handheld device like a smartphone) to the AR application. Other roles of sensors include providing information such as temperature, pH, lightness/darkness, or any other types of information about the environment to the AR application.

Tracking

In general, the primary function of sensors is to provide information about the real world to enable the application to determine the location and orientation of different things in the real world. For example, through the use of sensors, the application can determine where the participant is and his or her pose in the real world.

Optical Tracking Although there are many ways to do tracking in AR applications, by far the most commonly used technique, especially for indoor applications [see later for common methods for outdoor applications such as the global positioning system (GPS) and compass systems], is through computer vision, which is an example of one way to do optical tracking. The specific sensor used for optical tracking is a *camera*. The camera gathers light through a lens and provides a signal that represents an image of what the camera "sees." That image is then analyzed to determine the desired tracking information.

FIGURE 3.1

Most smartphones come equipped with a variety of sensors, including a camera. This smartphone contains a small, yet high-quality camera. *Photo courtesy of Michael Simeone.*

Just as there are many varieties of cameras used for taking photographs and videos, there are a plethora of cameras used for optical tracking in AR systems. The most common cameras used in AR systems are web cameras (webcams), smartphone and smart tablet cameras, and special-purpose cameras (Figure 3.1).

Note that optical tracking systems can be implemented by placing cameras in the environment and having them "watch" the entities being tracked or attaching them to the tracked entities and "watching" the environment. Some applications are more suited to the first case, whereas others are more amenable to the second technique (Figure 3.4).

Although many people are most familiar with cameras that operate in the visible light range, it is also possible, and sometimes desirable, to use cameras that operate in other frequency ranges, such as infrared or ultraviolet (Figures 3.2–3.3).

The Nintendo Wii system uses optical tracking as part of its technology. There are LEDs in the Wii sensor bar and infrared detectors in the Wii remote. This system, in conjunction with accelerometers in the Wii remote, provides information to the game system about the activities of the participant (Figure 3.5).

Optical tracking is also used for motion capture systems used to capture the performance of complex motions of multiple entities. This technique is typically used to achieve realistic motions for animated characters, but the same idea can be used for tracking multiple entities in an AR application. Typically, multiple cameras are placed in an environment and the character or objects

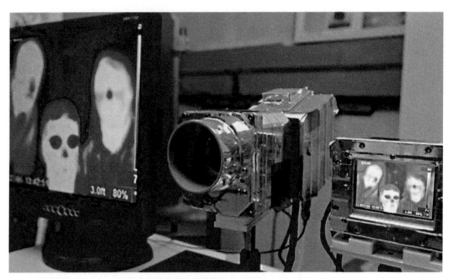

FIGURE 3.2
This infrared camera developed by NASA "sees" light in a different frequency range than conventional cameras. This enables the camera to detect things in the dark or that are otherwise not visible to cameras that work in the visible spectrum. *Photo courtesy of NASA.*

FIGURE 3.3
This small infrared camera can be used as a tracking sensor in AR systems. Note that there are LEDs surrounding the camera to bathe the scene with infrared light. *Photo courtesy of Liz Wuerffel.*

FIGURE 3.4

This pair of diagrams illustrates the difference between having sensors—in this case, cameras—in the environment watching what is happening in the environment and watching the participant(s) vs having a sensor(s) on the participant that watches the environment from the perspective of the participant. In the first of this pair of diagrams, there is a single sensor on the participant's head. There could be multiple cameras on the participant. In the second, there are multiple cameras in the environment, although there could, in some cases, be only one. There are advantages and disadvantages between having the sensors in the environment vs on the participant. In some cases, there is no choice. It may not be possible to place sensors in the environment, in that case—they must be connected in some way with the participant. However, it is often undesirable to force the participant to wear or carry any devices. In some cases, such as mobile augmented reality applications on smartphones, the participant might be carrying the sensor(s) anyway. *Diagram courtesy of Beverly Carver.*

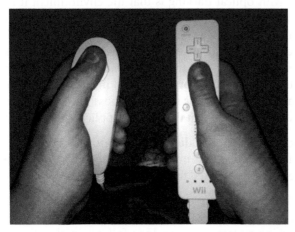

FIGURE 3.5

The Wii remote uses both optical tracking and an accelerometer to control the Nintendo Wii. *Photo courtesy of Holly McClain.*

being tracked are adorned with markers or other objects that are easy for the computer vision algorithms to identify. These might be spots, balls made of ret-roreflective material, or LEDs that provide a bright spots that are easy to follow.

Optical Tracking Advantages One advantage that optical tracking has over other types of tracking is that it can be done without requiring wires or any-thing else to be attached to the object being tracked. There is no need to have a physical connection between the object being tracked and the real world. Optical tracking also allows numerous entities to be tracked simultaneously.

Small, relatively high-quality cameras that provide a digital signal have become ubiquitous and thus are available very inexpensively. Additionally, cameras are already available in many devices used for augmented reality applications, such as smartphones. Optical tracking is inexpensive and, in most cases, doesn't require any alterations to the real world other than, in some cases, adding some markers to the world for the system to watch.

Optical Tracking Disadvantages One key disadvantage to optical track-ing is that it requires enough ambient light to "see" the real world in enough detail to provide suitable images to analyze by the computer vision software. Another disadvantage is that there needs to be a clear "line of sight" between the camera and the real world and the entities being tracked. Note that if there are multiple objects being tracked that are in motion, if one occludes the other from view of the tracker it can create problems tracking them indi-vidually. In some cases, cameras that operate outside the visible light spec-trum can be used to advantage in applications that require optical tracking in low-light environments.

Another issue with optical tracking is that the environment it is used in must provide information suitable for tracking. That is, if the environment is com-pletely the same color with no further information available, the system will not have adequate information available to determine anything about the loca-tion and orientation of anything in that environment. In situations that allow for them, fiducial symbols can be introduced in the environment to overcome this shortcoming. Of course, it is not always possible or desirable to place fidu-cial symbols in the environment that the AR application will be in.

Optical tracking systems introduce latency into the system. It takes time to acquire an image, deliver that image to the processor, and then analyze that image to determine the desired information.

Acoustical Tracking In much the same manner that cameras can be used as sensors in optical tracking systems, *microphones* can be used as sensors in acoustical tracking systems. The analogy follows in that the microphone(s) can be attached to the object being tracked or can be placed in the envi-ronment. With acoustical tracking systems, there needs to be a source of

FIGURE 3.6
An ultrasonic sensor can be used to do acoustical tracking in an AR system. This photo pair shows both the front and the back of the sensor. *Photos courtesy of Liz Wuerffel.*

acoustical information to be sensed by the microphones. Generally, *ultrasound* is used. Ultrasound is sound that is higher in frequency than the human hearing system can perceive. In general, ultrasonic tracking systems work by having the object being tracked emit sound, and an array of microphones in the environment to capture that sound. Based on the timing and amplitude of sound sensed in each microphone, you can compute the location of the source of the sound. Different objects can emit different frequencies of sound in order to track multiple objects in the same space. Conversely, objects can be tracked by having microphones attached to the objects and sound sources in the environment. In this case, however, the objects being tracked would need to be connected to the computing system in order to report the signals their microphones are sensing (Figure 3.6).

Acoustical Tracking Advantage Acoustical tracking systems have the advantage of not being affected by lighting conditions. They can function in the dark, as well as in bright sunlight.

Acoustical Tracking Disadvantages Acoustical tracking systems cannot be used in environments that are noisy with audio signals in the same frequency range that the system uses. Additionally, each object to be tracked must have a sound source attached to it. This means it can only be used in environments in which it is known a priori what objects will be tracked, and also that it is feasible to equip those objects with a sound source. Acoustical tracking systems can also have limited range.

Electromagnetic Tracking Another alternative to optical tracking is *electromagnetic* tracking. Because electromagnetic tracking systems are often utilized in virtual reality systems, they are well understood by those in that community, and there is software that is readily available to use such systems.

Electromagnetic tracking systems are able to track in six degrees of freedom. The most common way they are implemented is that there is a transmitter with three orthogonal antennas. There is a corresponding receiver attached to the entity you wish to track that also has three orthogonal antennas. The sensor is the receiving unit.

The transmitter emits a signal, sequentially through each of its antennas. The signal acquired by each of the antennas is then analyzed, and the level of signal reported by each antenna can be used to compute the location and orientation of the receiver (Figure 3.7).

FIGURE 3.7
This is the transmitting unit of an electromagnetic tracking system. The transmitter is in a fixed position, and the receiving units (small objects about the size of a die) are attached to the object being tracked. There are different sizes of transmitting units. This one serves a radius of about 12 feet. *Photo courtesy of Hank Kaczmarski.*

Electromagnetic Tracking Advantages Electromagnetic tracking systems can be very precise and accurate. They are not dependent on ambient light levels and, as such, can be used in completely dark environments, very bright environments, or anything in between.

Electromagnetic Tracking Disadvantages Electromagnetic tracking systems are sensitive to metal in the environment that they are in. Consequently, they must be calibrated and the effects of metal in the environment must be calibrated out of the system.

Electromagnetic tracking systems are limited in range. Although it is possible to use multiple transmitters to increase the range (by placing the transmitters throughout the environment), there are limits to the usable range. In general, the receivers need to be within a few meters of the nearest transmitter.

Electromagnetic tracking systems are costly. Because there is a limited set of customers for them, electromagnetic tracking systems can't achieve the level of mass production that cameras have.

Lower cost electromagnetic trackers couple the receiving sensors (with the antennas) to a larger receiver by a wire. This means that each entity being tracked is tethered to the receiver, which can be cumbersome. This disadvantage can be overcome by using a wireless system to communicate with the receiver, but then there needs to be a (potentially) bulky battery pack with each sensor.

Mechanical Tracking Mechanical tracking operates by attaching linkages to the object you wish to track. Those linkages have sensors at each of the joints that report the angle between the linkages. Often this is done by placing a variable resistor (potentiometer) at the joint and reading the voltage there. As the angle of the linkage changes, the amount of resistance in the potentiometer changes and a corresponding change in voltage (that you can measure) occurs. The voltage can then be used to determine the angle between linkages. This information, in combination with the angles between all other linkages in the system, can be used to compute the location and pose of the object (Figure 3.8).

Mechanical Tracking Advantages Mechanical tracking is very fast and very precise. It is used to best advantage when the area the tracking is done in is very compact and the need for accurate tracking is high. One example of this scenario is with medical applications. Although force feedback is actually an attribute of augmented reality displays (instead of sensors), mechanical tracking provides a very convenient mechanism that can integrate force feedback with an AR application. Motors can be placed at each joint in the mechanical tracking system, and the motors can be driven by the application to provide different levels of force and "push back" from the system. Hence, for example,

FIGURE 3.8

This image shows how mechanical tracking can be done by measuring the angles between articulated joints. The primary use for this particular arm is for digitizing objects. It does this by measuring where the tip of the arm is and reporting that location for each point on an object that you touch with the tip. It can also be used to track any object by attaching the object to the tip of the arm. The scene in this photograph looks out of focus, but it really isn't. The reason it looks that way is because it is a stereoscopic scene in which you are actually seeing two images. One of the images is computed for the perspective of the participant's right eye, and the other image is computed for the perspective of the participant's left eye. The participant is wearing glasses that ensure each eye sees the correct image. In this case, though, the camera sees both images, which is why it looks "double" or "out of focus" to us. *Photo courtesy of Hank Kaczmarski.*

if you are using mechanical tracking in an AR surgical simulator, you can provide the appropriate forces to the participant that a doctor would feel when doing surgery on an actual body. The force feedback provides another level of "realness" to the participant using the AR surgical simulator.

Mechanical Tracking Disadvantages In many cases, it is simply not possible to use mechanical tracking because the required mechanical connections can't be used. For example, if you are using a smartphone in an open field, it is not likely that the necessary mechanics will be available at any given moment.

Mechanical tracking is visually obtrusive. It will only work well in applications where the mechanical components can be hidden from view. Mechanical tracking can also be quite costly compared to other technologies. Because of the need to be connected physically to the mechanical tracking system, it is typically of limited range.

Depth Sensors for Tracking So-called depth sensors can be used for tracking in augmented reality applications. The term *depth sensor* is used to cover a number of different technologies that can be used to provide information about how far away an object is from the sensor. The underlying technologies can be optical, acoustical (ultrasound), radar, etc. The result from a depth sensor is a measurement of how far an object is from the depth sensor. This information can be used in conjunction with other tracking technologies to provide information about the location of an object.

Depth Sensors for Tracking Advantages Depth sensors are relatively inexpensive. Depth sensors do not require anything to be attached to the objects being tracked. That is, there is no need to know ahead of time what objects need to be tracked.

Depth Sensors for Tracking Disadvantages Depth sensors only report, as their name indicates, depth information. They don't supply location or orientation information directly. Hence, for use as a tracking system, they must be used along with data from other types of sensors. They also don't report what object they are "seeing." They merely report the distance they are from whatever object is nearest to them.

Depth sensors are really only useful for relatively close things. Resolution and accuracy fall off quickly the farther you are from the object you are sensing. Depth sensors also require a line of sight and may not enable you to track multiple objects that occlude each other.

Multiple Sensors for Tracking Some tracking schemes require more than one type of sensor for tracking. Each sensor can contribute to the overall goal of tracking. For example, *accelerometers* can be used to obtain information about relative motion but don't provide any information about an exact location. Additionally, many tracking systems that use accelerometers as their basis have a problem with error propagation. That is, any errors, instead of being corrected, tend to become worse unless there is something in place to correct them. Because accelerometers are inexpensive, small, quick, and light, they are useful as tracking sensors as long as they are paired with additional sensors. As described earlier, the Wii system uses a combination of optical tracking and accelerometers.

The Xbox Kinect uses a combination of a depth sensor, optical tracking, and an array of microphones (acoustical tracking) to achieve a remarkable system that tracks the actions of a participant with no encumbering devices. That is, the participant is not required to wear, hold, or do anything in particular for the system to be able to determine their location and actions (Figure 3.9).

Multiple Sensors for Tracking Advantages The advantage of using multiple sensors for tracking is that you can use each sensor to its best advantage. Also, by combining sensors you can create a solution to meet the needs of your specific application. For example, the combination of sensors in the Kinect allows the participant to engage with the game system without requiring the participant to wear or hold anything special.

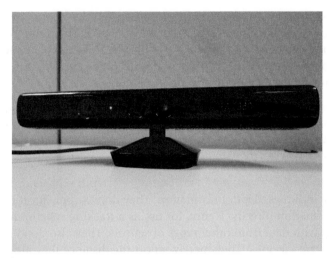

FIGURE 3.9
The Microsoft Kinect uses multiple sensors, including a depth sensor to track the participant. *Photo courtesy of Michael Simeone.*

Multiple Sensors for Tracking Disadvantages Using multiple sensors can become complicated when you need to integrate them all to provide a unified signal to report the information required by the system. Of course, using more than one sensor costs more than using a single sensor if everything else is equal.

Other Sensors for Tracking In addition to the sensors just described, other sensors are sometimes used as part of a tracking system. One of these is a *GPS receiver*. GPS provides a gross level of location information. Another sensor that can be used with tracking systems is a *compass*. A compass can be used to determine basic information about the orientation of the system. Further information about orientation can be discerned by using *gyroscopes*. Gyroscopes can determine data regarding relative orientation such as leaning, turning, and twisting (Figure 3.10).

Many sensors are becoming fairly ubiquitously available. As a point of reference, an iPhone 4 contains a multitouch screen, an accelerometer, a gyroscope, and a depth sensor (typically used to disable the touchscreen when the phone is placed near the ear). Additionally it contains a camera and a microphone. Hence, a typical smartphone provides a number of sensors that can be used for tracking or other purposes in augmented reality applications.

Other Uses for Sensors

Sensors are used in AR systems for purposes other than tracking as well. In general, sensors are used to obtain information about the real world so that

FIGURE 3.10
Small gyroscopes are available that will provide information about orientation. *Photo courtesy of NASA.*

the AR application can use that information. For example, if an AR application needs to respond differently depending on the temperature in the real world at that place and time, a temperature sensor would be used.

Processors

A *processor* is an essential component of an augmented reality system. Note that the term *processor* can refer to a single processor unit or multiple components working in tandem to provide a processing system.

Roles of Processors

Processors in augmented reality systems fulfill a number of roles. The processor is the "brain" of the technological system (of course, as mentioned previously, the magic of augmented reality happens in the brain of the participant). Hence, the core roles of the processor are to receive the signals from the sensors, execute the instructions from the application program based on the sensor information, and create the signals that drive the display(s) of the system.

In general, the processing system in AR applications consists primarily of one or more general-purpose microprocessors as the central processing unit (CPU) and perhaps one or more special-purpose graphics processing units (GPUs). GPUs are hardware specially optimized for executing three-dimensional graphics computations. Since three-dimensional graphics are one of the most common outputs from AR systems, GPUs are often used to good effect (Figures 3.11 and 3.12).

FIGURE 3.11
At the heart of most processor systems is one or more general-purpose microprocessor chips. *Photo courtesy of Liz Wuerffel.*

FIGURE 3.12
A graphical processing unit (GPU) is specialized hardware optimized to do computer graphics computations very fast. *Photo courtesy of Liz Wuerffel.*

Processor System Architectures

Several configurations/architectures are used for augmented reality applications. Some of the most common architectures for the processing functions include:

1. Application run on handheld system such as a smartphone
2. Application run on handheld system connected to remote server(s)

3. Application run on desktop/laptop computer
4. Application run on desktop/laptop computer connected to remote server(s)
5. Application run as a web application
6. Application run on a cloud with a thin client
7. Other combinations of local and remote systems

Handheld Modern handheld devices such as smartphones and smart tablets have a startling amount of computational power available in them. In general, most current generation smart devices have enough computational capability to execute the tasks required for basic tracking, interfacing with sensors, etc. They are not sufficiently powerful to compute complex simulations or other processor-intensive tasks. Where the handheld devices are weak is in the area of memory and storage (although current devices have more memory and storage than some desktop AR systems from 10 years ago). Every piece of software involved with the application, as well as all data (including graphical objects), must be resident on the handheld device. This can prove to be a rather severe limitation, as it can limit the number of virtual objects that can be displayed and the complexity of the objects, and limit the all-around utility of the system. However, it can be very advantageous to have the entire application that will operate on a handheld device without requiring being connected to any network or other servers. If the limitations are within what is acceptable for your application, this scenario is very useful for applications that must be mobile in areas in which there is little or no network coverage. So if your application needs to be run in a remote location without a network and where portability is of the essence, this model might be appropriate.

Always keep in mind that it is fully reasonable to expect handheld devices to gain in processor, memory, and disk capabilities as time moves forward.

Handheld Connected to Server To overcome the limitation of how much data a handheld device such as a smartphone can handle, it can be helpful to couple the handheld device to a server. This can be done via a wired or wireless connection, although in practicality a wireless connection is desirable. With a server connected to the handheld device(s), limitations on numbers, size, and complexity of objects available via the handheld can be curtailed. There will still be hard limits in terms of what can be resident on the handheld at any one time (i.e., having a server does not solve the problem if a single object is too large to handle on the handheld without serious trickery in the software environment), but by using clever caching and data swapping techniques, it is possible for the application to handle more objects than could be maintained directly on the handheld device.

Typically the server would handle such tasks as content management, collecting logging data on the use of the application, and fiducial marker management. In general, this architecture is appropriate for applications where the

FIGURE 3.13
A server like this Apple X-Serve has ample processing, memory, and storage to serve as a server for augmented reality applications. *Photo courtesy of Alan B. Craig.*

portability of handheld devices is essential and where a network connection to the server is available (Figure 3.13).

Laptop or Desktop Computer Modern laptop and desktop computers provide sufficient computational resources to be able to run typical augmented reality applications. The one case where such machines might prove inadequate is if the application program is especially computationally intensive. The most likely scenario for that is if the program must deliver results from high-fidelity simulations (perhaps they utilize complex physics or chemistry) that are typically run on supercomputers or other computers that are more powerful than typical laptop or desktop systems. Another scenario that might not be possible to execute on typical laptop or desktop systems would be if the program requires more memory than can be provided by the systems. For example, if the application requires a very large network graph to be constructed and analyzed, there may be insufficient resources available for such requirements. The downside to using a laptop or desktop system is its limited portability. Granted, laptops can be carried easily, but for applications that really require total mobility, they are cumbersome and awkward. This is not a limitation for all application scenarios though. In a case where there is a single point in space where the application is run, these types of systems can be fully adequate. For example, in a classroom, a museum, or an arcade where there is a kiosk where the application is run, it is perfectly reasonable and appropriate to use a laptop or desktop computer "behind the scenes."

Laptop or Desktop Computer with Server As noted previously, most laptop and desktop systems can handle the computational requirements for basic AR applications. There are, however, some scenarios where it is advantageous for the laptop or desktop system to be connected to a server. One of those scenarios is where many graphical (or auditory, haptic, etc.) objects must be managed or where it is unknown a priori what objects will be required by the system. The server system can maintain a library of objects and software for managing those objects. A server system can also help overcome the limitations noted in the previous section, such as if a computationally expensive simulation must be run. For example, a supercomputer could serve as a computational server to do the massive number crunching required by such simulations. The requirement for augmented reality applications to respond in real time, however, means that there must be virtually no latency in the time that it takes the supercomputer to respond. In order to be useful in this scenario, the supercomputer must be dedicated to the application (not running other programs) and must be connected by a high-speed, very low latency network.

Application Run as a Web Application There are many advantages to running AR applications as web applications. By "web application" I mean that the tool the participant uses to interact with the application is their web browser. The browser may or may not need a special plug-in to run the application.

It is very convenient to be able to access the application from any computer that has a web browser (plus any required sensors). This scenario is the closest implementation to a "cross-platform" augmented reality application. There are some difficulties in this scenario, however. In order to work effectively, the web browser needs to have some way of accessing the sensors that are either within or connected to the device. Additionally, this scenario requires the device to be connected to the World Wide Web. This may or may not be possible in some remote locations. Additionally, when using the web there is always the issue of latency. Thus, it is important to optimize the application for what tasks are handled on the server side vs what tasks are handled on the application side (client side). In general, as much as possible should be handled on the client side. As discussed earlier, objects can be loaded from the server to the client as needed and new objects can be loaded (and no longer needed objects discarded) on the client.

Application Run on a Cloud with a Thin Client This scenario is virtually identical to running as a web application with the exception that instead of using a browser as the mode of interaction with the application, a special-purpose application runs on the client side to interact with the application on the cloud. The client in this scenario is a lightweight "thin" client, meaning that it is only the minimal software that is needed to connect to the cloud. The bulk of the application runs on the cloud. Of course, latency is a serious consideration in this scenario. Many people are anticipating that the "cloud" is the way many applications will be handled in the future. Today, the vast majority of clouds are not designed to provide an option for consistent low-latency computing. It remains to be seen whether applications that require very low latency (such as AR applications) will be successful as a cloud service.

Note that any client/server model is a trade-off between the capabilities offered by the remote system and the latency involved in using it. No matter how powerful the remote resources are, if the round-trip latency between client and server is too great, it will outweigh the advantage of the additional resources. Hence, a client-server AR application requires careful design, testing, and tuning for a given combination of processor, network, and server.

Other Combinations of Local and Remote Processors Of course, all of the aforementioned architectures can be combined, mixed, and matched in many different ways. The important thing is to find the best possible combination for your particular application.

Advantages

Choosing the most appropriate architecture for your application is largely an issue of optimizing a number of trade-offs in a way that best suit your needs. The trade-offs include decisions such as portability vs power, portability vs the need for network access, or cross-platform performance vs the need for network access.

In general, the best solution where the need is true portability is a stand-alone application on a handheld device such as a smartphone or smart tablet. However, if the application requires more computation or memory than the device supports, it then becomes a question of whether it is better to use a larger system or to connect the portable device to a remote server via a network.

There are many advantages to using a web-based application if the specific application can be delivered this way, and if there is a connection to the web available.

Disadvantages

Most AR applications are rather hardware specific. That is, they are developed for a specific platform. The next chapter addresses software issues more fully, but it should be kept in mind that if you need to utilize specific features of specific hardware, today at least, will most likely require the software to be developed specifically for that platform. Times are changing and this is becoming less of a concern as standards are being developed and people are recognizing the need for more platform independence for augmented reality.

Summary and Comparison Chart

In summary, there is a variety of basic system architectures that you can choose from based on the needs of your application. Table 3.1 summarizes some of the advantages and disadvantages of the different system architectures.

Processor Specifications

A number of specifications indicate roughly how a processing system will work for a given application. Some of the more important specifications include:

1. Number of processors
2. Processor speed

Table 3.1 This Table Indicates the Capabilities of Several Different Architectures Available for Augmented Reality Systems

	Handheld	Handheld with Server	Desktop/ Laptop	Desktop/ Laptop with Server	Web Based	Cloud Based	Combination
Portable	Yes	Yes	No	No	No	No	Maybe
Portable with network	Yes	Yes	No	No	Yes	Yes	Maybe
Sufficient computation alone	Maybe	Yes	Yes	Yes	Yes	Yes	Maybe
Requires network	No	Yes	No	Yes	Yes	Yes	Maybe
Cross-platform solution	No	No	No	No	Maybe	Maybe	Maybe
Latency important	Maybe	Yes	No	Yes	Yes	Yes	Maybe

3. Available memory
4. Available storage
5. Graphics accelerator(s)
6. Network bandwidth
7. Network latency

Number of Processors

The number of processors is exactly as it sounds—the number of processing units that are available for the system. The "processor" in this case can represent any number of different processing *systems*. It may indicate the number of processor chips in the system, the number of cores (potentially multiple cores per chip), or the number of desktop computers, etc. In general, the basic processing required for carrying out "augmented reality" tasks, such as integrating inputs from sensors, executing computer vision algorithms (if used), and carrying out basic instructions from the AR application, can be handled by virtually any modern-day processor. The need for more processing capability comes if the AR application requires any heavy-duty computation, such as intense simulations or network analysis. In general, for most AR applications, there is not a need to concern oneself with the number of processors unless you are doing something particularly computationally complex.

Processor Speed

The processor speed is how fast a processor can operate. In general, you want the processor to be as fast as is available at a reasonable cost. The need for higher speeds is usually only warranted when doing computationally complex tasks. Graphics computations take considerable processor speed. However, graphics computations are usually handled by the graphics processing unit. If, however, you don't have a GPU, or a GPU is not available for AR applications, those calculations will need to be done on the processor.

Available Memory

More is better when it comes to memory for AR applications. Because latency is detrimental to AR applications, it is best to have as much data stored in main memory as possible as opposed to being available only from slower disk storage. Memory is the primary concern with handheld devices such as smartphones and smart tablets. As alluded to earlier, the limited memory on such devices limits the number and complexity of digital objects on the device. If there is need to have more data available in memory on a smartphone or tablet, then it becomes essential to have a scheme for swapping data in and out of main memory to and from a server. If using a GPU, the GPU needs its own memory available for graphics computations.

Available Storage

By *storage*, I am referring to disk space. This is where any data that can't be maintained in memory are stored. It is slower to access and retrieve data from a disk than it is to store and retrieve from memory. Consequently, it is important to decide what, if anything, can be relegated to disk storage. Often, with handheld devices, the disk storage is done on a remote server.

Graphics Accelerator(s)

Graphics accelerators are hardware that is optimized for doing the computations for three-dimensional computer graphics. In desktop systems, the graphics accelerator is usually in the form of a *graphics card,* but sometimes the graphics accelerator is part of the motherboard. Modern graphics accelerators have phenomenal performance. Smartphones and smart tablets have them built in. In general, the graphics accelerator drives the display system(s). Thus, it is important that the accelerator supports the types of operations and functions needed. For example, some graphics accelerators can support multiple display devices. This can be handy if you need to have more display real estate available than a single display can accommodate. Thus, if you are using a computer monitor as your visual display, with an appropriate graphics card you can use two displays that act together as though they were one single larger display or you can use the displays in different configurations. For example, if you need to drive a CAVE-like display, you can drive each of the different "walls" from different displays.

Another consideration for the graphics accelerator in the system is whether you plan to display stereoscopic imagery. In order to display stereoscopic imagery you need to compute different images for each of the participant's eyes and then ensure that each image is (somehow) displayed to the correct eye. For certain schemes for stereoscopic imagery you need special capabilities in the graphics accelerator. This is covered more thoroughly in the display section of this chapter. Note that I refer to a graphics accelerator(s) rather than simply a graphics accelerator. This is because in some cases it is beneficial to use more than one. For example, in the case of using more than one display, there is basically an option of using a graphics accelerator that has the capability of driving more than one display or using more than one graphics accelerator (one per display) (Figure 3.14).

Network Bandwidth

Network bandwidth is the rate at which data can pass in a network. It is expressed in bits per second. The network bandwidth is not as critical in AR systems as latency, but bandwidth becomes important if you need to pass large amounts of information, such as many high-complexity computer graphics models in a very short amount of time. This is especially important in scenarios where the AR application is loading data from a remote server.

FIGURE 3.14

This picture shows a single image that is made by tiling together multiple monitors. A couple of other things to note in this picture are that the graphics and text on the monitors look out of focus. This is because there is a separate image being displayed for each of the participant's eyes. One image is for the participant's left eye and the other is for the right eye. Because they are computed from slightly different perspectives, they look like a double image that is out of focus. The participant wears special glasses to ensure that each eye sees the correct image. The end result is that the participant sees an image that looks in focus and three dimensional. Another thing to note are the brightly colored balls on the participant's visor and handheld controller. These are observed by the tracking system cameras to determine the location and orientation of the participant's head and hands. *Photo courtesy of Alan B. Craig.*

Network Latency

Latency is the bane of all AR applications. Latency is the delay between the time something *should* happen and when it actually does. Latency is present in all aspects of an AR application (because it takes time to read sensors, compute what needs to be done with those, and then to display the results), but in situations where a network is involved, network latency is typically the most significant source of problems. It takes time for information to pass over a network. That time is *latency*. Simply increasing the bandwidth of the network doesn't solve the latency problem. If there are more data than the bandwidth can support, then the bandwidth does need to be increased, but even transferring one bit of information over a high bandwidth network still has latency (Figure 3.15).

Processor Summary

In summary, modern processors have ample capability for most AR applications. It is important to choose the proper system architecture. Latency is of prime consideration where a real-time response is essential for AR

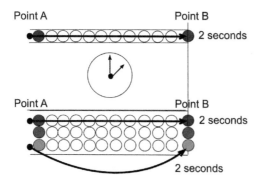

FIGURE 3.15

Latency is the amount of time it takes for something to happen. In the case of this diagram, it is the amount of time it takes for a piece of information to get from point A to point B. Bandwidth is the amount of information that can be carried at the same time. In the case of this diagram, it takes the red piece of information 2 seconds to get from point A to point B. Increasing the bandwidth allows more information to be carried in the same amount of time, but it doesn't reduce the absolute time that it takes for the red piece of information to get to point B. If it is necessary to get the red, blue, and green pieces of information all to point B, you can see that you can reduce the overall latency if you have enough bandwidth for all three to be carried simultaneously (as compared to one at a time), but there is still a latency in getting one piece or all the pieces of information from point A to point B. *Diagram courtesy of Beverly Carver.*

applications. Smartphones and smart tablets are at the lower edge of what is required for the proper operation of AR applications and, in many cases, will be required to be connected to server systems for data management and delivery.

Displays

The display is the device that provides the signals that our senses perceive. Displays provide signals to our eyes, our ears, our sense of touch, and our nose, and perhaps provide a sensation of taste. Additionally, some displays provide stimuli designed to cause other sensations, such as to our vestibular system. This book focuses primarily on displays for our eyes and ears and provides a much lighter treatment of other types of displays.

This section of the chapter is organized into the following sections:

- Visual displays
- Audio displays
- Haptic displays
- Other sensory displays
- Stereo displays (stereoscopic and stereophonic)
- Characteristics of displays that are in common to many display types

Within each of these sections I discuss different classes of displays, including different technologies that support these kinds of displays, followed by a section that addresses technological characteristics and specifications that apply to all displays in that category and then address advantages and disadvantages of different classes of displays and different technologies.

Visual Displays

The primary role of visual displays is to create signals of light that impinge our eyes that we perceive as visual imagery. We are all familiar with the typical desktop computer monitor. It is a classic icon of a visual display in that it shows digital information from a computer in a way that our eyes can see and our brains can perceive as visual images. In much the same way as different technologies [cathode ray tubes (CRT), liquid crystal displays (LCD), or plasma] can be used to implement a desktop computer monitor (with advantages and disadvantages of each), different technologies can be used to implement augmented reality visual displays.

The primary classes of visual displays used for AR applications include:

- Stationary visual displays
- Visual displays that move with the participant's head
- Visual displays that move with the participant's hand or other parts of his or her body

There are also displays that fall into more than one of those categories and are hybrids in that sense.

Stationary Visual Displays

Stationary displays are displays that, as their name implies, don't move during their typical use. They are placed in position, and they remain there. Of course, they can be moved to a new location, but, in a manner similar to a typical television set, you don't typically carry it with you wherever you go. In other words, *you must go to the display to use it.*

Kiosks. As mentioned previously, a typical desktop computer monitor would fall into the category of a stationary display.

A common usage of a computer monitor in AR would be in the context of a kiosk. A monitor could be placed with a camera mounted appropriately to allow individuals to walk up to the kiosk and present a document or some other object to the camera and see the AR-enhanced scene. This type of configuration can be used in museums, schools, libraries, public buildings, etc. A very popular example of a kiosk that uses a stationary display is the Lego Store AR kiosk (Figure 3.16).

In the aforementioned example, a stationary display is used to advantage by requiring the participants to come to the display and, as a consequence, to

FIGURE 3.16
In this picture, augmented reality is used in a retail setting. This particular installation is considered a kiosk and uses a stationary AR display. The participant holds up the product (in this case a Lego box) and can see an enhanced image of the box, as well as the box, on the display. The participant can manipulate the box to see the model from different perspectives. Note the fixed position camera above the display. This scenario can also be considered an example of an AR magic mirror, but magic mirrors are used normally to see an augmented view of the person rather than what he is holding. *Image courtesy of Intel Free Press.*

come to the point of sale. If someone wants to experience the augmented reality, she is required to come to the place where the augmented reality application designer wants him or her to be. In this example, in order to experience the AR application, the participant must come to the point of sale.

Not all kiosk-based AR systems are motivated by sales. Kiosks are found in libraries, schools, government facilities, and many other locations to provide an augmented experience to people who are at the kiosk.

Projection-based augmented reality. In the aforementioned kiosk example of stationary AR, the light that the participant sees emanates from within the display itself. It doesn't matter if the display uses a CRT, an LCD, or plasma display; the light comes from within. In projection AR, the participant sees light that is reflected on a surface. In other words, the participant is looking at a screen of some sort (or other surface) and seeing light that is projected onto the screen from a different place. In some cases, the projector is on the same side of the screen(s) as the participant. This is referred to as "front projection" because the projector is facing the front of the screen. In other cases,

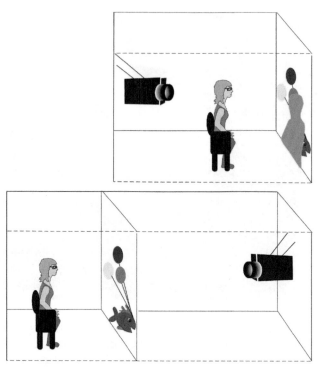

FIGURE 3.17

This diagram illustrates some of the trade-offs of front projection vs rear projection. Many common conference rooms use front projection for presentations. In AR environments, however, where the participant might be moving about in the room, shadows are caused when the participant passes between the projector and the surface on which it is projecting. Rear projection solves the shadow problem, but at the expense of requiring more space (typically) and with the requirement of a surface that allows for rear projection. Additionally, because many rear projection screen materials do not preserve polarization, you must use screen material that will preserve polarization if the AR system requires polarized light. *Diagram courtesy of Beverly Carver.*

the projector is on the opposite side of the screen than the participant. This is referred to as "rear projection" (Figure 3.17).

One advantage of rear projection over front projection is that you don't need to worry about the participant occluding the image by standing between the projector and the screen. The disadvantage of rear projection is that it requires space behind the screen for the projector, and enough space to accommodate the distance the projector needs to have between itself and the screen (hence they are not typically portable). Additionally, rear projection screens are a more specialized item than front projection screens. In a pinch, in the absence of a screen one can even front project directly on a wall or other surface. Another thing to keep in mind with rear projection is that one

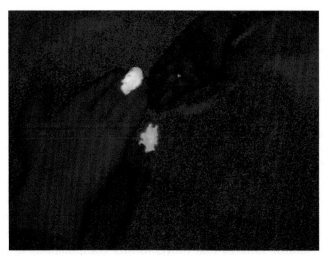

FIGURE 3.18

This example of projection-based AR uses a projector mounted above a sandbox. There is a simulation of virtual creatures that run around and interact with each other. Participants can interact with the creatures by altering the terrain by moving the sand around into hills and valleys or interact directly with the creatures with their hands. If a participant gets a creature in his or her hand he or she can carry it and release it in a different location. In this picture, one participant is handing a creature to a different participant. This particular application does not require the participant(s) to wear any technology. As many people can participate simultaneously as can stand around the sandbox. *Photo courtesy of Alan B. Craig. Application "Glowing Pathfinder Bugs" courtesy of Squidsoup; contributors: Anthony Rowe, Chris Bennewith, and Liam Birtles.*

must carefully consider the placement of other hardware, such as speakers, such that they don't cast shadows on the screen.

Projected AR systems may use one projector and one screen, multiple projectors on one screen (tiling the images together on the screen to achieve a single high-resolution image), or multiple projectors with multiple screens (one or more projector per screen). Another scenario is that there are no "screens" per se at all, but rather the imagery is displayed directly on the physical world. Recall from Chapter 1 the distinction between two modes of merging physical world and digital world information. In one scenario, the two worlds are merged inside the computer and then displayed. In the other mode, the digital information is not merged with the physical in the computer, but rather they are merged by simply projecting the digital information directly on the physical world. In this scenario, there may not even be a camera involved to collect what the physical world looks like. There will be sensors of some sort in order to determine where the participant is and how he or she is oriented in the physical world, but there is no video display showing the physical world. In this scenario, the physical world, in conjunction with one or more projectors, is the visual display (Figure 3.18).

The reason for potentially using more than one projector and/or more than one screen has to do with increasing different technical capabilities of one or more parameter with the display system. These are defined and discussed later in this chapter, but briefly, some of the reasons for using multiple projectors are to increase *brightness, resolution, apparent resolution, field of view,* and *field of regard.*

In the past, the most common surface to project onto was the projection screen. However, this is changing with a trend toward displaying on real-world surfaces. One advantage of displaying on a screen is that, in general, the screen is flat and located in a specific place. This is advantageous when determining the image to project onto the surface. Likewise, projecting onto other real-world surfaces that are flat and don't tend to move (such as the side of a building) is rather straightforward. When projecting onto irregular surfaces and/or surfaces that move, further computations must be done in order to achieve the desired result. Projecting an image that was created for a flat surface onto an irregular surface leads to distortion in the projected image. Thus, the image must be "corrected" for the surface it will be projected onto. There is a technique called *structured light* in which computer vision techniques are used to determine the topology of the surface and then the images can be corrected through computation to display on that surface distortion free. In lower end structured light systems, the system is calibrated a priori for the display surface, but at the higher end uses an IR projector and camera to be able to ingest (via the camera) the geometry of the surface and display the corrected image in real time. This allows the surface that is being projected onto to be dynamically changing yet allows the projected imagery to appear correctly, but requires significant computational resources. Similar techniques are used to project onto a surface that is moving in location. The system must determine where the display surface is and project the correct information for that location, corrected for distortion at that location. An example of this scenario would be to have a projector (and camera) in a fixed location but displaying on an object that someone is carrying in a region. To do this correctly, the system must determine where that object is and project the correct information where that object is, and only where that object is. Simultaneously, the projector must *not project* anywhere that the object isn't. As the object moves, the projected image must also move correspondingly, but typically not by the projector moving physically. One example might be when actors on a stage are wearing white costumes, but a projector in a fixed location projects the appropriate costumes onto the actors as they move around the stage. There is a lot of promise in applications that exploit structured light techniques. See the photos of the projected sand table later in this chapter to see an illustration of an application of structured light. In that example, (real) sand is used to represent the terrain of an area. Maps and other representations are projected onto the irregular sand surface. Structured light concepts are used to avoid the problems with distortion that occur with projecting onto irregular surfaces.

There are cases in which people wear projectors. In those cases, it is not considered a stationary display and will be discussed in the section that addresses displays that move with the participant's hand or other parts of their body. Structured light techniques can be used in this scenario as well.

Visual Displays That Move with the Participant's Head

Some AR systems use displays that are mobile and move with the participant's head and are sometimes referred to as *head-mounted displays* (HMDs). The most common instantiations of these are displays that are worn like helmets, glasses, or headphones (audio), with the trend being toward lightweight glasses. There are also displays that could be considered hybrids in that they move with the participant's head, but overall are stationary displays in which the participant places his head at the display and moves the display with his or her head in a limited range of motions.

Head worn. As mentioned earlier, the most common types of mobile displays worn on the head take the form of a helmet or glasses. Other types are variants of these two basic configurations. For example, some displays clip onto your own pair of glasses.

Head-mounted displays for augmented reality differ from HMDs for virtual reality systems in that in virtual reality systems, the participant does not see the real world. As a matter of fact, virtual reality systems depend on the user not seeing (at least in a distracting way) the real world. In augmented reality it is essential that the participant be able to see the real world. There are two basic scenarios with HMDs in how the participant sees the real world. One style uses optical means for the participant to see the real world, and the other uses video technology to allow the participant to see the real world. These two styles are referred to as *optical see-through* and *video see-through*, respectively (Figure 3.19).

Another distinction to be made between different HMDs is whether they display to only one eye or to both eyes. If they display to both eyes, another distinction is whether they display distinct images to each eye for the purpose of achieving stereoscopic 3D viewing or not. Stereoscopic viewing is covered in depth later in this chapter (Figures 3.20 and 3.21).

Eye worn. In the future, it will be possible to have a visual display embedded into a contact lens. Thus, other than the contact lens, no other bulky hardware would be required to be worn on the head. Already, researchers such as Babak Parviz at the University of Oregon and companies such as Innovega

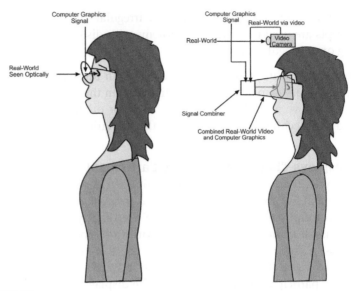

FIGURE 3.19

There are two basic types of see-through, head-mounted displays (or glasses). The first diagram illustrates the optical see-through type. In this type, the participant views the (real) world directly or perhaps through an optical lens. The computer graphics signal is then fed to the participant's eye(s) in conjunction with the optical signal, often by the use of a see-through mirror. The video see-through method illustrated in the second diagram generally precludes the participant from seeing the (real) world directly and instead provides a video camera (or potentially two video cameras for stereoscopic viewing) that is aligned as closely as possible with the participant's eye(s). This provides a video signal of the real world that can be combined with the video signal from the computer graphics system, which can then be displayed to the participant's eye(s). *Diagram courtesy of Beverly Carver.*

FIGURE 3.20

Helmet-style, video see-through AR display. *Image courtesy of Alan B. Craig.*

FIGURE 3.21
The nVisor ST50 from NVIS Inc. *Photo courtesy of NVIS Inc.*

(funded by the Defense Advanced Research Projects Agency and the National Science Foundation) are working on such devices. Of course, such a device would need to have power and the visual signals to be delivered to the lens. The power could potentially be contained within the lens itself, but the graphical elements from the AR application would need to be transmitted to the lens. By wearing a contact lens in each eye and delivering appropriate images to each lens, the contact lenses could be used as a stereoscopic display. Note that the contact lenses would only serve as a visual display. Other senses (hearing, etc.) would require other devices such as headphones, speakers, or earbuds. Contact lenses would be optical see-through displays because the participant would see the real world directly through the lens.

Some people may like the idea of wearing their visual display in their eyes, but others (people who don't already wear contacts, people who have had their vision corrected by surgery to avoid wearing contacts, etc.) may reject the idea of wearing contact lenses for the sake of augmented reality. One area where a contact lens display might be especially well suited is when it is important to have the AR content available in a stealth way. For example, spies might like the ability to have AR content available to them without other people realizing that they do. Other potential "customers" for such a device might be the military, trial attorneys, actors, athletes, and anyone who would gain an advantage by having AR content available to them without the necessity of wearing bulky displays (even glasses) and who don't necessarily want others to know that they are using AR (Figure 3.22).

Stationary. As mentioned earlier, there is another class of display that moves with the participant's head, but the overall display is stationary. One example

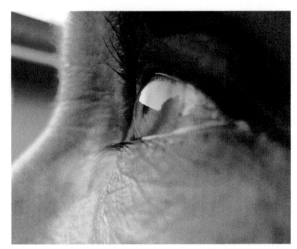

FIGURE 3.22

In the future, some people may choose to have their AR visual display as part of their contact lenses. By using a lens in each eye, a stereoscopic display can be made. *Photo courtesy of Alan B. Craig.*

of this is a viewing port similar in style to stationary binoculars present at scenic overlooks and landmarks. The display is in a fixed location, but the "binoculars" can move on two axes. They can rotate around the vertical axis and rock on the horizontal (azimuth) axis depending on how the participant moves his or her head. This concept has been brought to augmented reality and is especially useful in venues such as museums, schools, and libraries (Figures 3.23 and 3.24).

Visual Displays That Move with the Participant's Hand or Other Parts of His or Her Body

Currently, the most prevalent type of display for augmented reality applications moves with the participant's hand. This is due to the widespread adoption of smartphones (such as the iPhone and Android phones) and smart tablets (such as the iPad and similar devices). Many developers recognize that a huge fraction of the population carries sensors, processors, and display devices in their pocket or purse on a regular basis. Hence, even though they are more limited in some regards (processing, memory, screen size, etc.), their portability and ease of use make them a prime target for augmented reality applications (Figure 3.25).

This class of device is so important currently that Chapter 7 in this book, *Mobile Augmented Reality*, is dedicated primarily to the use of these devices for augmented reality applications. That chapter addresses different system

FIGURE 3.24

The view that a participant sees when looking through the digital binocular station "comes to life" in this museum application. *Image courtesy of www.DigitalBinocularStation.com.*

FIGURE 3.23

This display is a hybrid. It is a stationary display that tracks with the user's head. The participant looks into the viewer and sees the augmented world. Just like with this type of binoculars at scenic vistas, the user can move the binoculars around its axes to see different places in the world. This display also has the option of requiring the participant to deposit coins to use it, thus enabling a revenue stream. The display also provides mechanical tracking that reports the position of the viewport. *Image courtesy of www. DigitalBinocularStation.com.*

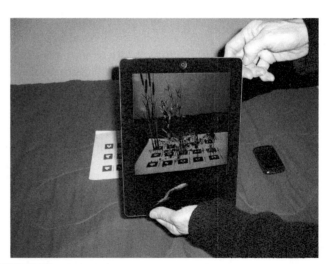

FIGURE 3.25

Smartphones and smart tablets can be used as a "magic lens" to allow the participant to see things invisible without it. Here, a sheet of fiducial markers shows a garden of different plants when viewed through an iPad. *Photo courtesy of Alan B. Craig.*

architectures, overcoming the limitations of those devices, and many more aspects of using them to maximum advantage.

In addition to handheld display devices that use a panel of some sort to display on (such as the screen of a smartphone or smart tablet), there are augmented reality applications that use mobile projectors. Projectors have become small and portable enough that it is possible to use them for mobile applications. They will continue to shrink in size, weight, and, to some extent, power requirements. The fallout of this will be projectors that can be placed as a button in a shirt, on a visor, on a pair of glasses, or on a cap. Likewise, they could be embedded in smartphones and pads.

Portable projectors can project onto surfaces in the real world that are present naturally (such as walls, the ground, and trees) but they can also project onto (real) objects that a participant provides specifically for the purpose of serving as a surface on which to project. For example, if the participant is wearing a projector on his or her head and is holding a surface in his or her hand covered with retroreflective material (retroreflective material reflects only in the direction that the light is coming from), the end result is that the participant can see a display on the surface (made of cardboard, plastic, or whatever), but other people can't see what is on that tablet.

Another scenario for a head-mounted projector is that it displays onto a surface that is transparent, but in front of the participant's eyes. In this way, the participant sees the projected image but can also see through the surface and see the real world.

There are also projection-based systems that are more or less permanent installations. In these scenarios, projectors are usually mounted in the environment and focused to project on different entities (Figure 3.26).

In order for mobile projection AR to be successful, a number of things need to happen. The environment must be lit appropriately (or darkened), as most projection images (especially low-powered ones) are washed out in bright sunlight. Additionally, because the projector needs to "know where it is" in the location, it needs to be tracked just like any other device. It must also be "aware" of what to project where and to compensate for the color and shape of the surface that it projects on.

Audio Displays

The second most common sensory display is the audio, or sonic, display. Analogous to visual displays displaying signals that our eyes can sense, sonic displays produce audio signals that our ears can sense. Our eyes and our ears convey different types of information to our bodies to help us perceive the world around us. These differences are explored more fully later in this book.

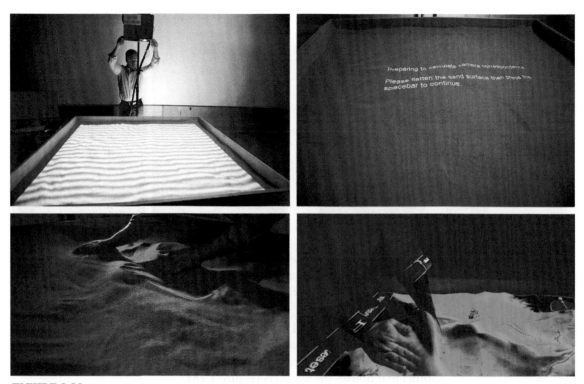

FIGURE 3.26
This series of four pictures shows the process of setting up a Simtable system that projects on a sandbox. The first step is to calibrate with the sand flattened, and then the system can project images that help build the terrain in the sand that you want to display on. This system uses the concept of structured light, described earlier in this chapter, to display on the irregular sand surface without problematic distortions. *Photos courtesy of Simtable.*

Similarly to visual displays, audio displays can also be classified into the following categories:

- Stationary audio displays
- Audio displays that move with the participant's head
- Audio displays that move with the participant's hand or other parts of his or her body

Stationary Audio Displays
Augmented reality displays are not limited to only visual presentations. The second most common sensory stimuli displayed is audio. The audio version of a stationary display is a stationary loudspeaker system, commonly referred to simply as "speakers." In general, home stereo speakers are an example of a stationary audio display (Figure 3.27).

FIGURE 3.27
These photos show front and rear views of a single high-quality speaker cabinet. In this case, the amplifier is contained in the same cabinet as the speakers, and the controls for the amplifier are on the rear panel. *Photos courtesy of Alan B. Craig.*

Headphones, earbuds, and the like, however, are examples of a mobile audio display system. In either case, an amplifier is also required by the system. In some cases, such as many computer speakers, the amplifier is built into the cabinet that houses the speakers (Figure 3.28).

Audio presents an interesting dichotomy in terms of stationary displays vs mobile displays. In general, sound comes from some location. The dichotomy in AR is whether the sound appears to come from a fixed point in the world as the participant moves about or whether the sound appears to come from a fixed point with respect to the participant as he or she moves about. In general, stationary speakers are conducive to sound appearing to come from a fixed space with respect to the world, whereas with mobile displays, such as headphones, the natural mode is for sound to appear to come from a fixed space with respect to the participant. In both cases, both modes are possible, but to cross over to the less natural mode of display requires tracking the participant (which is already happening in AR systems) and then doing computations to cause the sound to seem to come from the desired location.

In general, once speakers are placed in a location, you leave them there, much like you leave a typical television set in place. However, because most systems are at least somewhat portable, they can be moved when necessary or desirable, but they don't move during a typical application.

A very significant aspect of a stationary speaker system is the environment that it is placed in. Several issues must be addressed. One is the acoustics of the environment. Any given sound system of this nature is affected by its

FIGURE 3.28
This diagram shows the difference between using stereo headphones versus stereophonic speaker cabinets to deliver stereo audio. It is much more straightforward to present the left audio channel to the participant's left ear and right audio channel to the participant's right ear with stereo headphones than with speakers, especially if the participant is moving. However, sound, unless specially processed, typically seems to emanate from the location where the speakers are positioned, whereas the source of sound (unless specially processed to account for the participant's location and orientation) travels with the participant with headphones. *Diagram courtesy of Beverly Carver.*

location and the items in the environment that surround it. For example, if you place speakers in a large bare room with hard floors, and thus a lot of echo, it will sound quite different than if you place them in a small room full of cloth furniture and carpeting. Another issue is that of *noise pollution*, that is, how much other sounds in the environment affect the ability to hear the sound from the speakers clearly, and how sounds from the AR system speakers affect the ability to hear other sounds in the room for people who aren't involved with the AR experience. For example, in the case of a kiosk-type system in a retail setting, it is important to ensure that people using the kiosk for AR can hear the signals emanating from the AR system clearly without other sounds of the store, other customers, and so on interfering with the experience. Likewise, customers and staff in the store who are doing something other than the AR experience are not likely to appreciate the sounds from the AR system if they interfere with the sounds they need to attend to, and/or if the sounds from the AR system are simply annoying to those who are not involved with the AR. Sound is different than visual information in many ways. Two important distinctions that merit mentioning here include that sound exists around us, whereas visual imagery only impacts where we are looking. So, if we see something offensive in a specific place, we can easily "look away" from it. It is not as easy to "look away" from offensive sounds coming from a specific place. Likewise, we have no "earlids." With vision, we can simply close our eyes if we don't want to see something. With sound, we cannot simply shut off our sense of hearing.

Audio Displays That Move with the Participant's Head

Audio displays that move with the participant's head fall into two primary forms:

- Headphones
- Earbuds

Headphones and earbuds are actually the same type of device, but simply a different form factor and one other distinction. Headphones are typically worn *over* the ear(s), whereas earbuds are worn *inside* the ear(s). This distinction can affect how people perceive the sounds they are hearing. Earbuds take more advantage of sound traveling through our skeletal system in the head, whereas headphones are more limited to their impact on our eardrums (Figure 3.29).

FIGURE 3.29
Earbuds and headphones both allow for private listening. Earbuds (left) are worn in the ear and are fairly unobtrusive visually. Headphones (right) are worn over the ears. *Photo courtesy of Olivia Neff.*

Headphones and earbuds overcome many sound pollution problems and also offer more privacy to the participants wearing them. People who are quite close to the participant do not hear what the participant is hearing unless the volume of the sound is quite loud. Likewise, the person wearing the headphones or earbuds is unlikely to hear most sounds around them unless they are exceedingly loud. This can become a safety concern when using these types of displays because it is possible that someone wearing them might not hear a fire alarm or other sounds that are important to hear. Another safety concern with these devices is that they can cause hearing damage if the volume of the sounds they are displaying is too loud and/or for too prolonged of a time.

Headphones can be classified in two primary types: closed ear and open ear. Closed ear headphones have a goal of minimizing the amount of outside sound that the wearer can hear. Open ear headphones minimize the restriction on hearing outside sounds. One real-world application of open ear headphones is when singers are recording in sound studios. They wear the headphones to hear the music (without the music being picked up in their singing microphone), but they also want to hear the natural real-world sound of their own voice singing. This can be considered somewhat analogous to occlusive vs see-through head-mounted visual displays. In keeping with the idea of *not* isolating the participant from the real world, open ear headphones are a more natural match for augmented reality systems (Figure 3.30).

Headphones and earbuds of all types are not sensitive to room acoustics. Consequently, systems based on these devices can be deployed in virtually any sonic environment, whereas loudspeaker-based systems may or may not sound the same from one environment to another.

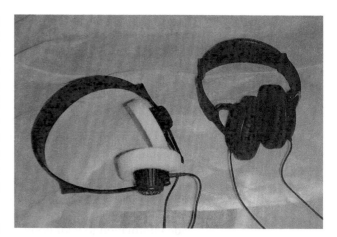

FIGURE 3.30
Headphones come in different types. The pair on the left is an example of open ear headphones, meaning that they are not intended to block the wearer from hearing sounds in the outside world. The pair on the right are closed ear headphones, meaning they are intended to block outside sounds. *Photo courtesy of William R. Sherman.*

Audio Displays That Move with the Participant's Hand or Other Parts of His or Her Body

Smartphones, smart tablets, and other handheld devices often have an audio display built in. They often also have a jack available to allow you to plug in a pair of headphones or earbuds. The key aspect about handheld audio displays is that they can be either private or not private depending on the participant's wishes. That is, with the volume turned up, it can be heard by anyone in the area within the limits of the available volume. Or, the volume can be turned down and the display held against one ear. Finally, for complete privacy, the participant can plug in a pair of headphones or earbuds.

Other Sensory Displays

In addition to sight and sound, augmented reality applications may display to other human senses. The most common of these are the haptic (touch) and olfaction (smell) senses. Neither of these is very common at this point in time, but work is being done regarding them, and there are examples of their use.

Haptics

Haptics, in general, refer to our sense of *touch*. This can roughly be broken into two components:

- Skin sensations (taction)
- Forces (kinesthetics)

Skin sensations include things such as temperature, texture, and pain. Forces are sensed by how our body responds to them. For example, when you lift a bowling ball, your body must overcome the force of gravity. Based on how much various muscles must react to do this, your body gains an understanding of the weight of the ball. Your body's sense of *proprioception* enables your mind to understand your bodily configuration even when your eyes are closed. As you move your hand over the ball, the muscles in your arms and fingers report information about its shape, and skin sensations tell you that the ball is smooth and cool.

Whenever you have real-world physical contact with something you are engaging with your haptic system. Some haptics are passive in nature, for example, the digital binoculars (shown in the visual display system section of this chapter) provide information to your body when you use it. You can literally feel when your face touches the viewport. You can also feel when the display has moved to the end of its range of motion and prevents you from moving it any further. When you hold a smartphone in your hand, you get a haptic sensation that is both from force (you feel its shape and weight) and from skin sensations (its texture).

Consequently, any display for any of your senses that touches your body in any way provides some sort of haptic display. Some, such as a heat lamp, can provide a haptic sensation even when they are not in contact with you.

In addition to these types of passive haptic display, augmented reality can provide active display for both forces and skin sensations. There are readily available transducers that can heat and cool rapidly based on an electrical signal. Consequently, participants could wear sensors of this nature on the tips of their fingers, and when one of their fingers intersects a virtual object they could feel the temperature of that object. As alluded to earlier, heat lamps, fans, and so on can be under computer control in an AR application to simulate different aspects of the environment (Figure 3.31).

Force sensations are a bit more complicated to achieve. One of the key problems with using devices to convey force feedback to participants is that it is difficult to "hide" the device being used. The major way force feedback is carried out currently is to use machinery of a physical nature to convey forces to the participant. Seeing that hardware can spoil the illusion of the AR application. In VR systems where the real world is occluded, this is an easier task. However, there are scenarios in AR where it is not necessarily problematic to see the haptic device.

An example of an AR application that makes use of force feedback could be one in which you are seeing an object (virtual) on a real table. A device such as the PHANTOM Omni from Geomagic is used in order to "feel" the object (Figure 3.32). The device is an articulated arm with a pen-type device on the

FIGURE 3.31

Skin sensations can be simulated with transducers that participants wear on their fingers. In this example (haptic canvas: dilatant fluid-based haptic interaction from the Bioimaging Laboratory, Osaka University), participants can "feel" sensations due to the transducers they wear on their hand and the fluid they interact with. *Photo courtesy of Alan B. Craig. Application from the Bioimaging Laboratory, Osaka University; contributors: Shunsuke Yoshimoto, Yuki Hamada, Takahiro Tokui, Tetsuya Suetake, Masataka Imura, Yoshihiro Kuroda, and Osamu Oshiro.*

FIGURE 3.32

This device from Geomagic is the Sensable PHANTOM Omni haptic device. It is a sensor that reports six degrees of freedom (*X, Y, Z*, yaw, pitch, and roll) as an input device (thus it is tracking your hand) and three degrees of freedom (*X, Y,* and *Z*) of output as force feedback. *Photo courtesy of Geomagic.* © *Copyright Geomagic.*

end. You move the pen around to probe into a space. If the device was in registration with an AR visual display, you could see the virtual object on the table and feel it by touching it with the pen. You could gain a sense of the shape of the object in much the same way as you could gain information about the shape of a real object by probing it with a pen. In this particular example, seeing the haptic device would not spoil the illusion because it would just appear to be exactly what it is—a device to probe objects with a pen.

Many smartphones have a vibrator built in. Hence one could use the internal vibrator to indicate different things. One example would be to indicate when the device has intersected with a virtual object. Thus, participants get an active haptic sensation regarding their activity in the virtual aspect of the world.

Smell (Olfaction)

Smell can be used to advantage in AR applications. One thing that makes the use of smell problematic is that it is difficult to "clear" a smell rapidly when it should go away (Figure 3.33).

Smell is generally administered globally as a mist from an atomizer under computer control or more specifically to a particular person via tubing, as will be shown in Figure 3.33. In general, smells are preformulated as a specific smell that is administered rather than a more general model where a set of scent "primitives" are combined to create new smells dynamically under the control of an algorithm in a way that would be analogous to using color theory to use red, green, and blue primitives (or another model) to create any color for display.

It is nontrivial to dispense smells/perfumes very rapidly, especially in large areas. It is even more difficult to "clear" an area of a scent that has been dispensed there. Hence, it is difficult to provide an environment in which different scents can be placed and eliminated rapidly.

Other Senses

While it is true that we have many other senses, including taste (gustation) and vestibular senses, they have not been fully explored in augmented reality as of this time. I believe people will continue to develop display technology and other support for other senses with time, but for now the focus is primarily on visual, sonic, haptic, and olfactory, with the lion's share of development in visual and sonic display technology.

Stereo Displays

This section addresses stereoscopic (visual) and stereophonic (binaural) displays. This section could be described more aptly as *multichannel* displays to

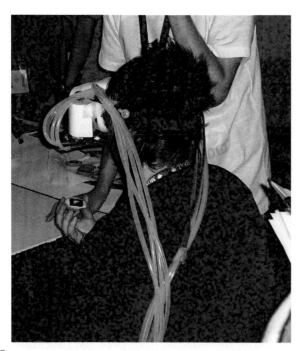

FIGURE 3.33

In this augmented reality application from Takuji Narumi of the University of Tokyo, a participant wears a see-through head-mounted display equipped with rubber tubing through which different scents can be presented to the participant's nose. In this example, the participant tries a bite of a tasteless cookie on which there is an imprinted fiducial symbol. With the AR system, the participant sees the cookie as a specific type of cookie and is presented with the smell of that type of cookie. The researchers are interested in how the visual and olfactory perception affects taste. This system also allows for interesting experiments, such as the participant "seeing" one type of cookie while "smelling" a different type. Note that the tubing is kept out of the view of the participant. *Photo courtesy of Alan B. Craig.*

be more general, but the most common use of displays is for stereo (two-channel) display. This section discusses most specifically how stereo display is carried out in the visual realm and in the audio realm. Many of the displays described earlier in this chapter can be used as stereo displays, but many cannot. Even within a specific display type, such as head-mounted displays, some can and some cannot. It is not always immediately obvious which can be used in stereo even though it might look like it is obvious. This section details how stereo displays work and how they can be used to advantage.

Visual

Stereo displays in the visual realm are referred to as *stereoscopic* displays. Stereoscopic displays take advantage of a depth cue referred to as *stereopsis*. Stereopsis was described in Chapter 2 of this book. This section explains

FIGURE 3.34

Before computers, photographers were able to take stereoscopic photos with a special camera with two lenses. In order to view the three-dimensional photos, people used a device called a *stereoscope* to ensure that each eye saw the image that was from the correct perspective for that eye. In this photo you can see the pair of images that the camera created and the viewport where you look to see the three-dimensional image. *Photo courtesy of Dave Pape.*

how to carry out the exploitation of stereopsis for augmented reality applications. Stereopsis, in brief, is the depth cue that we obtain because each of our two eyes sees a scene from slightly different perspectives. Note that the farther away an object is from you, the less important stereopsis is to understanding the three dimensionality of the world. Another way of stating this is that stereopsis is more important when you are observing and/or manipulating things that are close to you (less than 10 meters). Just as our sensory system uses stereopsis in the real world, we can simulate it in the virtual world. Hence, we can use stereopsis to great effect in augmented reality applications, especially when those applications involve observing or manipulating virtual objects that are close (Figure 3.34).

Ramifications on Computation of Imagery. In order to achieve stereopsis, you must have two images to look at—each one computed from the perspective of one of your eyes. That is, unlike in a movie where there is a single image for every time frame, if you are going to exploit stereopsis, you need a pair of images for every time frame. You need one for your left eye that was created for the left eye's perspective and one for your right eye that was computed based on where your right eye is with respect to the scene. When Hollywood makes three-dimensional movies, they use a special camera that has two lenses that are separated from each other the same amount that most people's eyes are separated from each other. This distance is known as the interocular distance. The two images that are created by such a camera (or other stereoscopic techniques) are referred to as a stereo pair. In the case of a movie, it is a stereo pair that is appropriate for the location of the camera. A major difference between creating stereo pairs of images for a movie vs. augmented reality applications is that with the movie, you can assume that the audience is viewing the movie from the perspective that the camera saw. Consequently, when a movie is displayed in a theater, the audience is in roughly the same location as the camera was with respect to the scene, and thus the images were created roughly for their perspective. I say roughly because the same perspective is used for everyone in the theater even though they are seated in somewhat different locations.

In augmented reality applications there is no way to know a priori what perspective the stereo pairs must be computed for. Hence, you must compute the images on the fly in real time in order for the participants to see the virtual object from the correct perspective for each of their eyes. As you can surmise, this requires tracking the location of the participant's eyes or the display through which they are viewing the scene. Since the interocular distance does not change on a person, if you can track any point on the participant's face you can infer the location of the two eyes at least approximately.

Computing a stereo pair requires more computational resources than computing a single image. Thus, if you have an application that can barely deliver a single frame in real time, you may have more difficulty creating a stereo pair in real time. I say you *may* have difficulty because some graphics processors have the ability to compute each image of a stereo pair in parallel, thus not doubling the amount of time required to compute two images.

Display Techniques. As mentioned previously, a critical element of a stereoscopic display is to ensure that the participant's left eye sees the image intended for the left eye and the participant's right eye sees the image intended for it. There are several methods to accomplish this with advantages and disadvantages for each depending on the circumstances. The most common include:

- Spatial multiplexing
- Temporal multiplexing
- Polarization multiplexing
- Spectral multiplexing
- Autostereoscopic displays
- Multichannel displays

Spatial multiplexing. Most head-mounted displays utilize spatial multiplexing in order to achieve stereoscopic display. *Binocular* displays provide an image to the participant's two eyes. Simply displaying to both eyes doesn't make a display stereoscopic. Some binocular displays are *monoscopic*. That is, they display the same image to each eye. Hence, they do not provide the cue of stereopsis.

Not all head-mounted displays are binocular, either. Some head-mounted displays provide an image to only one of the participant's eyes.

Some head-mounted displays are binocular (provide a signal to both eyes) but are not capable of providing a *different* image to each eye. In this case, it is a binocular, monoscopic display that cannot provide the depth cue of stereopsis.

In order for a display that uses spatial multiplexing (providing images separated by space) to be stereoscopic, it must be capable of displaying different images (each component of a stereo pair) to each eye. The stereoscope shown earlier in this section uses spatial multiplexing in order to ensure that each eye sees the correct image of the stereo pair. Each image is placed in front of the correct eye, and there is a small board that prevents each eye from seeing the other image. This is essentially how stereoscopic head-mounted displays work except that the images are displayed electronically rather than as static images on photographic paper, such as in the example of the stereoscope.

Some vendors sell head-mounted displays that they *imply* provide a stereoscopic experience, but the two image displays are, in fact, only capable of displaying the same image.

Spatial multiplexing is the most common technique used for stereoscopic display with head-mounted/head-worn displays.

It is worth mentioning that with head-mounted displays that have the possibility of providing a stereoscopic display, one must consider the stereoscopic display of the real world as well as the stereoscopic display of the digital augmentations. There are four potential combinations of stereoscopic and monoscopic display:

1. Real-world monoscopic, digital augmentations monoscopic
2. Real-world monoscopic, digital augmentations stereoscopic
3. Real-world stereoscopic, digital augmentations monoscopic
4. Real-world stereoscopic, digital augmentations stereoscopic

These different possibilities are most important when it comes to head-mounted/head-worn displays. The first thing to note is that with optical see-through displays, unless one specifically blocks off the view of one eye, the real world will be seen stereoscopically. This is because the participant sees the world through both eyes, with each eye seeing a different view of the world just like they do when they are not using a display at all. So, for optical see-through displays it really only makes sense to discuss options 3 and 4.

With video see-through displays, all four options are realistic possibilities and must be considered. The first thing to note is that in order for a video see-through display to show the world stereoscopically, it is essential that there be two video cameras positioned approximately where the eyes are. A single camera video see-through display is not capable of showing the real-world view stereoscopically. In general, displaying digital augmentations stereoscopically with the real world seen monoscopically does not lead to a compelling result, which is not to say that this configuration would not be suitable in certain circumstances/applications, but overall, it tends to work better to display the augmentations monoscopically if the real world is displayed monoscopically. Displaying augmentations monoscopically when the real world is displayed stereoscopically generally works out okay. As a consequence, if you have a single camera video see-through head-mounted display, it is probably best to display the augmentations monoscopically. There just aren't the stereopsis depth cues, and the augmentation might look somewhat flat. With optical see-through displays, showing the augmentations monoscopically or stereoscopically both work, again with the caveat that without the stereopsis cues the augmentations might look somewhat flat. However, other depth cues, such as head motion, can alleviate the flatness problems somewhat.

Temporal multiplexing. Temporal multiplexing refers to the idea of displaying images separated by time (rather than by space as in spatial multiplexing). The way this is done is that the image destined for the left eye is displayed and a filter blocks the right eye from seeing that image. Then, the image destined for the right eye is displayed and the filter for the right eye is opened and the filter for the left eye is closed (made opaque). This switching happens rapidly, with the net effect being that each eye sees the image that is intended for it.

The most common way that this is carried out in practice is that the computer generates and displays one image of a stereo pair and also provides a signal (either through a wire or wirelessly) to a pair of glasses that the participant wears. Most frequently, the glasses have liquid crystal filters in them that can be (independently) made opaque or transparent based on a signal provided by the computer (Figure 3.35).

The most common way to send the signal to the glasses wirelessly is via an infrared signal. Hence, there must be a clear line of sight between the glasses and the device that provides the infrared signal to the glasses. The glasses used for time multiplexed stereoscopic displays are often referred to as *shutter glasses*.

FIGURE 3.35

The glasses and the corresponding infrared emitter shown here work together to ensure that the image computed for the participant's right eye is seen by the right eye and the image computed for the left eye is seen by the left eye. The emitter provides a signal based on which image the computer is currently displaying. There is a sensor in the glasses above the nose that receives that signal and makes the lens over the incorrect eye opaque. The net result is that by the left eye and right eye images being displayed over time, each eye sees the image intended for it and the participant experiences the effect of seeing a stereoscopic image and senses the scene as a three-dimensional representation. *Photo courtesy of Michael Simeone.*

Time multiplexing is especially well suited to projected displays, especially when there is no specific orientation between the user and the image that is constant and known a priori. Shutter glasses with time multiplexing can provide a very compelling stereoscopic experience.

Polarization multiplexing. Polarization multiplexing works by passing one image of a stereo pair through a filter that is polarized one way and passing the other image through a filter that is polarized in a different orientation. The participant then wears glasses that have polarizing filters in them that match the orientation of the image intended for the eye that that filter is in front of (Figure 3.36).

Polarization multiplexing using *linear polarization* is often done by passing the signal for one eye through a *vertically* polarized filter and the other image through a *horizontally* polarized filter. Note that with linear polarization it is essential that the participant's head is always oriented the same way with respect to the image. If a participant is viewing a linearly polarized stereo pair and then tips his or her head such that it is parallel with the floor, the filter in his or her glasses that was

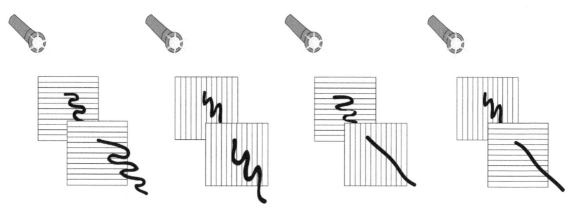

FIGURE 3.36

This diagram illustrates the concept of horizontal and vertical polarization of light. A light source with random polarization is passed through a horizontal polarizing filter. This causes only horizontally polarized light to pass. That horizontally polarized light is able to pass directly through another horizontally polarized filter but is blocked by a vertically polarized filter. Likewise, vertically polarized light can pass through vertical polarizing filters but is blocked by horizontal filters. This phenomenon can be exploited by passing the image that should be seen by the left eye through a filter. The participant wears a filter that is polarized the same way over his or her left eye. Likewise, the image that should be seen by the right eye is passed through a filter of the opposite polarization, and the participant wears a filter of the same orientation as that one over his or her right eye. In this way, the image that is intended for the left eye is seen by the left eye but is blocked from the right eye, and vice versa. *Diagram courtesy of Beverly Carver.*

polarized vertically is now polarized horizontally and the filter that was polarized horizontally is now polarized vertically. The net result of this is that each eye sees only the image that was intended for the *other* eye.

Many 3D movies use polarization multiplexing for achieving the stereopsis depth cue for the audience. This can be effective because the movie projector does not change its orientation during the movie, and it can reasonably be assumed that the audience is sitting with their heads upright. Hence, the polarization is not likely to be affected by people regularly changing their orientation. An example of where linear polarization is not likely to be effective is if the imagery is projected on the floor or the ground and there is no inherent "up" or "down" to the imagery and the participant potentially sees the imagery from any orientation of his or her body with respect to the imagery. If a participant is looking at an image on the ground and begins to walk around it, the polarization orientation of the filters in his or her glasses changes with respect to the orientation of the filters in the projector with the result of failure of the polarization multiplexing.

Another way to achieve polarization multiplexing is to use circularly polarized filters. One image is filtered through a clockwise-oriented circular polarizing filter and the other through a counterclockwise-oriented circular polarizing filter. The participant wears a pair of glasses with corresponding filters. Circular polarization overcomes the problem with changing orientation described earlier with linear polarization, but the end result is less compelling because there is the potential of "ghosting" (each eye seeing a muted version of the image it is not supposed to see), which causes the imagery to look somewhat out of focus.

Polarizing filters and glasses that use them are relatively inexpensive. Hence polarization multiplexing can be a good choice for scenarios where many people need to experience the stereoscopic display. This is why it is used commonly in movie theaters.

Spectral multiplexing. Another technique used for ensuring that each eye sees the image intended for it is to filter based on color. The old 3D movies from the 1950s that used the red and blue filters in cardboard glasses (other color pairs are possible) used a simple form of spectral multiplexing. With this scheme, the pair of images is filtered by color at the projector or at their creation, and a corresponding filter in the glasses is provided to "remove" the improper image from view. The downside of this method is that you are (largely) limited to two colors in your images and thus do not provide the participant with a full (or seemingly full) color experience. This technique is referred to by some as *anaglyphic stereo*, a term that could potentially be applied in a broader sense to stereo methods, but is used most commonly to refer to the two-color stereo technique.

A similar technique that is used applies the same idea yet preserves more color information. Instead of filtering on just two colors, a comb filter is applied to a more full spectrum image. For the other eye, a different comb filter is applied. With this scheme, many colors can be represented, yet the pair of images are distinct from each other from a spectral perspective. In simpler words, each image has all of the basic colors, but they have shades of each color filtered differently. For example, some shades of green are filtered on one image and different shades of green are filtered on the other, yet both images still appear to have green in them. Other colors are treated similarly. There are numerous different implementations of this idea that deal with different numbers of colors and different specific spectra. "Infitec" is an example of a specific instantiation of this idea. It uses six colors (two color bands each of red, green, and blue) yet the participants perceive a full color spectrum in their viewing experience (Figure 3.37).

Autostereoscopic displays. All of the previous techniques require the participants to have some sort of technology either on or near their face. The key

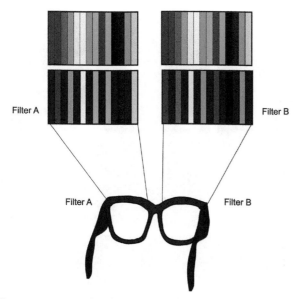

FIGURE 3.37

In early 3D movies, the movie was shown through red and blue or red and green filters. Audience members then wore glasses with the corresponding color filters in them to ensure that each eye saw the image intended for it. This worked but had the undesirable feature that the movie appeared to be basically two colors. The same principle can be used by applying a comb filter over one image source that incorporates all discrete colors of the spectrum, but not all the shades of those colors. The participants wear a corresponding filter on the eye that the image is intended for. The other image source is filtered through a comb filter that allows all the discrete colors of the spectrum, but different shades of them. The participants wear a corresponding filter over their other eye. In this way, the image intended for the left eye is seen by the left eye, and the image intended for the right eye is seen by the right eye. In this case, however, many more colors are seen. Not all shades of all colors are seen by each eye, but overall there is a wider range of colors represented than with the old-fashioned 3D glasses. *Diagram courtesy of Beverly Carver.*

differentiator of autostereoscopic displays is that they do not require the participants to wear any technology for the purpose of perceiving stereoscopic imagery correctly. Current autostereoscopic displays use either a parallax barrier or some type of lenticular lens system to ensure that each eye sees only the image intended for it. To work correctly, the participant must be oriented in a fairly specific way with respect to the display surface. Although the idea of autostereoscopic displays is exciting, at this point in time, applications that can use them effectively represent a tiny fraction of use cases for augmented reality (Figure 3.38).

Multichannel visual displays. Although most visual displays use two channels at most (because we have two eyes), as I alluded to earlier, it is possible to

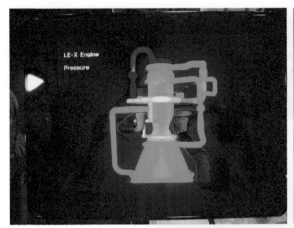
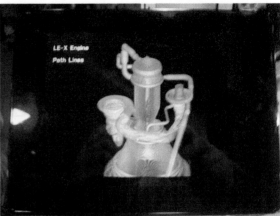
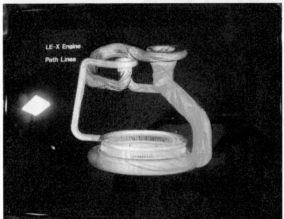

FIGURE 3.38

These three photos show an autostereoscopic display. In these photos it is not apparent that the images look 3D stereoscopic, but in the real world, if you stand in the sweet spot of the display, the images look quite three dimensional. Note that the display does not require the viewer to wear any glasses or other devices to see the three dimensionality of the images. The display is fed with an image intended to be seen by the right eye and one intended for the left eye. The nature of the display ensures that the correct image is seen by the intended eye. *Photos courtesy of Alan B. Craig.*

use more channels to advantage. The most commonly encountered scenario for more than two visual channels is when there is more than one participant who is experiencing the same imagery at the same time and it is important for each participant to view the imagery from his or her own perspective. In this case, rather than multiplexing over the location of each of a pair of eyes, you multiplex over the total number of eyes involved in the experience. For example, with temporal multiplexing, the images might be displayed sequentially to eye one, eye two, eye three, and eye four, with the shuttering glasses

Table 3.2 This Table Illustrates Some of the Similarities and Differences Among Different Techniques Used in Stereoscopic Displays

	Active vs Passive	Color Range	Dependence on Specific Orientation	Cost	Encumbrance on Participant
Spatial multiplexing	Passive	Full	Depends on how it is achieved	Varies	High
Temporal multiplexing	Active	Full	None	High	Medium
Polarization multiplexing	Passive	Full	Linear—very dependent Circular—less dependent	Low	Low
Spectral multiplexing	Passive	Ranges based on specific scheme	None	Low	Low
Autostereoscopic display	Passive	Full	Highly dependent	High	None

allowing exactly one eye to see the display at any specific moment. This means that there would be times when each participant sees nothing. This is either okay or not, depending on the rate at which the images are switching.

Summary chart. Table 3.2 illustrates some of the similarities and differences among different techniques used in stereoscopic displays.

Audio

Stereo displays for audio are much more straightforward than stereo visual displays. In order to display stereo audio (referred to as stereophonic audio) you need to create an audio stream for each ear. In almost all cases, spatial multiplexing is used to ensure that the correct ear hears the correct signal. For example, the audio intended for the left ear is delivered to the left earbud and the audio intended for the right ear is delivered to the right earbud. With loudspeakers it is a bit more difficult to ensure that each ear hears the correct sound, but in general, the audio intended for the left ear is delivered by the left speaker and the audio intended for the right ear is delievered to the right speaker.

Characteristics of Displays That Are Common to Many Display Types

There are a number of specifications that provide information about different display types and how well they will perform for the tasks you need them to do.

These can be described in several categories as follow.

Fidelity is a measure of quality and/or how well the representation replicates the real-world equivalent. This is largely measured in terms of *resolution*. Breaking that down further, we have *spatial resolution* and *temporal resolution*.

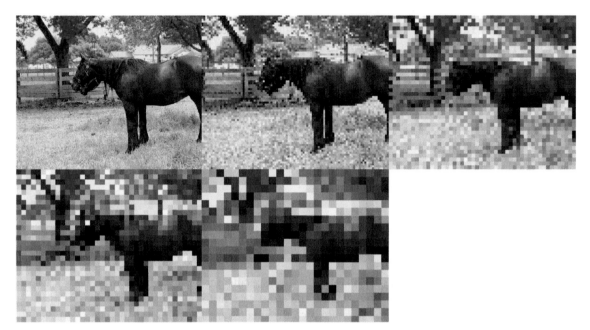

FIGURE 3.39
This series of photos illustrates the effect of different resolutions of images. The first in the sequence shows the photo at its original resolution. Each successive photo shows the picture at less and less spatial resolution. The result is a lower quality image, but at a reduction in storage space required for the image. It is a trade-off between size of data and quality of image. *Photo and sequence courtesy of Beverly Carver.*

These qualities apply to all displays whether visual, audio, haptic, or other (Figure 3.39).

Spatial resolution pertains to how much information is available over space. In a visual display, this is often described as how many pixels there are within a given area. The more pixels there are, the more information can be displayed. Likewise, in an audio display, this corresponds to the range of signals that can be displayed. Temporal resolution relates to how rapidly the display can update. Consequently, things that change in a high-frequency way require that a display with a high degree of temporal resolution be used.

Apparent resolution is how your senses perceive the system rather than exactly what the display is presenting. For example, a very large display screen may look very detailed but actually have poor resolution. The fact that you are a significant distance from it makes it so you cannot discern the blocky images. On a display that you are holding close to your eyes, the important measure of resolution is the number of pixels per inch rather than the total number of pixels.

Brightness is the amplitude of the visual signal.

Field of view refers to how much of your sensory system the display impinges on while you are in a fixed pose. For example, if you look through a narrow tube while you keep your head still, you have a narrow field of view. On the other hand, most projection environments have a very wide field of view. This term relates primarily to visual displays.

Field of regard is how much of your perceived world the digital portion covers. That is, if all the digital enhancements (whether visual, sonic, etc.) to your world occur only in front of you, it represents less field of regard than one in which you are totally surrounded by them.

Logistical properties are related to the weight, size, durability, energy requirements, and so on for displays. These must be considered in light of the potential augmented reality application.

Augmented Reality System

An augmented reality system, from a hardware perspective, consists of a sensor(s), processor(s), and display(s). In designing the overall system, one must consider the goals of the system: Who will use it? What is the required level of fidelity? Will it need to move from a single location? How many people must use it simultaneously? What sensory stimuli must be presented to the participant? And other questions of this nature. One must also consider the constraints that are placed on the system: Is there a size limitation? Is the Internet available? Is there power available or must the system function solely on batteries or some other energy source? Can the potential participants hear? See? Are there sanitary concerns that would preclude people from sharing head-worn displays, etc.? How robust must the system be against breakage? Is there a throughput requirement if multiple people use the same system (i.e., how quickly must a participant be able to "suit up" for the experience if using a head-mounted display)? If there are multiple installations, must the hardware be identical from site to site? What environmental constraints are there? Rain? Bright sunlight? Total darkness? There must also be serious attention paid to interoperability between the different hardware components. Will this display work with that processor? Will this sensor integrate with that sensor?

All of these considerations, as well as others, are addressed in subsequent chapters.

SUMMARY

This chapter has taken a very hardware-centric look at the components of an augmented reality system. The three core elements of an AR system—sensors, processors, and displays—were discussed based on the specifications and affordances they offer to application designers and experience participants. The next chapter focuses on software. Software and hardware are very closely related to each other in that there must be compatibility and interoperability between a number of disparate pieces of the complex augmented reality system.

CHAPTER 4

Augmented Reality Software

INTRODUCTION

Regardless of the hardware platform available, it is the software that will make the hardware do what you want/need it to do. The software is the piece of the puzzle that turns that hardware into a powerful system capable of making your ideas for how to apply augmented reality (AR) to your area of interest come to fruition. There are software components that are part of the AR infrastructure that is required regardless of the application being used, there is software specific to the application, and there is software used to create the content for your application. This chapter addresses each of these categories of software.

MAJOR SOFTWARE COMPONENTS FOR AUGMENTED REALITY SYSTEMS

The software involved with creating and using an augmented reality application can be divided roughly into four categories:

- Software involved directly in the AR application
- Software used to create the AR application
- Software used to create the content for the AR application
- Other software related to AR

Another way to conceptualize the software components for augmented reality systems is:

- Low-level programming libraries (e.g., tracking software)
- Rendering and application building libraries
- Plug-in software for existing applications
- Standalone applications (e.g., content building, complete AR authoring)
- Software to create the content for the AR application

There are software components that serve many different roles with respect to an augmented reality application. As noted before, different ways can be

125

used to implement the various functions. One thing that is fortunate for augmented reality application developers is that there are software libraries available that are bundled together to provide a number of these functionalities without the developer needing to worry about all of the details of all of the components of the library.

Before looking at specific aspects of the software, for the sake of grounding these ideas in some form of reality, let's consider a simple, typical augmented reality application and the pieces of software involved with it. Consider a simple augmented reality-enhanced game that uses optical tracking. The key components involved in such a game would include the following:

- Tracking library (to recognize the fiducial markers or features)
- Model loading and animation (to provide the AR elements of the game)
- Game logic/game engine (i.e., something that provides the actual "game" of the application)
- Rendering software to provide the images (visual, audio, etc.) to the display(s). Note that many game engines include rendering software as part of the game engine.

As we look at the software in further depth it might help to think about how the different pieces are related to the simple AR game.

The first set of software functions to look at is the software involved directly with the AR application. By that I mean that the software plays a role at the time that the application is being used by one or more participants. This is as opposed to software (such as compilers) that are used when you are creating the application, but aren't used directly during the application, and software to create content, fiducial symbols, etc.

Software Involved Directly in the Augmented Reality Application

The software that is involved directly in the AR application includes the following functional components:

- Environmental acquisition (sensors)
- Sensor integration
- Application engine
- Rendering software (visual, audio, etc.)

These components are often bundled together in an AR library (to be discussed later in the chapter). One of the major differences between different AR software libraries is how the creator of the library chose to carry out and integrate those functions. Currently, it is not a straightforward thing to pick and choose among different components from within different AR libraries. That is, in general, you pick a library and that then constrains you to use the components that come with that library. Note that even the platform that a library works with can constrain you as well. Hence, you must be certain that the software library you choose will work with all the different delivery platforms you plan to support (Figure 4.1).

Efforts are being made to develop standards that will make it easier to pick and choose different components with a reasonable belief that they will work together. Unfortunately, because none of the popular libraries do everything that any given developer might need, there is a tendency for AR application developers to create their own library and/or simply create all the modules they need from scratch rather than use a library. That said, there are several AR libraries that are among the more popular libraries to use. The details of what is contained in any given library and which are the most popular libraries change at a rapid rate and would be out of date by the time this book is published. Hence, that information is posted on the companion website for this book.

There are some frameworks, such as openFrameworks (http://www.openframeworks.cc/), that make it easier for developers to combine different library modules, including AR library modules. openFrameworks, for example, includes AR tracking libraries such as ARToolkit.

Environmental Acquisition

The software that supports environmental acquisition is the software that interfaces between the AR system and the sensors used to gather information about the state of the real world. For example, there is software required to take information from a camera and make it available as an image that the rest of the software can make use of. This is handled differently in different AR libraries that are available. It is important that the system is able to gather information from the camera very quickly.

Likewise, in the case of gathering audio information from the real world through the use of a microphone, how well and how fast the transition is made from the analog signal from the microphone to the digital signals needed by the AR system can affect the overall quality of the AR experience.

This is also the case for other "image"-based signals such as RADAR, as well as compass, global positioning system (GPS), and depth sensors, along with input devices such as physical buttons. Other sensors, such as temperature sensors, deal with much less information and are not generally a problem for acquiring information. Of course, the next issue is how to make use of the signals that each of the sensors provide.

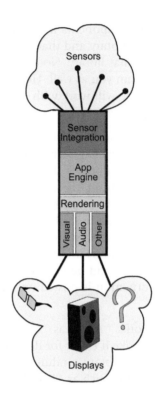

FIGURE 4.1

This diagram shows the relationship between the core components (hardware and software) of an augmented reality system. The state of the environment is assessed by the sensors—the results of those are combined and fed to the main AR application. Based on the state of the total environment, the system renders the information as signals that are then fed to the various displays. This process repeats constantly, and the displays are updated anytime any piece of information changes. This might include the participant changing his or her position slightly or some other aspect of the environment or AR application changing. *Diagram courtesy of Beverly Carver.*

Sensor Integration

Sensor integration is the step in which signals from the sensors are processed and integrated to make them suitable for the AR application. That is, the low-level sensor signals are converted into a piece of information that is required for the AR application. The most obvious instance of this is the use of camera data to provide tracking information to the AR application. The camera images alone don't tell the application directly any information about where the camera must be in order to provide that image. The information must be (potentially) combined with another sensor, such as GPS, to tell the application where the camera must be; also, the imagery the camera is providing must be processed to determine the camera location and pose in the environment. This step, as described in Chapter 2, typically involves the use of computer vision techniques—specifically, camera-based computer vision software.

Most often, once the camera image is acquired, the computer vision algorithm (software) "looks" through the image to find any fiducial markers and/or natural feature tracking (NFT) information. That information provides information to the system about where the camera is with respect to that marker or other data. It determines this information through a complex set of processes that "look" at the size of the marker (to determine distance), how the marker is oriented with respect to the camera, distortions present in the image (it uses these distortions to determine the orientation of the marker with respect to the camera), and other entities in the scene and their relationship to the marker. This step could also be considered *image processing*. This process must occur continuously (at least 15 times per second) because the application needs to "know" whether the camera has moved with respect to the marker. If so, it needs to recalculate where it is and how it is posed with respect to the marker. Note that in practice, the vision algorithm runs continuously whether there is any movement or not in the scene. The application updates at each time step whether anything has changed or not.

Another process that occurs during sensor integration is to combine the signals in meaningful ways. For example, sometimes it is necessary to use the signals from multiple sensors to accomplish a single task. Sometimes tracking can be enhanced by combining the vision results with data from accelerometers, GPS, a compass, etc. The combination of multiple sensors can be advantageous to determining the camera location and pose accurately and speedily.

Any participant-generated signals, such as a button press, are also captured and integrated here. The result of the sensor integration with the application is a digital model of the world and/or the participant as determined by the sensors, including the geometry of the scene and the orientation of the objects. This model is continuously updated with new information from the sensors, both the environmental sensors, as well as any explicit actions the user has taken via button presses or other interactions.

Application Engine

The application engine is the core structure and framework for the AR application that the participants will interact with. The application engine gathers the inputs from the sensor integration component(s) and the participant(s) and generates the information that will be given to the renderer(s) to generate the signals for the display device(s). It also provides a simulation loop supporting user interaction (Figure 4.2).

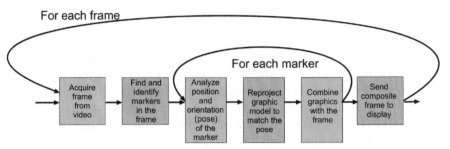

FIGURE 4.2
This diagram illustrates the basic flow of an augmented reality application. *Diagram courtesy of Robert E. McGrath and Beverly Carver.*

The application engine enforces the "rules of nature" for the augmented environment. That is, it supports any simulations or rules that take place in the combined virtual/real world of the AR environment. For example, if you "pick up" a virtual ball in the AR world and then let go of the ball, the ball could be made to do any number of things. It could fall to the ground, stay exactly where you let go of it, float to the ceiling, explode, change color, take off like a rocket ship, or anything else the application designer wants it to do. The possibilities for these types of reactions are addressed chapter 5 (Content is Key!—Augmented Reality Content) and chapter 6 (Interaction in Augmented Reality). Suffice it here to say that those desired actions are handled in the application engine.

The application engine will also have a component for content management. That component might be a very simple table that keeps track of the digital assets, such as objects, sounds, and other content elements involved with the AR experience, or it might be a very involved section that keeps track of what assets are currently available on a mobile device (recall that there are limited resources on many mobile devices) and handle the swapping of currently needed assets for those that can be removed from the device at least temporarily. The content management component also relates the digital assets with any fiducial markers or other resources that they are associated with and handles the loading of content.

For some AR applications, the role of the AR application engine could be handled by a computer game engine. Many AR applications resemble computer games, even though it may not appear that way at first blush. Many games have the same kinds of issues, including utilizing user input (perhaps from a joystick or buttons on a controller), content management (keeping track of the graphical and sound elements of the game), managing simulations (that perhaps govern how a brick wall falls when it is destroyed), and so on. Many game engines also include the rendering components described later in this chapter. Thus, the game engine could potentially interact with the AR sensors and displays and provide an overall framework for the AR application (Figures 4.3 and 4.4).

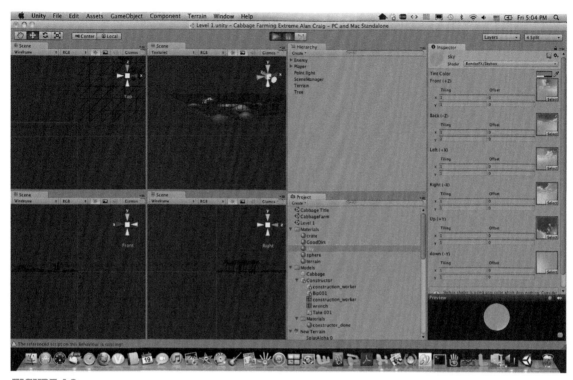

FIGURE 4.3
This screenshot shows the Unity Game Engine from the game developer's perspective. *Screenshot courtesy of Alan B. Craig.*

Some game engines, such as the Unity Development Tool, are available for free download with a "Pro" version available for a fee. Some of these types of systems offer full development environments (and content development environments) as well as just the game engine component.

In many AR applications, it is the application engine that is written "from scratch." That is, a developer makes use of components contained in an AR library (to be discussed shortly) but writes their own "application," which really amounts to writing the application engine and using modules contained in an AR library to handle the "AR-ish" aspects of their final product.

The application is written in the language of the developers' choice, often C or Java, within the constraints of the AR library being used. The choice of programming language matters when it comes to deciding on what AR library to use. As you can see, choosing an AR library impacts what language you write the application in and vice versa. Bear in mind that the platform you choose to deliver the application on has an impact on your choice of programming language (Android requires Java, Apple iOS requires Objective C).

FIGURE 4.4
This screenshot shows the perspective a game player sees when playing the game that was created using the Unity Game Engine. In this case the game takes place on a terrain among trees. *Screenshot courtesy of Alan B. Craig.*

Rendering Software

As discussed in Chapter 2, rendering software is the component that converts the information from the AR application into signals to drive the AR display(s). There is rendering software for graphics (visual output), for sound (audio output), for (potentially) haptics (tactile and force output), and, although rare, for smell output, taste output, and any other sensory output. Different AR libraries use different renderers and thus handle graphics in different ways. From the AR application developers' perspective, the primary things to think about in the case of the visual aspect are the types of graphics that the system supports (such as polygon-based graphics) and the file formats used to support them (such as .obj, .wrl, or others) and, in the case of audio output, what types of sound synthesis and/or sample playback the system supports, as well as the file formats used to support them (such as .wav, .aiff, .mp3, or others). File formats and other details regarding sound and visuals are discussed in the content chapter, Chapter 5.

Many computer graphics programs are built on a base library called OpenGL (http://www.opengl.org/)(stands for Open Graphics Language). OpenGL is an open graphics platform that many software applications and hardware (hardware accelerators optimized for OpenGL) have at their core in order to provide a standard software interface to different graphic devices to simplify the development of applications. Many graphics developers are very comfortable working with OpenGL in their development efforts. Consequently, OpenGL is used very often as the core piece of a renderer for augmented reality applications.

Augmented Reality Libraries

Augmented reality libraries are available commercially, as well as for free download from various sources. Each library brings with it a set of capabilities, and a philosophy for developing AR applications. Hence it is important to pick your AR library wisely, taking into account the capabilities the library offers, the needs of your application, the target deployment platform, the level of support available, the development methodology and cost of the library.

Some of the questions to ask yourself when deciding on what AR library to choose include: "What platform(s) am I developing for?"; "What sensors do I need to integrate?"; if planning to use computer vision for tracking, "What kinds of fiducial symbols do I want to use, or do I want to use NFT or something else?" and "How many markers do I need to track simultaneously?"; "What kinds of graphics and audio are supported?"; "How much can I afford to invest in development time vs cost to purchase a higher end AR library?"; and so on.

Cross-Platform Support

One benefit from using an AR library, as opposed to developing all of the software yourself, is that in addition to some of the development work already having been done by the library developer, AR libraries offer the current best hope for an application that can be deployed on different hardware and software platforms (Figure 4.5).

I say "the best hope" for being able to create a cross-platform application because even with the best of AR libraries, cross-platform capability is not a given. At the first cut, you can only hope that your application will work on a given platform if there is a version of the library available for that platform. Not all libraries work for all platforms. Even with that caveat, it is still a wise idea to use an AR library rather than build your own library if there is one available that will meet your needs, even if it isn't perfect.

With augmented reality applications, being "cross platform" isn't as simple as being across different operating systems such as Windows, OSX, and Linux.

FIGURE 4.5
Developing software for multiple platforms is a nontrivial task. This photo shows a very small number of the different kinds of devices you might want to have your software support. In this photo there is a laptop, a tablet, and two varieties of smartphones. You might also want your software to run on other operating systems than represented in this photo and other types of displays and controllers. *Photo courtesy of Michael Simeone.*

Because the AR application needs to interface with specific hardware in specific devices, even if you are using an AR library it may require you to do specific coding for specific devices. Additionally, different libraries offer different performance on different platforms. Hence it might be necessary to do some testing and benchmarking of different libraries on your platform of choice to assess their capabilities and performance for your application.

The Rapidly Changing Landscape

Anyone who has been paying attention to AR libraries over the past several years has noticed how rapidly the libraries are undergoing change. New libraries are constantly emerging, some libraries disappear, and others get merged into each other. It is very difficult to keep up with the rapid changes. It is very tempting when an upgrade is made to a different library than you are using to "jump ship" and use the new library because it appears to match your needs better than what you are using. This can become an exercise in futility as you are constantly redeveloping your application to take advantage of a different library. There is a significant learning curve to using any of these libraries, so it is a considerable investment to develop for one library and another investment to convert to a different one.

Although most AR applications of the type discussed in this book use three-dimensional (3D) graphics objects for the visual component, there is also a set of applications, and thus, AR libraries, that make it straightforward to use two-dimensional animated graphical elements pasted onto (or "texture mapped") the 3D graphics for the visual display. This can be done with any of the libraries, but there are libraries created specifically to exploit this capability in a more straightforward way. The FLARToolKit is an example of this type of AR library. The FLARToolKit is a flash version of the popular ARToolKit library. This library makes use of graphical elements that are enhanced with (potentially) data-driven animations using tools such as Adobe Flash to create the animations. This opens the development of content to developers who already create content in programs such as Flash.

Comparing AR Libraries

At some point it becomes necessary to make comparisons of different AR libraries to see how they match up with your needs. Although some AR libraries have been around for a long time (e.g., the ARToolKit has been around for over 10 years), the landscape of AR libraries and library specifics is changing so fast that anything included in this book would likely be out of date by the time it hit the shelves. Hence, I will provide a list of some of the things to consider when comparing libraries and refer the reader to the companion website of this book for more specific information.

Some of the basic questions you should ask about any library you are considering include:

- What is the licensing arrangement? (Free?, Free for education? Fee?, etc. One-time purchase or ongoing license?, etc.)
- What is the level of support? (Commercial support? Open source community? None?, etc.)
- What platforms does it support? (Windows? MacOS? iOS? Android? Linux?, etc.)
- How difficult is it to use?
- Is training available for how to use it?
- What is its performance level?
- What input and output devices does it support?
- What types of content does it support?
- What kinds of interaction does it support?
- How widely is it used by other developers?

Software Used to Create the Augmented Reality Application

Beyond the AR libraries, or the same functionality from other sources, creating an AR application is not significantly different than any other interactive, media-intensive application. Of course, efficiency is of the utmost concern to minimize lag and latency, but the same types of tools and resources used for other types of applications are also used for developing AR applications.

In the same way as compilers, software development environments, debuggers, and so on are used for creating any type of software, those same tools can be used to develop AR applications. There are, however, some environments that are especially conducive to developing AR applications. For example, the free AndAR AR library (for Android devices) exists as a plug-in for the (free) Eclipse software development kit (SDK). Eclipse was written primarily in Java with plug-in support for other languages. Hence, it is friendly for development using the Java language. If you are doing development for applications that run on Apple iOS environments, you will use Apple's Xcode development environment and you will need a connection to the Apple developer site. You can't do this development in Eclipse. Applications developed in Xcode cannot run on Android. If you wish to develop for other platforms such as Sony PlayStations and Nintendo devices, you will need to be a licensed developer for them.

I mention these specific examples of tools that work together to make the more general point that there are a number of considerations to make when embarking on an AR development project. Your choice of AR library may be influenced by or influence your choice of programming language, software development environment, and other software libraries, as well as the hardware platform you're targeting. Changing AR libraries can be a bigger task than simply unplugging one library and plugging in another (Figure 4.6).

SOFTWARE USED TO CREATE CONTENT FOR THE AUGMENTED REALITY APPLICATION

The software used to create the content for AR applications is discussed in more detail in Chapter 5, *Content Is Key!—Augmented Reality*, but it is good to provide a very high-level overview of the software in this chapter on AR software. Although there are software tools for creating fully multimedia content in one package, more often content creators use tools built and optimized for creating one type of content. Because the vast majority of AR applications use visuals and/or sounds, this section covers the following types of software:

- Software for creating and editing three-dimensional graphics
- Software for creating and editing two-dimensional graphics
- Software for creating and editing sound

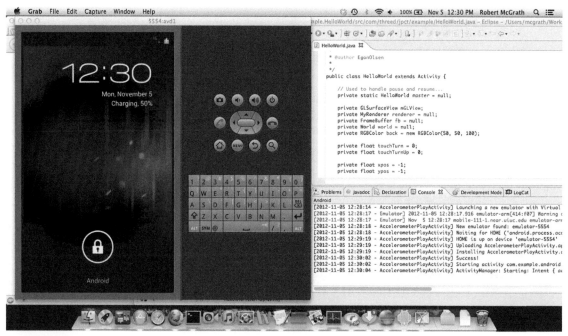

FIGURE 4.6

This screenshot shows the Eclipse development environment being used to develop an Android application. The Android emulator at the left of the screen is used during development when you do not have a physical Android device attached. *Screenshot courtesy of Robert E. McGrath.*

Software for Creating and Editing Three-Dimensional Graphics

There are two basic categories of software for creating and editing 3D graphics. One is used to create computer graphics from scratch. The other is software that helps you "import" real-world objects through some type of a three-dimensional scanning process or by analyzing photographs of 3D objects and creating graphical models of the object in the photos. First, let's take a look at software tools that are primarily used for creating objects from scratch.

There are a number of 3D modeling packages used by scientists, engineers, movie producers, architects, and so forth to create three-dimensional computer graphics. These packages may be used to create augmented reality content as well. The main criterion is being able to generate the types of files that your AR library requires. Because most of these types of packages can export and/or convert between many different graphics file formats, this is not usually a problem. File formats and related information are covered in Chapter 5 in this book.

In general, the graphical content elements for an AR application are made as a separate process from the development of the AR application itself. The AR

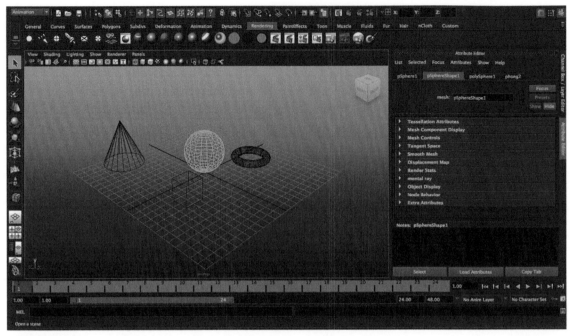

FIGURE 4.7
This screenshot shows one view of the user interface of a 3D graphics modeling program. In this case, the screenshot is from Autodesk Maya, which is a widely used program for creating content for movies, virtual reality, augmented reality, engineering, and many more uses. This type of program offers the capability of creating anything you can imagine. In this screenshot, a cone, sphere, cube, and torus are shown in wireframe mode. Objects of much greater complexity can be created and modified. Also, it is straightforward to attach "materials" to the objects to give them colors, surface and reflection properties, textures, etc. Ultimately, the graphics objects are written out to a file that can be read by the AR application. *Screenshot courtesy of Alan B. Craig.*

application then reads the graphical elements from files to be used in the application. The exception to this is if the graphics are generated algorithmically from within the application based on data provided by the application. An example of this exception would be an application that creates a virtual thermometer that shows the temperature at the location the application is being used. In this case, based on temperature readings from a temperature sensor, the application could draw a thermometer that shows the current temperature.

Although computer graphics can be described in a file directly by writing graphics commands and information into a file using a text editor, it is much more common to use a graphical user interface to create objects. The software then creates the graphics file automatically. This is a much friendlier way to create graphics files.

Although different programs offer different features, and a different user interface, most of the 3D computer graphics modeling programs work in much the same way. It is beyond the scope of this book to teach you how to

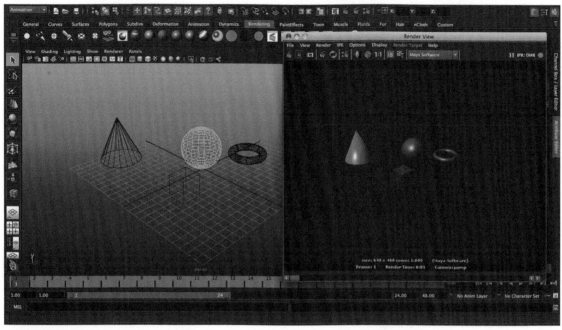

FIGURE 4.8

This screenshot shows the scene that was made in Figure 4.7 with a window showing a quick rendering of what the objects will look like. Note that the objects are rendered very simply. The objects can be made far more complex with far more surface properties, colors, textures, etc. *Screenshot courtesy of Alan B. Craig.*

use these packages in an expert way, but I hope to give you an idea of what these programs are like (Figures 4.7 and 4.8).

In addition to standard graphical packages, there are also some free software tools that provide somewhat of a similar functionality in a free, open-source mode of distribution. One of the more popular free modeling tools is called Blender (Figures 4.9 and 4.10).

If you are trying to create a three-dimensional model of some object that exists in the real world, instead of creating the computer graphics from scratch, you can (depending on the size of the object and many other criteria) scan the object with a 3D scanner and then use or modify the resulting computer graphics file. Usually, 3D scans require some "touching up" in order to be useful. Software for this purpose is often included with the 3D scanner. It is beyond the scope of this book to describe the scanning process in detail, but if you have the need to create graphical objects representing specific real-world objects, it would be worthwhile to learn more about the process, capabilities, and limitations of such an approach (Figure 4.11).

A growing trend is to make 3D computer graphics models by providing software with photos of the object taken from all sides of the object. The software

FIGURE 4.9

Blender is similar in many ways to Maya but is available as a free download. It does have a higher learning curve though. *Screenshot courtesy of Alan B. Craig.*

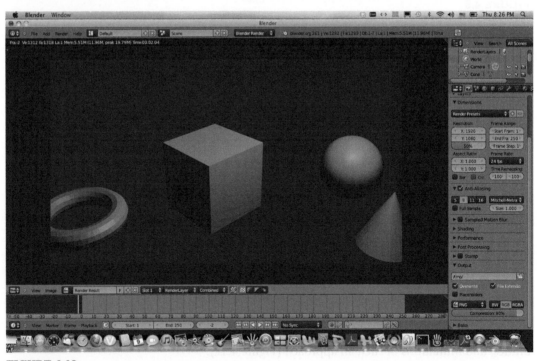

FIGURE 4.10

This screenshot shows a basic rendering of some simple objects in Blender. *Screenshot courtesy of Alan B. Craig.*

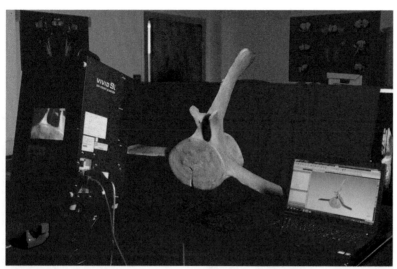

FIGURE 4.11

This 3D scanner (Konica Minolta Vivid 9i) is capable of scanning large objects. In this case, a large bone is being scanned. The resulting model can be seen on the laptop on the right. *Photo courtesy of Nicholas Homer, Idaho Museum of Natural History.*

stitches the photos together and extracts clues from the images about the three dimensionality of the object. The software then creates a file that is in a computer graphics format that can be used with AR applications. One example of a program that does this type of operation is Autodesk 123D Catch (http://www.123dapp.com/catch).

In a somewhat related activity, one can also capture motion from the real world for animations. In general, if you require the animation of objects or other things, the process is either to use a computer program to compute where every entity needs to be at any given moment or to use animation software that allows you to specify the paths and timing of any animation. In a manner analogous to scanning real-world objects to create graphical objects, real-world movements can be imported through a process called *motion capture*. In brief, motion capture systems work by "observing" a real-world entity and recording its motion over time, which can then be used to drive computer graphics objects in a similar way. One of the most common ways of doing motion capture is for an actor to wear a suit that has retroreflective markers on it at various critical locations on his or her body. Cameras then record the locations of those markers over time, and software turns those paths into a description of motion that can then be applied to computer objects. This is done most typically when there is the need to create complicated motions that are difficult to achieve through programming or directly via an animation software package (Figure 4.12).

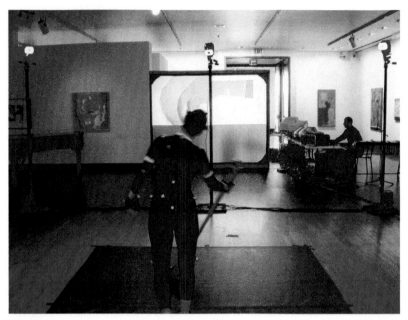

FIGURE 4.12

Motion capture systems use optical tracking to capture the motions of multiple objects. In this photo, there are a set of cameras and lights surrounding the area in which the tracking is done. The dancer is wearing small retroreflective spheres at each point their body is being tracked. In this case, the dancer's motions are controlling the computer graphics. *Photo courtesy of Hank Kaczmarski.*

Software for Creating and Editing Two-Dimensional Graphics

In addition to creating three-dimensional graphics, it is often important to create two-dimensional graphical elements. Two basic types of software are used for creating and modifying two-dimensional graphics: vector graphics programs and raster graphics programs. Vector graphics programs are used mostly when creating imagery from nothing. That is, vector graphics programs are a tool often used by illustrators. Raster graphics programs allow you to modify the pixels in a two-dimensional image. Hence, they are often used for retouching photos, for modifying images, and for processing color maps or anything that is done to all or part of an image. They are not typically used for creating an image from nothing. Both of these types of graphics programs are discussed in detail in Chapter 5.

Software for Creating and Editing Sound

Sound is an important aspect of an augmented reality application. Although most current AR applications focus on visual elements, many incorporate sound in interesting ways. It is likely that as the field of AR matures, sound will play a more important role in AR applications.

Sound can be created "on the fly" in AR applications or it can be created separately from the AR application and then made to play at appropriate times under the control of the AR application. By "on the fly" I mean that computations are performed from within the AR program to synthesize the sounds that are displayed. There are numerous techniques for synthesizing sounds, and it is beyond the scope of this book to explore the different methods by which sound can be synthesized in real time within an AR application.

Other primary ways that sounds are created for AR applications are as follows:

- Record sounds from the real world that can be played back by the AR application at the appropriate time(s)
- Precompute (synthesize) the sounds using software outside of the AR application for later playback in the AR application
- Edit sounds from other sources using editing software

Before delving into the software used to generate sounds outside of the AR application, it is important to know the format that is used to represent sound digitally. In almost all cases, AR applications that play sounds are using some form of digitally represented sound. The file formats used to carry digitally represented sound are covered in Chapter 5 with the discussion of AR content. At this point, however, it is important to know that the basic idea is that a sound is represented as a stream of numbers. A monophonic (single channel) sound can be represented as a single stream of numbers, whereas a stereophonic sound (two channels) requires two streams of numbers. Multichannel sound can be represented by the same number of streams of numbers as there are channels of sound. A channel can be thought of as an independent playback mechanism for the sound. Most modern computers (including handheld devices) have hardware capable of playing stereophonic (two channel) sound. One channel is presented to the left ear and the other channel to the right ear. Note that it is also possible on the same systems to present identical information from a single channel to both output channels. Doing so will eliminate any of the desirable (and undesirable) attributes of stereophonic sound.

Each stream of numbers actually represents an abstraction of a voltage that will be used to drive a speaker. That is, it is a list of numbers that represents a voltage that changes over time. The voltage causes the cone of the speaker to move back and forth to produce a sound. By choosing (or computing or recording) the numbers carefully, any waveform (sound) can be represented. The goal, then, is to create the list(s) of numbers to represent the waveform desired. The waveform that is then later played by the AR application can sound like a natural sound, a musical sound, noise, or anything the creator desires. One of the two most common ways to arrive at the lists of numbers is by computing the desired list(s) or recording a real-world sound digitally.

A digital recording is a direct translation from a real-world sound captured by a sensor (most commonly a microphone) and passed through an analog-to-digital converter to change the analog voltage produced by the sensor into a number, which is then stored in a list for later playback.

Record Sounds from the Real World
Outside the AR Application

The most straightforward way to support your AR application to make very realistic sounds like those in the real world is to record real-world sounds and then use those sounds to play back in your application. In much the same manner that you can record your voice on your computer, which can then be played back by your computer (and sound like the original sound), you can record any real-world sound, including the sound of voices, birds chirping, a gunshot, waves crashing at the ocean, or any of countless sounds. Because it is not often convenient or possible to record sounds yourself (perhaps you don't live near the ocean to record waves), and it is a difficult task to make *good* recordings, some AR developers instead choose to purchase sounds from a third party for use in their application.

Precompute (Synthesize) Sounds Using Software
Outside the AR Application

Another common mechanism used to acquire the sounds that your AR application will play back is to use a computational algorithm to generate the numbers. A plethora of algorithms can be used to generate waveforms for sounds. Fortunately for the AR developer, a number of powerful tools can be used to create your sounds from an (or many) algorithm(s). The home recording industry and the DJ industry have produced a number of very powerful tools to compute interesting sounds. Some algorithms are meant to be used to mimic real-world sounds, whereas others are used to more easily to create sounds that have no counterpart in the real world.

One key type of sound creation environment is what is known as a "soft synthesizer" or "softsynth." Softsynths are software programs that run on your computer and offer a variety of sound synthesis algorithms that allow you to provide a variety of parameters in order to vary the sounds that are made. These synthesizers are often connected to a keyboard (that looks like a piano keyboard), and the sounds are programmed to play different pitches based on which key is pressed. Any number of controllers (in addition to the piano-like keyboard) can be connected to alter any of a number of parameters used in the synthesis. Note that if you want to be able to control your sounds in real time based on parameter values determined by the state of the AR application, the sounds must be computed in real time ("on the fly") on your AR device (Figures 4.13 and 4.14).

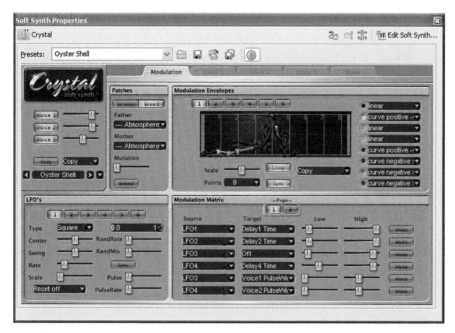

FIGURE 4.13

This screenshot shows the user interface to the Crystal softsynth (http://www.greenoak.com/crystal/ indexDesktop.html). The sliders and buttons correspond to the types of controls you might find on a real, physical sound synthesizer, but this one exists purely in software. *Screenshot courtesy of Alan B. Craig.*

FIGURE 4.14

This screenshot shows the user interface of a sophisticated sound sample library and player (http://www .garritan.com/ and http://www.native-instruments.com/#/en/products/producer/kontakt-5/). This particular one is loaded with samples that are recordings of traditional orchestral instruments such as violins, cellos, and clarinets. This interface also provides a virtual keyboard that you can play the instruments with, or you can attach a physical keyboard via a midi connection, or you can play the sounds via a computer program. *Screenshot courtesy of Alan B. Craig.*

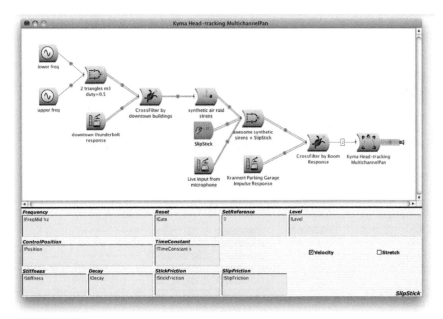

FIGURE 4.15

In the Kyma sound design signal flow editor, you can combine synthesis, signal processing, sample playback, and live audio sources and easily map the sound parameters to external controllers and position sensors via MIDI or Open Sound Control (a protocol for communication among computers, sound engines, and controllers over TCP/IP networks). Note that Kyma provides modules to integrate tracking information that can be used to determine the placement of the sound. *Screenshot courtesy of Symbolic Sound Corporation.*

There are very sophisticated "sound design" packages that focus on providing incredible control to the sound designer. One such system is the Kyma system from Symbolic Sound Corporation (http://www.symbolicsound.com/). Systems such as Kyma allow total flexibility and control over the process of creating sounds. This particular example (Kyma) of a sound design environment provides a graphical user interface that allows the sound designer to piece together a variety of sound sources, filters, modulators, and so on and allow each element to be controlled in any manner that the sound designer desires (Figure 4.15).

Editing Sounds from Other Sources Using Editing Software

Because a sound is represented as a stream of numbers, it is a straightforward process to alter that stream of numbers by any algorithm the sound designer desires. There are a wide variety of editing programs that let you slice, dice, filter, and apply sonic effects to existing sounds. Many such filters are built into sound design and other sound synthesis programs, but they also exist in specialized sound editing programs. Thus, you can begin with some sound and enhance that sound, destroy that sound, or apply effects to that sound and the resulting sound will be some derivative (that may or may not resemble

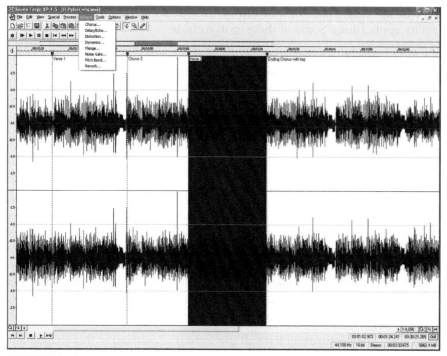

FIGURE 4.16
This screenshot shows a sound-editing program with a two-channel (stereophonic) audio stream loaded. The stream destined for the left ear is on the top, whereas the stream destined for the right ear is on the bottom. A portion of the streams are highlighted, and a menu is chosen to add an effect to the highlighted portion. *Screenshot courtesy of Alan B. Craig.*

the original sound in any way) sound that can be used. A common example of applying an effect to a sound is to give a sound an echo. An echo algorithm computes a new stream of numbers that represents the original sound with an echo. Note that the echo algorithm can have many different parameters that you can specify based on your desires. For example, most echoes allow you to choose how many repeats are created, how fast the repeats happen, or whether the sound fades away, continues, or gets louder and louder. Many of the effects that you can use with sounds allow you to change the character of a sound that is in keeping with the environment in which the sound is played. (This is AR, after all.) That is, a sound might be made to sound different if you are in a desert versus in a cave (Figure 4.16).

Other Software Related to Augmented Reality

Augmented reality applications are complicated and can be difficult to develop. Other general-purpose tools typically used for developing any other type of interactive applications can be utilized when developing augmented reality applications. Some of these tools include:

- Simulators and debuggers
- Tools to manage multimedia assets (e.g., in a database)
- For network applications, tools for creating, managing, and delivering web content
- Packaging and license management technology, for both the application and the multimedia content

Putting It All Together

There are some AR authoring environments that assist you in putting together AR applications. Some of them hide details from you so that nontechnical people can put together an AR application. There are limitations to these types of environments, but they can be used in very powerful ways even today for basic AR development. Over time, these types of tools will become more and more powerful. A couple examples of these types of tools that would be worth taking a look at include buildAR (https://buildar.com/) and Metaio Creator (http://www.metaio.com/products/creator/).

Of course, just because you have all the software described in this chapter and the hardware described in the previous chapter, you don't have an augmented reality application. Creating a compelling application requires careful integration of the hardware, various pieces of software, and content. How these pieces work together is covered more fully in Chapter 8, *Augmented Reality Applications*.

SUMMARY

This chapter focused on the variety of software involved with AR applications, whether it is the software actually running at the time the AR application is being used or the software used for the creation of content for an AR application.

The software involved in creating content for the AR application is covered from a different perspective and a different level of detail in the following chapter (Chapter 5).

The good news for AR developers is that very powerful tools are available to them that address the different aspects of application development. AR libraries are becoming more and more powerful. Unfortunately, as of the writing of this book, there is little standardization between different AR libraries and software components. Hence, it becomes necessary for a developer to "buy in" to a particular library or suite of software tools. In the future (hopefully near future) it will be possible for a developer to pick and choose among, for example, computer vision algorithms, image rendering tools, and so forth and have them work together seamlessly. Until then, developers must use the software and algorithms that are implemented in the AR library they are using, choose a different AR library, or create their own AR library.

At some point, authoring AR applications will be supported by easy-to-use tools that will create AR applications that can be used on a variety of hardware platforms. These tools will make it as easy to create AR applications as it is to make other types of software, and will be suitable for use by designers, teachers, kids, and so forth. We have seen that some of these types of tools already exist, but we expect to see tremendous improvements in capabilities and ease of use from these types of programs.

CHAPTER 5

Content Is Key!— Augmented Reality Content

INTRODUCTION

The reason that augmented reality (AR) applications exist is to provide content that the participant(s) in the augmented reality experience interacts with. Indeed, without compelling content, augmented reality becomes nothing more than a technological novelty. It has been said that someone will go see a movie exactly once because it is a movie. After that the reason to go a second time is because of the compelling content that is conveyed in the movie. With the resurgence in popularity of three-dimensional (3D) movies, some people will go to see a movie once because it is 3D. They want to see what a 3D movie is like. But unless there are good movies being made that use 3D in a compelling way, most people won't go to see a movie just because it is in 3D.

The same is the case with augmented reality. Augmented reality is new enough that people are interested in it just because it is augmented reality. This will wear off very quickly. As discussed in Chapter 1, AR is a medium, and as such, the medium is judged by its content. It is also important that the content is used in a way that takes advantage of the affordances of the medium. It is a mistake to think it is optimal to directly transfer content from one medium to another. For example, if you were interested in making a movie, it would be a mistake to simply place a camera at the audience perspective of a stage play. Only by exploiting the affordances that film provides, such as multiple camera angles, editing, and other possibilities, are you able to utilize the medium of film to its full potential.

Augmented reality is new enough that it is not obvious yet how to make the most of this new medium. As such, this is a time to explore, to experiment, and to try new things. It is also the time to keep tabs on other applications being developed to gain an appreciation of what is working, what is not, and why. Chapter 8 of this book (*Augmented Reality Applications*) takes a look at some successful AR applications, as well as some principles for application design. The companion website to this volume also contains links to applications and demonstration videos and other links of interest.

151

It is important to understand that the technology of augmented reality is not yet fully developed and, as such, AR applications of the future may be able to do things that today's technology can't support. In much the same way that movie making has evolved as the technology of filmmaking has evolved (such as the creation of powerful editing technology) so will augmented reality applications. The technology of AR is still undergoing rapid development, and it is not fully clear what capabilities will be available in the future for sensing, processing, and displaying AR information. Likewise, new technologies will be available to aid in creating content for AR systems. Hence, like the early days of filmmaking, when it was not possible to synchronize an audio track with the visual portion of the movie, we are in the early days of AR application development, and it is reasonable to assume that AR systems of the future will have capabilities that we don't understand today. In the same manner that audiences learned to "read" or understand movies in new ways, it is likely that consumers of AR applications will learn to interact with and interpret AR applications in new and different ways as the technology, and the content, matures over time. We have witnessed this same evolution of people learning to "read" and interact with virtual reality (VR) applications (and the evolution is still occurring). In VR we have seen people adapt to technology and adapt technology to their needs. It is reasonable to believe that the same will occur in the medium of augmented reality.

This chapter addresses conceptual aspects of content (in the medium of AR), as well as some of the technical aspects of how that content is represented within an AR application (such as file formats).

WHAT IS CONTENT?

With respect to augmented reality, content is any and all elements of the *virtual world*, or the enhanced physical world that is part of the augmented reality application. What, then, is a virtual world? Simply put, a virtual world is an idea that is represented through some medium. The virtual world can be manifested in any number of different media. For example, the fictitious character "Pinocchio" exists in a virtual world. That world can be expressed as a story in a book or as a movie, or it could be implemented as a virtual reality experience or an augmented reality experience. That is, the virtual world exists regardless of the medium that it is represented in. Note the importance of the word *represented* in the aforementioned sentence. Ideas can be represented in many different ways in many different media. The idea of Pinocchio can be represented as a painting, as a description using words on paper, as a motion picture, as a verbal story, or as a woodcarving. Note that each of the *representations* of Pinocchio given is virtual. All of the *media* are physical. For example, the woodcarving is a fairly direct representation of Pinocchio that you can see, touch, and potentially hear. The "description using words on paper" exists as a physical medium, but the words are not a direct physical representation of the idea. You can see the paper and the words, and you can touch the paper (the medium), but you can't directly touch what is being represented (Pinocchio).

In all of the representations noted earlier, the actual idea of Pinocchio exists only in our minds. Different media are capable of carrying representations that stimulate different senses of ours, but in all cases, our understanding of the idea of Pinocchio exists only in our minds. Because these media only convey certain elements of the idea of Pinocchio, different people create different images of Pinocchio in their minds. Different representations (via different media) convey different amounts of information about Pinocchio. A representation can be very general or can contain very specific details. The more information that is conveyed, the more likely it will be that the consumer of the representation gets the same idea that the creator of that representation intended. The person creating the representation may very deliberately keep the representation vague to allow the consumers of that representation to fill in their own details or he may choose to be very specific. For example, if I simply represent the idea of Pinocchio by the word "puppet," someone may interpret what Pinocchio looks like, sounds like, and feels like differently than I do. If I represent Pinocchio by the words "a wooden marionette puppet with red pants, a yellow cap with a red feather, and white gloves, then the mental image you create will have those attributes but you and I may have different ideas of what color shirt Pinocchio is wearing. If I give you a color drawing of what I think of as Pinocchio, you may get a closer feel to what I think Pinocchio *looks* like. But you and I might have completely different ideas of what Pinocchio *sounds* like. A movie (with sound) of Pinocchio represents not only how Pinocchio looks and sounds, but also how Pinocchio *moves* and interacts with the world around him. If I make a wood carving to represent Pinocchio, I can convey how Pinocchio *feels*. This discourse of different ways to represent Pinocchio could go on and on and what we would learn is that different representations are appropriate for communicating different kinds of information for different types of purposes.

Attributes of Different Ways of Representing Content

There are many different ways that we can classify different types of content and different ways to represent that content. This section considers representations that are perceived by our senses, the differentiation between the real world and the virtual world, realistic representation vs abstract representation, representations meant to convey physical attributes vs representations to communicate emotion, the idea of representing content to tell a story, and some unique representational methods and unique characteristics of content in augmented reality applications.

Representation and Our Senses

In grammar school we learned that we have five senses:

- Sight
- Sound
- Smell
- Taste
- Touch

We actually have more senses than that (such as our vestibular system), but in general, we gain our understanding of the world around us by interpreting what we perceive through each of our senses. We *see* things, *hear* things, *smell* things, *taste* things, and *touch/feel* things. We sense all of these things over time and integrate the information that each of our senses provide in order to understand where we are, what is around us, what is happening, etc.

As discussed in Chapter 3, AR systems can provide stimuli to each of our senses, with the most common being sight and sound. Some senses are more difficult to provide synthetic stimuli and/or are less important in many applications (such as taste).

It is important to bear in mind that one of the defining characteristics of the medium of augmented reality is that the virtual world coexists within the real (physical) world. Thus, it is reasonable to raise the question of where the virtual world ends and the real world begins and vice versa. Indeed, one must address the question of whether physical world elements are a part of the virtual world or not and/or whether digital elements of the virtual world are a part of the physical world or not.

Consider a television set. The television set is clearly part of the physical world, but what about the content being displayed on that television set? Is the content of a television show a part of your real (physical) world?

Now instead of a typical situation comedy or newscast playing on the television, imagine that the content is a video recording of a home aquarium playing on the television, complete with the sounds of the aerator and filter, the bubbles, etc. Is this object (television playing the role of an aquarium) part of your real world? Indeed it is. Is the virtual world of the ecosystem that makes up the content displayed on the television part of your real world? What if the fidelity is raised to the degree that you can't tell that it is not a real fish tank? What if you can feed the fish in the tank, and if you touch the top of it you can feel the water on your fingers? At some point, if the simulated aquarium, including the behavior of the occupants, is presented at a high enough level of fidelity, the way we perceive the (television) aquarium becomes the same as if there was an actual aquarium with real water and real fish in it. Our mind takes the stimuli from our senses and builds our own mental understanding of what is taking place in the spot where the television portraying a virtual aquarium is. What, then, if we introduce something into that (virtual) aquarium that couldn't possibly exist in a real aquarium? Perhaps a fire-breathing dragon. Such a component in the aquarium would likely place us in a *cognitive dissonance*, where our mind is confused because our senses are telling us something that can't possibly be happening. However, we have learned over our history with technology to resolve many cognitive dissonances. Consider someone from the early 1700s witnessing a modern television with a newscast on it. This would present a cognitive dissonance because they wouldn't understand the technology and would be confused by how someone's head inside that box could be telling us about the events of the day. In fact, if they were to break open the television set they would not find a person's head at all, but rather wires and electronic components that they had never seen before. How do they make sense of this? As we experience augmented reality we face similar dilemmas in interpreting things that appear to be the case, but we know can't possibly be the case.

This dilemma leads to a dichotomy in terms of augmented reality content between that content that falls within our understanding of the real world and that content that does not fall into our understanding of the real world (and sometimes a combination of both).

The point at which something crosses that barrier of when we accept it to be something other than what it actually is can be referred to as *presence*. Presence can be divided between *object presence*, when we accept something as being an object that either doesn't actually exist (and is presented as a digital representation) or is different from what it actually is (e.g., accepting a television as an aquarium), or *user presence*. User presence is when participants cross the line between believing/acting as though they are watching something vs believing/acting as though they are actually present in the virtual or combined virtual and real world. Presence is a difficult concept to define, and also a very difficult concept to measure. People's behavior is often different than their stated level of presence. That is, sometimes people *act* like they are present more than they *say* they are present.

Content That Falls Within Our Understanding of the Real World

Recall the example in Chapter 1 of the (real) table with the (digital) vase on it. We are all accustomed to seeing objects sitting on other objects, such as a vase sitting on a table. In fact, with an augmented reality system of sufficient fidelity, we may actually believe that the vase is a real object. It only begins to create a dissonance as we use our senses to explore the vase and some aspect of the vase does not behave the same as our idea of what a real vase behaves like. Perhaps the visual representation portrayed on the display is of such high fidelity that we believe it is a vase. But then, we reach out to pick up the vase and our hand passes right through it. Our mind is confused and can only be appeased by believing the object is not real or that we are being tricked in some way. However, if we reach out and touch the vase and there is some type of display that can represent the feel of the vase to high fidelity, we may still have no idea that the vase is not "real." If our hand passes through the vase, we may be startled enough to then wonder if the table is real, so we reach out and touch the table. In short, we generally believe what our senses are telling us unless there is some reason to believe otherwise.

One of the most compelling cues that something is not real is if the representation of it is too low in fidelity, that is, some aspect of the representation or the display does not provide enough verisimilitude to the real object. Early computer graphics were "blocky" and "clunky." Hence, it was quite easy to recognize whether you were looking at a real object, a photograph of that object, a painting of that object, or a computer graphics rendering of that object. Today, however, both representation and display of computer graphics objects can be highly realistic, and thus a participant may not realize that he or she is looking at computer graphics as opposed to a real object. Many people today do not recognize when computer graphics have been used in movies as opposed to filming a real scenario.

In today's world we have become sufficiently aware that technology can fool us that it is not always a given that we will even raise an eyebrow when we see something that seems to be unreal in some way. This idea actually makes it easier for people to accept the idea of augmented reality in their everyday world.

Content That Does Not Fall Within Our Understanding of the Real World

Perhaps the more interesting content for augmented reality applications exploits areas that are not meant to only replicate what would happen with the equivalent real-world content. Moviemakers have already taken these ideas to create virtual worlds that are manifest as movies that can't possibly exist in the real world. Whether the virtual world contains alien creatures from outer space or animated animals that talk and behave like humans, audiences are willing to "suspend their disbelief" to enjoy the story that the moviemaker presents.

Because the virtual world in an augmented reality application can take full advantage of synthetically created imagery (not limited to visual imagery), the content creator can embed any types of objects or behaviors in his or her augmented reality applications, as long as they don't conflict with the (real) content provided by the real world.

The Dilemma of the Virtual World and the Real World

The thought question provided earlier in this chapter that asked whether real-world entities are part of the virtual world and vice versa has some very practical fallout for the AR content developer. As already discussed, the content creator can make anything in the virtual world. For example, if the content creator wants the (virtual) vase on the table to morph into a three-headed monster, no problem! However, if the content creator wants the participant in the AR application to be able to walk through the (real) table, the physics of the real world rear their ugly head. Try as we may, an AR application (today) cannot allow the participant to break the real-world laws of physics. This precludes the AR content creator from doing certain things he or she might like to do, such as remove the law of gravity, teleport a (real) object from place to place, or allow the participant to (really) fly.

Recall that the magic of AR is in the mind of the participant. Hence, it may be possible to circumvent or at least give the appearance of circumventing some aspects of real-world physics. For example, if one wants the participant to feel like he or she is hovering in the air when he or she actually is standing on the floor, one can create visual imagery that looks like there are objects, trees, and ground far below the participant when he or she looks down. The visual clues provided can (sometimes) overcome the real-world cues (such as the participant feeling the floor on the bottom of his or her feet) to cause his perceptual system to "believe" he or she is hovering in midair.

Realistic Representation vs Abstract Representation

In much the same manner that other media (painting, some music, etc.) have explored realism vs abstract representation, the same ideas and capabilities are available to the AR content creator. Beyond exploring abstract representation for artistic purposes in AR, abstract representation can be used to communicate ideas for which there is no real world (physical) counterpart. For example, if part of my AR application is to convey the idea of complex chemical or physical processes taking place in the air around the participant, there is no real physical entity that can show that. Hence, it is up to the content designers to create abstract representations to communicate the ideas or feelings they are trying to communicate (Figure 5.1).

Likewise, the content creator might want to add additional information to some object (either real or virtual) to show invisible aspects of that object. For example, if the goal was to show the stresses and forces involved when two objects are in contact with each other, the AR content developer could create abstract representations, such as color maps, to show what happens to both the vase and the table when someone places the (virtual) vase onto the (real) table.

FIGURE 5.1
This AR application from Inition shows a scientific visualization of flow fields around a model of a building. This one is particularly interesting because it shows the visualization around a 3D printout of the building design created by Zaha Hadid Architects. *Photo courtesy of Inition.*

It is important also to differentiate between content elements that are specifically meant to be *photorealistic* (i.e., to appear to look **exactly** the same as some physical counterpart with respect to its visual appearance, as well as all other aspects of that entity) and those that are important to the application, but it is not necessary (and, in some cases, not desirable) for the entity to replicate a specific real-world equivalent. For example, in some cases, it may be important that the (virtual) vase on the (real) table be a photorealistic rendering of some specific real-world counterpart vase, whereas in other cases it may just need to be a simple, generic vase meant to communicate just the idea that there is a vase on the table. The difference might be made more clear if the intention of the AR application was to show a historically accurate view of what the table in Abraham Lincoln's home looked like at a specific time in history vs an AR application with the goal to allow the participant to see how his or her new kitchen might look if he or she remodeled it in different ways.

Representations Meant to Convey Physical Attributes vs Representations to Communicate Emotion

In much the same way that a painter might want to convey the idea of the physical attributes of some object or other entity, the AR content developer can, too. For example, medical illustrators draw images to show the layout of muscles in our bodies or the veins and arteries in our body. The illustrator strives to make the image clear and easy to understand. It is a factual representation that says "this is your anatomy" (Figure 5.2).

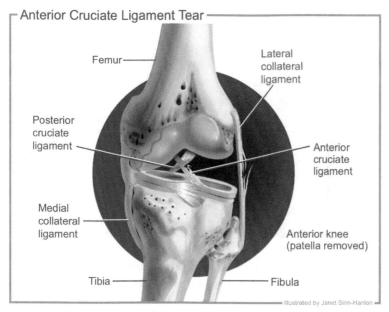

Anterior Cruciate Ligament Tear

Femur

Lateral collateral ligament

Posterior cruciate ligament

Anterior cruciate ligament

Medial collateral ligament

Anterior knee (patella removed)

Tibia

Fibula

Illustrated by Janet Sinn-Hanlon

FIGURE 5.2

This illustration of a knee is clearly intended to communicate factual information about this aspect of the human anatomy. The knee is a physical object that is represented in a realistic way. *Illustration courtesy of Janet Sinn-Hanlon.*

However, an artist may not be interested in communicating factual data clearly. He or she may instead be interested in communicating an emotion such as sadness, heartbreak, shock, or glee. In this case, the artist uses whatever tools he or she has to evoke a desired response in her audience whether or not it conveys anything factually (Figure 5.3).

The AR content developer has all of these options available as well. The content of any media, including AR, is directly informed by the goal of the creator. If the goal is to communicate factual information or physical attributes, then the content developer must choose representations to support that goal. If the goal is to evoke an emotional response or communicate feelings, then the representations he or she chooses will be chosen to evoke that response in the audience/participant (Figure 5.4).

Physical Representations vs Conceptual Representations

John Ganter (Ganter, J.H. "A Comparison for Complex Earth Volumes" Auto-Carto 9: Proceedings of the Ninth International Symposium on Computer Assisted Cartography, 1989) distinguishes between representations meant to portray something that has a physical counterpart vs those that have no physical counterpart but are conceptual in nature. Ganter dubs the

FIGURE 5.3

This image was created to not resemble a real-life counterpart, but rather to communicate emotion. The medium in this case is computer graphics. *Image courtesy of Jason Chaney.*

FIGURE 5.4

The Norwegian artist Edvard Munch clearly intended to communicate an emotion with his painting "The Scream." This painting is an interesting example of using a somewhat realistic representation that is clearly not intended to be photorealistic.

physical representations P-Reps and the conceptual representations C-Reps. Augmented reality applications, unless they are meant to only portray realistic renderings of virtual world entities that have a direct physical counterpart, utilize both P-Reps and C-Reps. Our (virtual) vase that sits on a (real) table is an example of a P-Rep. C-Reps are useful for conveying content intended to evoke emotion or other ideas that have no physical analog. So an AR application that has content that portrays the idea of temperature would use a C-Rep. C-Reps are especially useful for conveying emotional content such as fear, glee, or others.

Unlike many other media, including paintings, maps, and other static material, AR is an interactive medium. Hence, the content can change not only over time, but also based on the position of the participant. Although movies can convey the passage of time, and illustrate motion, they do not allow the viewer to actively participate as the content unfolds. Hence the AR application developer has both the good fortune and the burden to take this feature of AR into account. It is good fortune because time-evolving content that allows the participants to choose their own physical point of view can be very powerful. It is a burden, in a sense, because the creator must consider all the possibilities of the medium. That is, the content developer must consider issues such as "What if the participant does this? What if they go there?" Because the participants could conceivably go anywhere, there must be some limit to the domain that the content of the virtual world covers. This could be limited by some physical constraint, such as a room that the participants are in, or by some limitation in the virtual world, such as a (virtual) fence. The content could simply end at some point and nothing "magical" (in an AR sense) happens when the participants leave the space in which there is AR content or the augmented reality experience could simply end.

Content That Tells a Story

As with many other media (film, novels, stage plays, etc.), the medium of augmented reality can be used to tell a story. Using AR to tell a story, though, requires some special care on the part of the AR developer and an understanding of the meaning of "story" in an interactive medium.

Recall that you *read* a book, you *watch* a play, and you *listen* to a concert. Also recall that AR is an *interactive* medium and that you *experience* an AR application. As with any interactive media, AR presents interesting challenges and possibilities to how you tell a story. Additionally, AR has some characteristics that set it apart from other interactive media.

Typically a story has a plot that takes shape as some sort of a narrative. A story usually has a beginning, a middle, and an end. In most noninteractive (immotive) media, the creator of the work determines the narrative of the story and the audience experiences the unfolding of the story according to the wishes of the author of the content. That is, the audience does not participate actively in how the story is told and how the story comes out. There is a certain element of active engagement on the part of the audience in that as they read, watch, and listen, they generate internal mental images and interpretations of the content, but they don't actively affect the narrative of the story. For example, if one is reading a novel and the author describes a "dashing young man with an inner strength that comes only from decades of experience in the cut-throat corporate world," each reader creates his or her own mental model of what that character looks like, their personality, etc. However, the reader is not actively involved in the creation of the narrative of the story.

With interactive media, including AR, the participant takes an active role in determining the narrative and how the story plays out. In many cases, the participant *is* a protagonist of the story. He or she is also the director and, in some cases, either partially or fully the content creator. The narrative is created by how the participant engages with the virtual world. The participant can be given the choice of how engaged he or she is with the AR experience. For example, he or she can choose to simply sit back and observe his or her surroundings or he or she can be actively engaged with the environment he or she is in and make events happen intentionally. Note that simply walking around in an AR environment generates a narrative. That narrative can be captured and documented by the computer and represented in other media. For example, returning to our vase on the table example, if the participant sees the vase on the table, walks around it to see it from different vantage points, and then picks it up and drops it on the floor, the computer could generate a written narrative story from that activity: *Jim saw the vase on the table. He walked to his right to see the vase from a different perspective. He walked all the way around the table and saw every side of the vase. Then, he picked up the vase and dropped it on the floor. The vase shattered when it hit the floor.*

Hence, the simple actions that one takes in an AR environment create a narrative. The participant is actively engaged in creating the narrative of the experience. This is a separate action from creating the content of the experience. Hence, in this short story example, the story was collaboratively authored by contributions from the content creator and the participant in the experience.

In many ways, telling a story in AR is similar to creating a story in VR. The primary difference is that in AR, the real world is part of the content of the virtual world. One way to think about content and storytelling in VR and AR is expressed by Mike Adams of Virtuality Group PLC, who says that VR doesn't exist as a storyline, but rather a place to explore (Adams, 1995). Consequently, the content creator provides a "space" and the participant creates his own narrative.

However, there are things the AR developer can do to encourage the participant to take certain actions in the environment. For example, the developer can place signs and instructions in the world or have objects in the world beckon the participant to do certain things. Another issue the AR content/story developers must address that isn't an issue in novels and other non-interactive media is that they must provide content that supports any path the participant wants to take through the "story" unless they make clever restrictions on the activities and paths the participant can take. With augmented reality in particular, certain aspects of any story must abide by the laws of physics of the real world. Consequently, if the participant picks up a (real) rock and drops it, the rock will fall to the ground regardless of the participant's wishes. A virtual rock, however, is not constrained by Mother Nature. If one desires to have some real-world activity take place that would not be naturally feasible, it can be possible to fool the participant into believing something is happening that is not (after all, AR is all about fooling our perceptions). Suppose the content creator wants the participant to have the ability to float in the air. As mentioned earlier, one could create AR content that would cause the participant to see objects that are below him or her as though they are hovering. If the scene is compelling enough to overcome the participant's disbelief and the natural cues that are telling him or her that they are not floating, then the participant may, in fact, get the feeling that they are hovering above the ground.

Don't forget that the digital elements of the content don't need to conform to real-world expectations. They can, but they don't have to. Consequently, if you as a content creator want an old gnarly stick to "come to life" and become a snake in the participant's hand, you can create that illusion. This type of content can potentially shake up your participant. But, after all, many good stories shake up the audience. Do keep in mind, though, that the participant may never even encounter that stick unless you cause it to appear right in front of him or her. Telling a story in AR (and other interactive media) does not provide the content developer the luxury of knowing all of the content the participant will encounter and in what order. If someone writes a novel, or produces a movie, it is reasonable to assume the audience has encountered the content that came in the previous pages of the novel or the earlier parts of the movie. It is possible to keep track of what the participant *has* encountered in an AR experience and use that information to help guide the experience appropriately, but it is more difficult to force the participant to encounter specific things in the order you hope he or she will. If you do use tricks to do this, you run the risk of losing one of the features of AR, which is the ability for the participant to explore and choose his or her own paths through the content.

Content for AR Games

Augmented reality is a medium well suited for supporting games. One of the key issues for the AR content creator to address is to have a good idea for the underlying game. This is no different than any other content issue in AR. If AR is used to tell a story, the story must be good without AR. If AR is used to convey information, the information must be good in its own right. In order to use AR to support a game, it is important to exploit the capabilities that AR provides, as otherwise it may be more prudent to create the game in some other medium.

One of the key advantages of the medium of AR for gaming is that it can combine the best of the real world with the best of digital worlds. Consequently, the most compelling AR games are those that take place in an interesting real-world setting (as opposed to in an empty room). A trade-off to consider is between making the game very specific to an absolute location (such as the base of the Eiffel Tower) or to make it more generic to work well in any location such as a park. Being specific to a location allows you to take advantage of the affordances of that particular location. For example, one aspect of the game might require you to go to the top of the Eiffel Tower. However, if one wants to play that game elsewhere it would require a digital representation of the Eiffel Tower and require a way to simulate going to the top of the tower.

Another important content element for AR games is other players. Note that those other players might be digital entities, they might be other real people in close proximity to you, or they might be real people who are located in some other place, perhaps on the other side of the world from you. A design decision for the content creator is to determine whether the other players *seem* to be near you, in the same place that you are, or whether they seem to be in some other location.

The method of interaction used has high importance when using AR as a game platform. Interaction methods are covered in depth in Chapter 6, but when using AR to support a game it is important to realize that you can interact with the game in many different ways and the choice of interaction schemes can help, or hinder, the game experience. In brief, one can use physical buttons or sliders on a device such as a smartphone or smart tablet, one can use virtual buttons or sliders on that same device, or one can use virtual controllers in the real world [e.g., a (virtual) slider on a (real) rock] or even virtual controls just "hanging" in the air. Another option is to use other physical devices, such as a toy gun or a toy sword (that may or may not look the same in the AR environment) as part of the game play. Going to the further extreme, one could create custom controllers for a game that are made specifically only for that game.

FIGURE 5.5
Street signs convey information via text and sometimes images. The signs often have information on both sides. *Photo courtesy of Kevin Fedde.*

Content for Conveying Information

At its core, all AR content conveys information of one sort or another. In some cases, though, the goal of the AR application designer is to convey factual information about some specific idea at some specific place. In its simplest case, simply overlaying an object that is text, such as a label, could work. However, a problem could arise if one were to walk to the other side of the text. The text would then appear to be backward. In the real world, one can make signs with text on both sides of them. A street sign, for example, has text on both sides of it (Figure 5.5).

In AR, however, there are additional options. For example, the sign can rotate automatically as you look at it from different perspectives such that it is always perpendicular to your line of sight. Alternatively, that same content can be conveyed in many different ways. For example, the name of the street could be made to appear on the street itself, oriented for easy reading, or it could be spoken to you.

Other kinds of information can be overlaid on the real world in many different ways. For example, if one is using AR to help someone find a location, the AR application could make it appear as though there are lines on the ground that you can follow to your location. In the real world, an example of this is a stripe on the floor that you follow to get to the appropriate room. Usually there is a different color stripe for each destination and you follow the appropriate color.

In AR, however, you could have a truly customized stripe to follow to your destination. Alternatively, you could have the AR application overlay

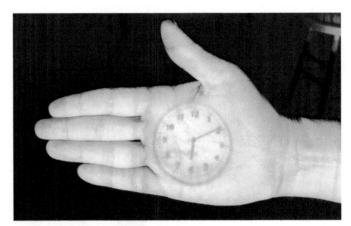

FIGURE 5.6

With projection-based AR, information can be projected on any surface. Here, a clock is projected on the palm of a hand. *Photo courtesy of Beverly Carver.*

footprints on the ground that you can follow to your destination. Still another thing that you could do in AR is to have a hand floating in space that continuously points toward your destination.

Any number of pieces of factual (or fictional) information can be overlaid on the real world with AR. For example, one could provide the names of the different types of trees that are in view. Or one could overlay color on a running engine that depicts which areas are hot vs cool. In order to do this, however, sensors are required to provide that information to the AR application.

Augmented reality can also be used to summon a set of virtual "gadgets" to provide information about the real world. For example, there could be a clock gadget that displays the current time and a weather gadget that provides information about the temperature, humidity, etc. (Figure 5.6).

Because AR can provide a digital representation of something with a high degree of verisimilitude, if the idea that someone is trying to convey is "What will the skyline look like when the new building is built?" then AR can be used to convey that information visually. Unlike "Photoshopping" the new building into a photo of the skyline, AR offers the opportunity to see the building in the skyline from all perspectives, at real-world scale, on all sides of the building. AR can be very handy for many sorts of visualization tasks in which it is important to be able to see, hear, or sense some phenomenon that can't normally be seen, heard, or sensed in the real world at that point in place or time.

CREATING VISUAL CONTENT

Regardless of how well you understand the concept of content and even if you have strong ideas of what content elements you need for your AR application, at some point the rubber meets the road and you (or a member of your team) will need to go through the process of creating the pieces of content needed for your application. Visual content for AR applications can be categorized as three basic types:

- Three-dimensional (3D) objects
- Two-dimensional (2D) images (including text)
- Visual elements that vary with time (animation, video clips, etc.)

Note that these are the same types of visual elements used when creating content for other types of digital media, such as web pages, computer games, and digital movies.

Three-Dimensional Objects

As learned in Chapter 2, 3D computer graphics objects can be obtained in one of four ways, or any combination of these ways:

- Created from scratch using a computer graphics modeling program
- Created dynamically from an algorithm that generates the objects
- Created from a real-world object by scanning an object with a 3D scanner
- Obtained by purchasing or otherwise obtaining an extant 3D model

Created from Scratch Using a Computer Graphics Modeling Program

One of the most common methods used to obtain the 3D objects needed for your applications is to create the necessary models using 3D computer graphics modeling software. The majority of these tools work as standalone applications that run on a personal computer. There are modeling programs for Windows, Macintosh, and Linux systems. Some of the more common 3D modeling packages include Maya from Autodesk, 3ds Max, also from Autodesk, SketchUp from Trimble, and Blender, which is an open source 3D modeling and animation package. Anim8or (freeware 3D modeling and character animation software) and Art of Illusion (free, open source 3D modeling software) are also useful tools.

Maya and 3ds Max are commercial products that are very full featured and are used in fields including special effects for Hollywood movies, architectural modeling, animation and scientific visualization, video games, and rapid prototyping. SketchUp has a free version as well as a paid "Pro" version.

SketchUp is known for being very easy to use. Blender is a full-featured modeling, animation, and rendering package that is free and open source.

The basic workflow for all of these packages is to first create the 3D shapes required for your object(s) and then apply information regarding the surface features of the objects, such as textures, colors, and information about reflectivity. Finally, the object is saved in a file in a format that your AR system requires. Some of the most common file formats for 3D graphics objects include:

- .obj—The Wavefront (now Autodesk Maya) object format. This is a very commonly used format.
- .max—The format used by Autodesk 3ds Max
- .skp—The format used by SketchUp
- .blend—The format used by Blender
- .wrl—The format used for Virtual Reality Markup Language (VRML) files. VRML used to be a common format used for 3D objects on the web and other applications but is less widely used today. The early ARToolKit library used VRML for specifying objects.
- .x3d—Replaces VRML/.wrl files
- .dae—Digital Asset Exchange is a file format created by COLLADA to support content in interactive 3D applications

Each of these file formats has its own characteristics and strengths and weaknesses. The overriding factor that will cause you to choose one or the other is the format required by the AR library that you are using for your application. In general, it is relatively straightforward to convert from one format to another, so if your AR library requires one format and the tool you are using creates a different type, it is possible to convert the object file to the type of file you need. In fact, many 3D modeling packages allow you to "Save As..." whatever file type you need and will allow you to set a preference to make your desired file format the default. Be aware, though, that sometimes conversions do not result in a perfect transfer of your model. Sometimes, due to quirks in the modeling software and conversion software, some artifacts from the process of conversion must be addressed. That is, your model may require some "touch up" after the conversion process. The amount of touch up required can vary from nothing to extensive repair work. Deep Exploration from Right Hemisphere and Polyglot from NCSA are a couple examples of tools that can be helpful for file conversion.

Scene Graphs

Another concept important to the issue of 3D content is the idea of scene graphs. A scene graph is a data structure that provides information about the relationship between different graphical entities. For example, it provides information about the spatial relationship between entities as well as other relationships, such as the impact that moving one object has on moving another object. So if our virtual vase has virtual flowers in it, when I move the vase, the flowers move too.

The scene graph is expressed exactly as it sounds. It is a graph in which objects (or parts of objects) are nodes in the graph, and the relationships are expressed by the edges in the graph.

OpenSceneGraph (OSG) (http://www.openscenegraph.org/projects/osg) is a free, open source implementation of scene graph functionality that uses C++ and OpenGL. This allows the content creator to worry more about their content and less about low-level details of the graphics involved with the content. The OSG library has plug-ins that allow it to read from different common file formats. This allows you to build the scene graph from multiple sources and also to use the scene graph in different applications.

Created Dynamically from an Algorithm That Generates the Objects

This technique was described briefly in Chapter 2. In short, instead of using a high-level user interface with a modeling program such as Maya or Blender, the content creator creates computer code that executes during the runtime of the AR application and that code generates the graphical elements based on the output of the algorithm. The earlier thunderstorm example would be a case where the graphics objects are not created a priori, but rather are created on the fly. In the case of the simulated clouds, it would not be possible to predict the shapes of clouds that would be needed. Hence it is not really feasible to use a modeling package to create every possible shape of a cloud that might be needed. Rather, the code that the developer wrote takes conditions of the world as inputs and then generates the appropriate graphical representation.

Computer games often use algorithms to create content dynamically. For example, smoke, explosions, rippling water, and fire are often created from underlying algorithms. Likewise, there are algorithms to create flocks of birds, schools of fish, crowds of people, and so forth.

Created from a Real-World Object by Scanning an Object With a 3D Scanner

A shortcut to creating some types of graphics objects is by using a 3D scanning system to (somewhat) automatically create a graphics object from a real-world object. There are multiple technologies by which this can be done. Some involve touching the object physically with a probe that then reports where that location is. The person doing the scanning touches the object in

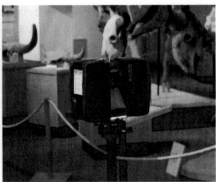

FIGURE 5.7
This pair of photos shows a 3D scanner suitable for scanning small objects (NextEngine 3D Scanner) and one suitable for scanning large objects (Faro Edge). *Photos courtesy of Nicholas Homer, Idaho Museum of Natural History.*

many different places and that information is used to generate the computer graphics object automatically. It is important to not only generate the geometry of the object, but also the look of the surface. Hence, some scanning systems create a polygonal mesh as well as an image that can be applied to the mesh as a texture.

Other 3D scanning systems use cameras to "look" at the object from all sides and to generate the 3D graphics object from that information. Today, there are even systems that let you simply photograph an object from multiple perspectives, and then the system uses that data set (multiple photographs) to create the 3D graphics object automatically (Figures 5.7 and 5.8).

Obtained by Purchasing or Otherwise Obtaining an Extant 3D Model

Some types of 3D graphical objects can be purchased from catalogs of 3D objects. If you need content that is available as such it can be expeditious to simply purchase the objects. Of course, it is critical that you obtain the objects in a format that you can use in your application or that you can convert reliably to the needed format. It is important that the technical aspects of the object (file format, resolution, number of polygons, file size, etc.) are suitable for your project, but also that any licensing restrictions and terms of use are appropriate. For example, some objects can be used for any purpose, whereas others might not be allowed to be used in commercial applications.

Some objects can be obtained for free by downloading them from a website that is for that purpose. Sometimes designers want to get their objects used in applications and hence make them available for free. Sometimes objects are

FIGURE 5.8

This facility, the Idaho Virtualization Laboratory at the Idaho Museum of Natural History, is equipped to scan 3D objects of all shapes and sizes, both within the lab and in the field. Pictured here from left to right are Jesse Pruitt, Robert Schlader, and Nicholas Clement. *Photo courtesy of Nicholas Homer, Idaho Museum of Natural History.*

free for educational purposes. Just like with purchased content, it is important that any free objects meet the technical requirements of your application and that the licensing allows the type of use required.

One disadvantage of using third-party content of this nature is that it is possible that the same object could be used in someone else's application. This may or may not matter to you for your particular application, but it is something to consider. Sometimes the objects can be modified, color changed, and so on to make them a bit more specific to your application, but at the lowest level it is still the same object.

Some sites where you can obtain 3D models of varying types, formats, quality, and so on include 3DModelFree.com, Archive3D.net, 3Dxtras.com, Artist-3D.com, and TurboSquid.com. These aren't recommendations (it is impossible to recommend without knowing your needs, formats required, etc.) but merely show you some examples of these types of resources.

Two-Dimensional Images

Two-dimensional images can be used to great advantage in AR applications. They can be used as somewhat standalone entities as backdrops, signs, and so on or can be used as "textures" affixed to the surface of a 3D graphical object. The term *texture* might be a bit misleading because it sounds like the image gives the object a texture. This is one use of this technique, and images that give the appearance of a texture can be used for that purpose. However, any 2D image can be "pasted" onto a 3D graphical object. As stated previously, this can be helpful in making it appear that the 3D object has a texture. So if you have an object such as a (virtual) table, instead of simply relying on the surface properties that you define to designate what the surface looks like, you can attach an image that is a photograph of wood grain so that it appears like the table is actually made of wood (because what you see is actually a photograph of real wood). The use of images attached to 3D objects isn't limited to the idea of conveying textures though. You can use this idea to create photorealistic looks with any object that can benefit from attaching an image to its surface. For example, to create a realistic-looking soft drink can, one could model a cylinder and then wrap an image around the cylinder that looks like what the can looks like.

Another benefit of using 2D images to texture a 3D model is to save the expense (time of creation and additional file size) of a 3D model by using an image to put additional detail onto the surface of a model. For example, if you are modeling a museum building that has intricate surface detail, you could simply model the building as a cube and attach an image of each side of the building to the appropriate face of the cube. Seen from a distance, this will probably look more "realistic" than if all of the detail had been built into the model. Seen up close, however, it may appear to be merely a photo on a box.

Two-dimensional images used for any purpose (textures, backdrops, etc.) can be procured in many of the same ways as 3D graphical content (created from scratch using a computer graphics program, created dynamically from an algorithm that generates the objects, created from a real-world object by scanning an image or taking a photograph, or obtained by purchasing or otherwise obtaining an extant image).

Two-dimensional images are one of two basic formats:

- Vector images
- Raster images

Vector images are made of points, lines, and curves and are generally created with a vector image program such as Adobe Illustrator or the open source Inkscape. Vector graphics are often used when creating illustrations (Figure 5.9).

Raster images, however, are a matrix of pixel values that represent an image. Your digital camera, for example, takes pictures as raster images. Software such as Adobe Photoshop is useful for creating and modifying raster images (Figure 5.10).

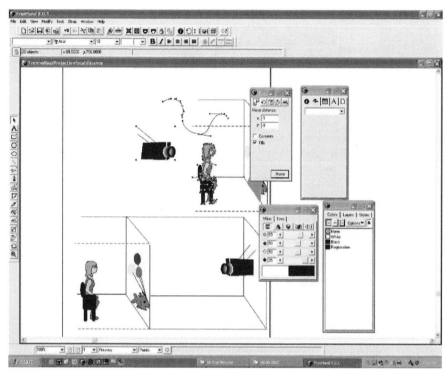

FIGURE 5.9
Vector graphics programs are used to create two-dimensional computer graphics images. The artist has a variety of tools that can be used to create and modify his or her illustrations. *Screenshot courtesy of Beverly Carver.*

Some of the more common file formats for 2D images include

- Vector:
  - .svg—Scalable Vector Graphics
  - .cgm—Computer Graphics Metafile
- Raster:
  - .tiff—an uncompressed raster image format
  - .jpg—a compressed raster image format
  - .gif—a compressed raster image format
  - .png—an open source successor to the .gif format
  - .bmp—a Windows bitmap file

Visual Elements That Vary with Time (Animation)

Animation can bring a scene to life with motion that is independent of the motion of the participant. The motion can be interactively related to the actions of the participant, it can simply be a motion sequence that either

FIGURE 5.10
This screenshot shows a raster image created by taking a digital photograph of a horse. A raster graphics program, in this case Adobe Photoshop Limited Edition, can be used to alter and modify the image in different ways. In this screenshot, the artist has used the tool to cut out just the horse's head and also to apply a filter to the original image to modify the original photograph to look more impressionistic. *Screenshot and photo courtesy of Beverly Carver.*

plays once and then stops or repeats over and over, or it can be animation that is driven by other elements in the real and virtual world. For example, in the case of a high-end simulation, one could see clouds growing and other items in the world being blown in the wind, and ultimately a tornado could be born when all conditions are conducive to it.

These different categories of animation have differing degrees of complexity to create. In the simplest case, one could have an animated texture (movie) on the surface of an object. The object appears to animate because the texture changes over time. For example, one could have a model of a school building in the distance where the texture attached to one side of it has a movie of two schoolchildren bobbing up and down on a seesaw over and over as a movie of the children playing loops repeatedly.

FIGURE 5.11
An animation can create the appearance that an object in the virtual world explodes based on some triggering condition, such as someone throwing a rock at it. It is also possible to have a computer program control the action based on the physics of the scenario. *Diagram courtesy of Beverly Carver.*

The next level of complexity is the movement of an object following a preprescribed path in the world. If one modeled a toy electric train, one could have it follow the (modeled) train tracks around and around the path of the tracks. This could also include modeling the wheels to go round and round and the pistons on the engine pumping over and over.

The animations can be triggered by actions the participant takes, so one could animate a vase shattering anytime it collides with another object at a certain velocity. The shattering animation could begin because the vase falls off of the table, because the participant throws it at the wall, or because the participant throws a rock at it and hits it (Figure 5.11).

Another level of complexity is objects that are created dynamically on the fly based on an algorithm. The algorithm can be dependent on any number of different inputs/data items. For example, with the storm scenario, the cloud objects are created on the fly with every time step based on the current conditions in the overall application. This can also be informed by real-world conditions. Hence the (virtual) clouds change appearance throughout the duration of the use of the application and could potentially be different every time the application is used.

Some animation scenarios (such as movie texture and animated objects) are created using animation software, but the scenario where the objects are created dynamically according to the conditions of the application requires customized programming for that particular application.

CREATING AUDIO CONTENT

In much the same way that visual content is created for AR applications, audio content can be created as well in analogous ways. For example, there is sound design software that can be used to create and edit sound elements from scratch. Recording a sound is analogous to scanning a visual image. Sounds can be created algorithmically and sounds can also be purchased.

One way that sound is fundamentally different from visual information is that sound exists primarily in time (although it can have a spatial element) and visual imagery exists primarily in space (although it can have a temporal element in the case of animation). Consequently, the tools used for creating sounds are somewhat different than those used for creating visual imagery.

Basically, sound creation software falls into a few different categories with respect to creating sound content for AR applications:

1. Sound design/sound synthesis
2. Sound recording/editing
3. Sound processing

Additionally, just as with visual imagery, custom code can be written to create sounds on the fly in real time in response to the current state of the AR application.

Sound design and sound synthesis are very closely related. In both cases, sounds are created from the ground up. Sound design and sound synthesis may have recordings of sounds involved, but this is not necessary. Sounds can be created from basically nothing at all using either a mathematical formula or some other way for specifying what the sound content creator wants the sound to sound like. There are many, many different procedures and algorithms that can be drawn on to generate sounds. Many of them have different parameters that can be varied to alter the sound. These parameters can be preset by the AR developer or the parameters can be altered dynamically in real time during execution of the AR application.

Sound recording is analogous to scanning a physical object. By using a microphone to capture a real-world sound for later play and/or modification by other processing algorithms, very realistic sounds can be incorporated into the AR application.

Sound processing is something that is done to some other sound signal whether that signal was synthesized or recorded. Common processing algorithms do things such as filter the sound in different ways or place an echo or other effect on the sound. One of the more interesting processes applied to sound in AR is the idea of sound spatialization. That is, the sound is processed to *appear* to emanate from some particular location in the virtual/real world. That location **may** be different than the location of the speaker or headphones that the sound is coming from. 3D placement of sound is a complex phenomenon that requires an understanding of psychoacoustics to carry out properly. As is the case with many aspects of AR, spatializing sound is another example of the AR developer trying to *fool the perception* of the participants so that they believe something that isn't truly the case (that the sound is coming from somewhere other than where it is really coming from).

Different aspects of the technical representation of digital sound in files were addressed in Chapter 4. There are several common file formats for the storage of audio. The most common that the AR developer will encounter include:

- .wav—common uncompressed sound file format for Windows
- .aiff —common uncompressed sound file format for Macintosh
- .mp3—most common compressed sound file format

As with graphics files, software is available that can be used to convert from one file format to another.

CREATING CONTENT FOR OTHER SENSES (TOUCH, TASTE, SMELL)

Because the use of other senses for AR is currently not very prevalent, I will not address creating content for those senses. However, because these sensory elements are present in the real world, they will automatically be a part of any AR application that you build. For example, if you have an AR application that takes place in the woods, the real world will automatically provide the smells that go along with being in the woods, such as the smell of trees and flowers and perhaps bug repellant.

The sense of touch is a special case in AR applications and because the real-world provides objects that you can touch, they can be exploited in AR applications. Some examples of the use of real-world objects that you can touch are discussed in Chapter 6. Note that the sense of touch (haptics) is composed of different aspects. There is force feedback (i.e., something pushing against us or something having weight that gravity causes to push against us) that is sensed mostly by how our muscles have to respond to forces. There is taction, which is typically skin sensations such as temperature sensed primarily by nerve endings. We also have our own sense of proprioception, which is how we can understand our body pose even without seeing it. That is, even with your eyes closed you can tell where your various joints (elbows, knees, etc.) are in space. All of these senses can be exploited by creating content to provide stimuli to your body. In order to provide that stimuli you must have appropriate devices available to do that. Some of those devices are discussed in Chapter 2, such as the Sensable Phantom Omni haptic device. A device such as that can help you feel content by "probing" it with a stylus. It can also give a sense of texture by dragging the stylus across a virtual surface. This is sensed by participants in the same way as if they were dragging a light stick across a textured surface. Sony has recently patented a device to provide temperature (heat/cold) feedback on a controller device. Real-world objects, of course, provide haptic feedback without any special technology. For example, if you pick up a (real) rock that is cold, it feels cold.

REPRESENTATION AND PERCEPTUAL ISSUES

Representation and Our Senses
Sight
In the real world we see things because those things reflect light that impinges on our retina. Our brain then deciphers the signals from the nerves in our retina to allow us to see. The light that reaches our retina has already undergone tremendous transformations from the source of the light. For example, when we see an apple in the sunlight and see that the apple is red, it is because the physical characteristics of the apple cause it to reflect the red components of the sunlight. Other colors in the sunlight are not reflected by the apple. However, we may also see other things that tell us something about the apple, the light source(s), and the environment that the apple is in. Shadows, for example, tell us something about the location of the light source vs the location of the apple. Surface reflections and highlights also tell us about the characteristics of the light and the surface of the apple. These things happen automatically in the real world, compliments of the laws of nature. In the virtual world, however, it is up to us, the content creators, to define the "laws of nature" for the virtual world and to implement those laws. Many computer graphics systems already have many of these types of capabilities built into them, but even then, we need to choose how we want to apply those laws in the virtual world.

Imagine for a moment that we decide we want the laws of nature in our virtual world to be exactly the same as in the real world and that we have a system that can implement those laws perfectly. We still need to make decisions and implement such decisions as "Is the sun in the same place in the virtual world as it is in the real world?" If so, we need to be able to sense and determine where the sun is in the real world with respect to where we are in the virtual world and provide that information to the graphics system so that the system will display the virtual objects as though the sun (in the virtual world) is in the same place that it is in the real world. This will be necessary to obtain the correct visual images that are congruent with the rest of the real world. Shadows, for example, must be computed appropriately, taking into account where the light source is, as well as where other objects are that might be casting shadows on the virtual objects and so forth. Additionally, any shadow that the (virtual) objects should be casting on (real) objects will need to be created in the graphics system and displayed appropriately.

Occlusions (where you can't see something in the world because it is hidden behind something else) also need to be considered. To do this properly requires that the system knows what all objects (and parts of objects), whether real or virtual, should be seen from the particular vantage point that the participant is at at that moment. The system must then present the appropriate image to the participant. Creating a convincing occlusion of real and virtual objects can be difficult. It is a more straightforward problem if you are using a video see-through display than an optical see-through display (see Chapter 3), but both can be tough. The reason it is easier with a video see-through display is because you have complete control (electronically) over what the participant sees. With an optical see-through display the participant sees the real world unmediated by the AR system. It is difficult to "block out" objects in the real world that people are seeing optically. With the video display it is more straightforward to create an image with a virtual object "blocking out" (occluding) a real-world object.

Hearing

Sound is an incredibly rich medium for transmitting information, emotion, and more. If you don't think so, try watching a movie with the sound turned off or playing a video game with the sound turned off.

Next, turn the soundtrack of a movie off and play a song while you watch the silent movie. Then, watch the same movie while it is shown over a different song. The emotive content of the movie varies radically depending on the soundtrack that is placed behind it.

When developing content for an augmented reality application it is critical for the developer to consider all aspects of the content, including sound, as well as (most importantly) how the different content elements (such as sounds and visuals) interact with each other and create more than the sum of the parts.

Sound can be used in augmented reality in the same ways it is used in the real world as well as some additional ways. In the real world, sound is used in a number of ways:

- To communicate spoken information
- To tell our eyes where to look
- To communicate emotion
- To provide information about the characteristics of an environment
- To understand time-varying information

These same purposes can be used in an AR application. The more difficult issue is how to address real-world sounds that you don't want the participant to be able to hear. The most straightforward way to address isolating the participant from real-world sounds that you don't want them to hear is to have the participant wear closed ear headphones. (See Chapter 3.) While not perfect at isolating the participant from real-world sounds, they are the best solution at this point in time. Another technique is to have the virtual world provide sounds that mask real-world sounds. That is, while wearing the closed ear headphones, the participant could hear relatively loud, constant ambient sounds from the AR application. However, if this is done, consideration for safety is important. If the AR participant is isolated from real-world sounds, then it is important that the participant has some other way of hearing important warning signals (such as a car horn honking) from the real world.

Indoor AR applications have a better chance for limiting interference from real-world sounds. If an AR application is executed in a low-noise, indoor environment, then the participant will hear primarily AR application sounds. In the extreme, the AR application could be executed in a very quiet sound-proof room such as a recording studio.

If one wants the participant to hear *some* real-world sounds, but not others, things get much more complicated. The best strategy is to isolate the participant from real-world sounds as much as possible, but to have sensors (microphones) near the real-world sounds that you desire the participant to hear and to feed the sound from those microphones to the participant via headphones or other sound transducer.

As mentioned earlier, in the real world, one of the important purposes of sound is to tell our eyes where to look. Consequently, if sound in AR is to fulfill that purpose it is important to be able to cause the participant to perceive that the sound is emanating from a certain location, or at least a certain direction. Human beings have the ability (in the real world) to *localize* sounds to a certain extent. That is, in the real world we can tell more or less where a sound is coming from. I say "to a certain extent" and "more or less" because research shows that we are less accurate in our ability to localize sounds than we might think. Consequently, if it is a difficult thing in the real world, it is even more difficult for an AR developer to synthetically cause a participant to perceive that a sound is coming from a certain place.

The best way to cause sounds to appear to emanate from a specific location is to have the sound actually emanate from that location. In some AR applications it is possible to place speakers or other sound devices in locations (perhaps hidden from view) such that the participant will perceive the sound coming from that location.

World-Referenced
Sound Stage

Head-Referenced
Sound Stage

FIGURE 5.12

The idea of *sound stage* refers to whether the source of sound appears to be fixed to a specific place in the world vs fixed to the listener's head. In this diagram, a world-referenced sound stage is denoted by a trumpet affixed at one position in the world. If the listener is looking at that point in the world, the sound seems to be coming from in front of him. However, if he turns his back to that point in the world, the sound seems to be coming from behind him. In the diagram depicting a head-referenced sound stage, in this case depicted by listening in headphones, the sound seems to come from whatever direction the person is facing. That is, as he moves his head around, the source of sound moves with him, as opposed to a world-referenced sound stage where the sound stays in a fixed place with respect to the world. *Diagram courtesy of Beverly Carver.*

In some AR applications, however, it is not possible to place sound sources in the environment, or the sounds need to be able to move. For example, if the tiger that is creating a roaring sound is walking around, then the source of the roar needs to move as well, or at least it needs to seem as though it does. In this case, it is important for the AR developer to exploit the sonic depth and location cues discussed in Chapter 2. In order to do this appropriately, the AR application must have data about where the sound is supposed to be coming from as well as the location and orientation of the participant's ears. That information can be utilized by sound spatialization software that the AR application is using to provide a signal that the participant perceives as emanating from the appropriate spot. Note that those locations (where the sound should be coming from and where the participant's ears are) must be updated constantly as the participant moves and/or the desired perceived location of the sound changes (Figure 5.12).

SUMMARY

There's no mistaking it. Without good content an AR application is nothing more than a technological novelty. The content, the interaction, the sensors, the displays, and all other components of your AR application must work together to communicate the desired content to the participant, and the participant's actions must communicate to the AR application their intent and goals.

There are aesthetic, communicative, and technical aspects of AR content and all must be addressed fully to achieve a compelling AR application. There is some compatibility between different content file formats, but overall, at this time, you make content choices based on all aspects of your AR system and AR system choices based on your AR content.

It is not fully clear whether to consider the real world as part of the virtual world or the virtual world as part of the real world. Indeed, when you start creating AR applications, the notion of what is and isn't "real" can become a bit clouded. It is important to consider the philosophical ramifications of your work in AR, but it is not good to get totally sidetracked in philosophical dilemmas if your goal is to get an AR application out the door. However, the more you consider and understand the ramifications of what AR really is and really isn't, the better the position you are in to exploit the capabilities of AR for your goals.

The more that AR application developers can learn about other media, especially interactive media, the better they are equipped to use AR as a medium in a compelling way. Although other media are more or less evolved in terms of the language of the media, AR is at the very beginning of its use as an interactive communication medium. Consequently, the language elements of AR aren't yet clearly defined or even invented. Thus, as an early AR application developer, you are in the position to invent new uses and new constructs in the AR medium.

Due to the potential complexity of content for AR applications, one should consider the cost of creating the content. Content creation can be time-consuming and costly—much like the cost of creating compelling content for any medium (such as movies and computer games) is high. The potential payoff is also high.

CHAPTER 6

Interaction in Augmented Reality

INTRODUCTION

One of the key features of augmented reality (AR) is that it is an interactive medium. As such, interaction plays a key role in the overall user experience. AR is a relatively new medium and, as such, not all the details are worked out regarding the capabilities and affordances of the medium. This means that what we see in current AR applications is not the full suite of possibilities that will exist in the future. Some aspects of AR will only be possible with new developments in hardware and software.

One of the obvious places to begin studying interaction in augmented reality is to study interaction in other media, especially closely related media such as virtual reality (VR) and interactive fiction. This is extremely useful, although it would be very unfortunate to stop there. AR will provide the best experience only when its unique capabilities and affordances are taken advantage of. This chapter explores interaction techniques that can be borrowed from the real world, from other media, and also those that have already emerged and are emerging in current augmented reality applications. Some techniques are more suitable to certain AR paradigms (EG projection environments vs head-based displays vs handheld AR) than others. What we will seek are underlying principles that can be built on to take the best advantage of interaction schemes that are being used in current AR applications, some of which are becoming somewhat "standard" in AR applications, as well as providing a platform on which we can conceive new interaction methods that will be appropriate for new and different applications.

WHAT IS INTERACTION?

Interaction can be defined roughly as a mutual influence of one thing on another. That is, one entity does something, and the other entity responds in some way.

For example, in the real world I might press a button and the doorbell rings. Or, I drop a quarter in a vending machine and a pack of gum comes out. Or, I might carry on a conversation with my friend, or click on a hyperlink in a web document to see a new page. Many real-world interactions are much more complex. I see a light change from red to green. I then look to see if the intersection is clear and then I remove my foot from the brake pedal and slowly press it on the accelerator, which causes the car to move ahead slowly and gain speed while I hear the sound of the engine and the tires rolling on the road increasing. Likewise, there can be many levels of interaction in an augmented reality application. A noncomplete list of potentially interacting entities in an AR experience could include the following.

Interactions can be between:

- participant and AR application
- participant and another participant(s) via the AR application
- virtual world and real world
- participant and virtual world
- participant and real world

Augmented reality as a medium enjoys the advantage that it is situated in the real world. Consequently, certain real-world interaction elements are automatically available in AR. For example, in virtual reality if I want a ball to fall when I let go of it, I must program the explicit "law of gravity" to cause a (virtual) ball to fall when I let go of it. However, in AR, if I drop a (real) ball, the real-world law of gravity will cause the ball to fall.

FIGURE 6.1
These two boys play a game where they interact with each other. This game would be impossible to play without the interaction. What one boy does affects what the other does and vice versa. *Photo courtesy of Alan B. Craig.*

Interaction in the Real World

"Knock knock"
"Who's there?"

In the real world, any child who grew up in the United States understands this interpersonal interaction very well. If another kid approaches and says "Knock knock" you know that your part in the interaction is to say "Who's there?" and then the knock knock joke/interaction can proceed from that point forward. A knock knock joke doesn't work unless there are two parties involved (Figure 6.1). At least it is not very fun.

As can be seen from the knock knock example, interaction is (at least) a two-way street. One entity does something and a different entity does something in response and vice versa. One entity lets go of a ball and another entity (gravity) makes the ball fall to the ground. What happens next is up to the different entities involved.

Even in the real world, there are many different ways to interact to do the same thing. For example, if I want someone to know that I have arrived at their house, I may walk to the door and ring the doorbell, I may walk to the door and knock, I may stay in my car and honk the horn, or I might throw rocks at their window.

The word *interaction* is made up of two components, both of which are essential to interaction. *Action* means that something is *done*. It is *active*. Even seemingly passive activities such as listening are actions. In fact, anything described by a verb is an action. *Inter* means *between in a reciprocal way*. Thus, an interaction is something that is done between two things.

Taking a look at the action part of interaction, consider some of the actions we take in the real world:

- We *press* a button.
- We *flip* a switch.
- We *speak* to others.
- We *listen* to a bird sing.
- We *kick* a ball.
- We *choose* what we want to take.
- We *select* between options.
- We *travel* to the store.
- We *issue* a command.

Of course, this list is endless. As we begin to list the kinds of actions that we can take, it becomes apparent that virtually any action is really an interaction between two or more things. When we *flip* a *switch*, there is an interaction between ourselves and the switch, and potentially something that the switch controls. We flip the switch and the switch is changed to a different state. That new state may cause a light to come on, an engine to start, or any number of different things. Even seemingly passive activities, such as listening, are actually an interaction between two things. We listen to the radio. This is the action of listening between ourselves and a radio. But where is the *interaction*? We listen and, based on what we hear, we may choose to change the station or turn the radio off. This is one level of interaction. However, if we listen to the radio and as a result of that listening we call the radio station and request a certain song be played, it becomes much more of the class of interaction where each entity is affecting the other. The station played a song. I did not like that song. I call the station to request a different song, and the station plays my request. There has been a reciprocal action that has taken place. The station probably would not have played my request unless I was involved in an interaction with the station.

As described earlier, most actions can be considered interactions, but not all interactions are at the same level. It is important to note this when it comes to designing interactions in AR applications. For most practical purposes, any action taken by the participant(s) in an AR experience can be considered *interactions*. So if I press a button in the AR application and the application responds in some way, that can be considered an interaction.

Since augmented reality exists in the real world, we can borrow interaction schemes from the real world. We can also offer interaction possibilities that aren't possible in the real world. For example, if I want to retrieve an object from across the room in the real world I must get up, walk to the object, and then pick the object up. This interaction scenario could be emulated in the AR application as well. If I want to retrieve a physical cup from across the room I follow the same actions. However, if I want to retrieve a virtual cup from across the room, I can do anything that the application designer allows. He or she could require that I get up, walk over to the virtual cup, and then pick up the virtual cup or he or she could offer different possibilities for me to get the cup. I might just point at the cup and the cup would fly to me, or I could issue the verbal command "Cup—come to me," and the virtual cup would come to me. It is truly up to the application designer's imagination what interactions are possible and how they are implemented.

A number of interaction paradigms have become customary in the desktop computer arena. One widely adopted interaction scheme is the *WIMP* paradigm. WIMP stands for *Windows*, *Icons*, *Menus*, and *Pointing Devices*. On tablet computers, a common interaction scheme that has become popular is to spread your fingers apart to scale up (enlarge) what you are looking at. Most interactions, on these types of devices, involve some form of mouse, track pad, or touchscreen to allow you to select items, press a "button," or drag something around the screen. Interactions on handheld devices are in many ways similar to those of a desktop WIMP scheme, only made to work in the absence of external devices such as mice, and also adding some beneficial elements such as reorienting the screen automatically when the device is rotated (Figure 6.2).

However, in AR applications, it may or may not be possible to implement those more common interaction schemes. It largely depends on the devices available. Also, it is not fully clear exactly how these types of interactions would be done best in AR. For example, with a desktop computer, it makes perfect sense to use pull-down menus. The user knows this paradigm and knows where to find the menus. In AR, however, it is less obvious how to use menus effectively. If the participant has a tablet with him or her, it might be

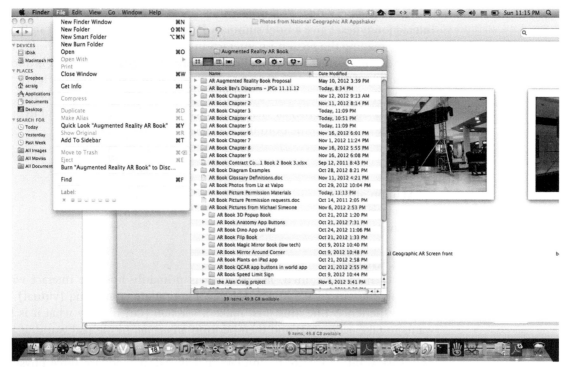

FIGURE 6.2
This screenshot shows a typical WIMP (Windows, Icons, Menus, Pointer) interface. Several windows are open, and a menu is pulled down from the top of the screen. Numerous icons are shown at the bottom of the screenshot. *Screenshot courtesy of Alan B. Craig.*

possible to use the menus on the tablet. If there is no tangible display, should the menus be placed such that they are always at the same physical location, thereby requiring the participant to return to that location to make a menu selection, or should the menus be positioned such that they are always in front of the participant? That might get very annoying. Should the participant be able to summon a menu on command and then place it wherever he or she wants? This might be a good solution, but the participant would need to know that it is even possible to summon a menu at any given point in the application. These sorts of questions surround all currently used interaction schemes, not just WIMP interactions.

Working in a full three-dimensional environment, such as an augmented reality experience, requires thinking about interaction in new ways.

It is useful to break down interactions into a few categories to help us consider interactions that we might want to support in an AR application.

Virtual reality application designers have already faced the dilemma of how to support interactions and have broken out a set of interaction possibilities.

In *Understanding Virtual Reality*, Sherman and Craig provide a breakdown of interaction types. I give a brief summary here, but interested readers can learn more by reading the section on interaction in *Understanding Virtual Reality* for further details. Virtual reality applications have the advantage, which is also a disadvantage, in that the participant is isolated from the real world. Hence, in general, all of the interaction possibilities are virtual interactions, whereas in AR there is the possibility of virtual interactions, real interactions, and hybrid interactions that combine both the real and the virtual.

Interactions in the virtual world can be boiled down to three primary categories:

1. Manipulation
2. Navigation
3. Communication

Manipulation

Taking each in turn, then, *manipulation* is primarily how we interact with things in the virtual world. In order to manipulate something (virtual) in an AR experience, one must first make a *selection* (i.e., identify what it is he wants to take action on) and then perform an *action*. In the real world, if we see three objects and want a specific one of them, we reach out and grab the object we want. If we are to emulate that in AR, if there are three physical objects, and they are within our reach, we have the option of doing the same thing. However, if the objects are virtual, we must somehow indicate to the system which object we are interested in and then must indicate we want to take it (whatever *take it* means in this context).

Mark Mine (Mine, 1995), a VR researcher, provides three ways that manipulation can be used in virtual reality applications and, by extension, in AR applications. These are:

1. Direct user control—in which participants manipulate the virtual world in a manner that is directly analogous to how they do it in the physical world.
2. Physical control—where participants use a physical device that they can hold and touch, such as a tablet computer or a physical push button.
3. Virtual control—where participants interact with virtual versions of a physical control, such as a (virtual) button, that they can press in the virtual world.

Sherman and Craig add a fourth category to this list:

4. Agent control—where participants issue commands to some agent in the virtual world to carry out the action on behalf of the participants (Figure 6.3).

FIGURE 6.3

These four images illustrate, in a virtual reality application, the ideas behind different levels of physicality involved in different types of control systems in VR and AR systems. (A) Direct user control, (B) physical control, (C) virtual control, and (D) agent control.

These interaction paradigms are discussed in detail in *Understanding Virtual Reality*.

The trend in AR applications is to mimic real-world interactions to the degree that is possible while using a handheld device such as a smartphone to provide inputs to the system that are not part of a natural world interface (i.e., to choose which AR application to start, etc.). This trend, however, doesn't take full advantage of the capabilities of AR. For example, a real-world interaction to fetch something at a distance requires the participant to travel that distance to carry out the task. However, AR has the capability to allow participants to engage in activities they couldn't in the real world, such as to

FIGURE 6.4

A child accustomed to reading on a device with a touchscreen that enables clicking on words for more information might try to press on a word in a (real) book to get more information. This is because when we are used to certain interactions working in one medium, we sometimes expect them to work in other media. *Photo courtesy of Beverly Carver.*

"magically" summon distant objects to them without having to travel to the object. As this type of interaction becomes more common, and as the virtual world *becomes* the real world, people will begin to accept those capabilities as normal, and potentially be bothered when those types of interactions aren't available, even in the real world. We have seen evidence of acclimation to new interactions that become natural to become expected even in real-world interactions. For example, when people read books in the past, they never even thought to point at a word on the page to get more information, a definition of the word, etc. However, now that the web has become pervasive and people are accustomed to hyperlinks, many people lament that they can't do the same with a physical book (although with augmented reality enhanced books these types of interactions become possible) (Figure 6.4).

With the pervasive presence of tablet computers such as the iPad, the two-finger gesture to make something bigger has become a part of many people's daily lives. I have witnessed young children trying to enlarge what they see on the television by doing that type of gesture and their disappointment when it doesn't work. One child, after trying to enlarge the image on a television by this gesture, turned to his parents and said: "It's broke" (Figure 6.5).

Physical control depends largely on what devices are available to the participant. In general, most devices used currently for augmented reality have some sort of physical interface that participants can interact with. Laptop computers have a keyboard and mouse (or trackpad or some type of mouse

FIGURE 6.5

It is common to expect a method of interaction to work on many different devices. Some people are accustomed to using two fingers to expand an image and are startled that it doesn't work on all devices. Here, a young boy is familiar with the two-finger gesture to expand an image on a tablet device and tries to do the same on a television set. *Photo courtesy of Beverly Carver.*

substitute). Smart tablets often have a touchscreen; some have physical keyboards and physical buttons, and some do not. Some have a virtual keyboard that behaves just like a physical keyboard and can be used as such (except that it takes up potentially valuable screen real estate). Some have physical volume controls and on–off switches. Smartphones have many of the same affordances as smart tablets in the way of physical controls.

There needs to be a distinction between physical controls vs virtual controls that are part of a physical device vs virtual controls that are purely virtual. To help understand this differentiation, one could consider the difference between pressing a physical button on a physical device to change the state of something vs a "physical" button on something in the environment, but that physical button is really just an image in the environment, vs a virtual button on a display such as an iPad vs a virtual button just hanging in space in the environment (Figure 6.6).

As displays such as eyeglasses and contact lenses become more ubiquitous (and with other head-based displays), there will be fewer obvious physical controls to use with AR applications unless the participant carries an additional device with which to interact. In this case, virtual controls become much more important to the application. This will rely most likely on very sophisticated computer vision software to interpret hand gestures and other actions on the part of the participant.

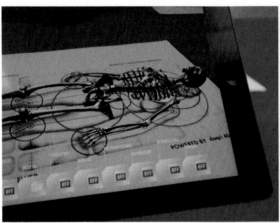

FIGURE 6.6

This pair of images shows an anatomy AR application from daqri that uses virtual buttons on the device to allow the participant to change the scenario. In the first picture, the participant has touched the button labeled "SKELETAL," which has toggled on the skeleton in the view shown. The button is highlighted in blue and labeled as "ON" until the participant toggles it off. In the second photo, the participant has touched the button for the muscular system. Thus, both the skeletal system and the muscular system are displayed until the participant takes a different action by pressing either of those buttons (to turn off the corresponding system) or pressing any of the other buttons to display additional systems. The slider seen by the participant's thumb in the second photo alters how transparent or opaque the skin (integumentary system) is displayed. In both these photos that slider is placed in the fully transparent position. *Photos courtesy of Michael Simeone; application courtesy of daqri.*

FIGURE 6.7

Smart tablets provide a keyboard that is manifested as virtual buttons on the physical device. The touch-sensitive screen interprets the keys that the participant is pressing. *Photo courtesy of Alan B. Craig.*

There are combination physical/virtual controls in the sense that a virtual keyboard on a smart tablet consists of virtual "keys" on the keyboard, but the touchscreen (physical) is actually used as the mechanism to indicate which key is being pressed (Figures 6.7 and 6.8).

An example of agent control would be a voice interface in which a speech recognition system (the virtual agent) interprets the participant's spoken commands and issues those commands to the AR application on the participant's behalf. Another example would be if the AR application provided a virtual "assistant" that the participant could prompt to carry out activities for him or her. For example, the assistant could execute high-level commands and carry out the low-level operations for the participant—the participant

FIGURE 6.8
This pair of photos shows a physical keyboard being attached to a smart tablet. *Photos courtesy of Michael Simeone.*

could gesture to the assistant to gather up the objects in the environment and the agent would carry out the duties required to fulfill that task.

As the real world and the digital world merge, it becomes less apparent when we are interacting with something or someone real and something or someone virtual. Sometimes people disagree with me that they will ever come to accept that something that is virtual is real; however, those same people are willing to accept that a song on the radio is actually a band playing physical instruments, whereas in many cases they are hearing digital simulations of instruments and there may be no "band" at all, but simply a computer programmer who created the work they are hearing. Likewise, in movies and television, many people are able to accept digital simulation as being "real," and many people are unaware that anything they are seeing is not real. Hence it is not a very strong leap to believe we might lose track of what we are interacting with—whether it is something from the physical world or something from the virtual world. Indeed, interaction, if done appropriately, can affect our perception of our environment and actually add to our sense of realness of the virtual world.

One interesting example mode of selection interaction that can be done in augmented reality is called *aperture selection*, or *aperture select*. In this technique, participants use their fingers to create an aperture through which they can see the object they are trying to select. The technique uses computer vision to determine what object in the scene that the participant is surrounding with their finger aperture. That object is then the selected object that the user can take action on. Note that this technique uses the image that is formed that combines the real world, the virtual world, and the participant's fingers. In

FIGURE 6.9

Aperture selection allows participants to select something in the scene by viewing it through an "aperture" made by their fingers. Computer vision interprets what in the scene is selected by that aperture and allows the participants to take some action with the object that is selected. In this particular example, the participant is indicating that he wants to select the (real) jacket that is hanging on the (real) coat rack by positioning his fingers around the jacket to form an aperture around it. The fingers are between the camera and the object being selected. *Photo courtesy of Michael Simeone.*

addition to using this technique to select an object, it is possible to also use the same technique to move or to delete virtual objects (or different actions can be taken on the selected object via other interaction techniques). For example, when an object is selected in the aperture, the participant could be allowed to essentially "pick up" that object and move it to a new location in the scene or may choose to delete the object by making the aperture smaller and smaller by closing their fingers closer and closer together until the object is fully crushed. At this point the system can delete the object (Figure 6.9).

A very common way of selecting objects is to point at the object you are interested in. Again, computer vision is used to determine which object the participant is trying to select. Of course, the object you are selecting needs to be a virtual object unless your application program is prepared to do some very serious image processing and alteration. By this I mean that the computer must be able to recognize real-world objects in the camera view, which can be quite difficult to program (Figure 6.10).

It is possible for the application program to keep track of all the objects that are available for selection in any given scene in the application. The participant could then pick the object from a list of objects by either using a physical button or slider or summoning the list as a virtual object in the scene and

FIGURE 6.10

In this photo, the participant is selecting the jacket that is hanging on the coat rack by pointing to it in the real world. *Photo courtesy of Michael Simeone.*

FIGURE 6.11

Another way to select an object is to point at it on a touchscreen. In some cases, you touch the object directly on the screen. Another alternative is to point at an object (rather than touch it directly) on the screen to select it. *Photo courtesy of Michael Simeone.*

then selecting an entry on the list by pointing to it, or some other means. If the participant is using a smartphone or tablet with a touch panel on it, the participant could just touch the desired element in the list to select it. A common technique used to help the participant understand when an object is selected or activated is to overlay a box or circle on the object (Figure 6.11).

Navigation

Navigation is related to how we move through the world. Some people equate navigation specifically with the act of moving through the environment, but navigation actually has two components: (1) travel and (2) wayfinding. *Travel* is the actual physical act of locomotion through the world. *Wayfinding* is related to how we know where we are in the world, and what we need to do to get to the place we want to go. For example, if I want to go to the store, and my chosen method of locomotion is walking, I need to figure out where I am and the path that I am going to take to get to the store. As I walk toward the store I must adjust my course, make turns, and so on to cause myself to end at the store. In this particular example, I am the combined navigator and locomotor. If I am driving to a place that I don't know how to get to, a passenger in the car may serve as the *navigator* and read a map and tell me where to make turns, even though I am the person actually manipulating the steering wheel.

Travel in Augmented Reality

Travel in augmented reality is accomplished the same ways as it is in the real, physical world. Because you are constrained by the real-world laws of physics, you are not able to fly, for example, without an airplane or some other flying machine, although in some cases it is possible to simulate such an experience. Hence, modes of travel in augmented reality include typical real-world modes of travel, including walking, running, riding a pogo stick, driving a car, taking a taxi, or flying in an airplane or any other mode of travel.

One concern about travel in augmented reality is that it is possible to travel to places where the AR application, via its sensors, is unable to track you and your location and pose. Likewise, it is possible to travel to places where there are no augmented reality enhancements in the world. One technique used to assist the participant in the AR experience to know when he or she is about to leave the boundaries of the enhanced world or the range of his or her tracking is to display a virtual fence that defines the boundary. Alternatively, one could display an audible alarm, or other warning signal (visual, audio, or otherwise), indicating that the participant is about to leave the range of the AR application. Of course, if there are AR enhancements tied to the participant's own body or the region around it, the AR enhancements travel with the participant to wherever he or she is at the moment. However, if those localized enhancements require any type of proximity to something in an absolute location in the real world (such as something that is part of the sensor system), then the participant still cannot travel without the potential of leaving the range of the AR application.

Because the limitations of the real world are in effect only when you are *in* the real world, one way to avoid those limitations (although it is not possible to overcome real-world gravity) is to experience the AR application in an empty space with no real-world objects to speak of. This could be an open field, an empty warehouse, or any number of scenarios. Once you are in a space devoid of real-world entities, then options for "travel" become much more flexible. For example, if the empty space is laid out with various virtual objects, it becomes possible to "travel" to an object by having that object appear to fly toward you. If the object's locational relationship with all the other objects remains the same, then the whole world will have traveled to you. Of course, although we know that the objects moved, in this particular frame of reference you perceive, and can act, as though you moved through the world to that object.

Overall, application designers must concern themselves with any mismatches that occur between the virtual world and the physical world. For example, if one sees an open virtual door on a real-world wall that is solid, one needs to consider what needs to happen if the participant tries to walk through that door. Of course, the real world will prevail and prevent this action. Likewise, if one overlays a flat surface on a real-world terrain that actually contains holes, one must think about the ramifications for the participant who may be unaware of the holes in the real-world surface. As can be seen from these examples, these types of mismatches between the real world and the virtual world can be particularly hazardous when it comes to traveling in augmented reality.

Again, if there is nothing in the world except virtual objects and entities, then there is a multitude of options for travel. However, in the case of an AR application where the world is composed only of virtual objects and entities, it is a case of virtual reality and, as such, the reader should consult materials related to navigation (travel and wayfinding) in a text such as *Understanding Virtual Reality*.

Navigation in Augmented Reality

Like travel, navigation in augmented reality can be done in the same ways that it is done in the real world. However, a multitude of additional things can be done in augmented reality to assist in navigation that are not possible in the real world.

In the real world, we use many things as navigation aids. These aids range from the simple use of landmarks to technological solutions such as global positioning system (GPS) applications that help us find our way. Since one key ingredient for an AR application is that the system must know where the user is, it is a relatively simple matter to add navigation aids into an AR application, and it is a compelling application of AR to *use* AR *as* a navigation aid in the real world.

Some methods that can be used as navigation aids in an AR application (or to use AR as a navigation aid in the real world) include:

- Provide a virtual map, including showing your current location on that map
- Provide a virtual assistant that walks (or hovers) beside you to show you the way
- Provide indicators of a path to follow, such as providing a (virtual) line or (virtual) footprints on the ground for you to follow
- Issue spoken directions to you, such as "turn right at the next opportunity" or "head east for another 100 feet"
- Provide (virtual) landmarks in the environment that can help you know where you are and how to find your way
- Allow you to drop (virtual) "bread crumbs" that you can use to find your way back to where you came from
- Provide you with (virtual) binoculars so that you can see long distances, and perhaps through objects to help you find your way

Note that in order for the application to help you find your way, it must know where you are currently (which it does via its sensors), know where you want to go (you will have to indicate this to the application one way or another by typing it in or speaking the goal location, etc.), and have a database of locations and objects in the world so it can determine a reasonable route for you to take that is possible for you to take (i.e., it doesn't try to have you walk through a brick wall to get to your desired location).

A handheld GPS device that shows you where you are on a map and helps you find your way by showing a path on a map on the screen is an example of an AR application for wayfinding. If, instead of showing you a path on the map on the device, it somehow superimposed that path on the real world [either by projecting it on the environment or by drawing the path (or arrows telling you which direction to go, etc.)] on a screen in registration with the real world on your display device, then it would be an example of an augmented reality wayfinding application.

Communication and Multiperson Augmented Reality Applications

Although most current AR applications are single-user experiences, there is no reason why they can't be (and some of the most compelling applications are likely to be) multiperson experiences. In a sense, any AR application that takes place in a space where other people are is a multiperson experience—it just happens that the other people are engaged in only the physical part of the experience. However, it is entirely possible, and often desirable, to have multiple participants in *both* the physical and the virtual world (and hence in the AR experience).

Many questions arise when there is more than one participant in an AR experience. For example, do all the participants see all the same elements in the virtual world from their own point of view? The answer to this is that it is up to the application designer to determine what each participant in the experience can see, hear, do, and so forth. It is entirely possible, of course, to allow each participant to choose what he or she sees or hears and/or what other participants are able to see or hear or not.

But what does this have to do with *communication*? Clearly the participants can communicate with each other in any of the typical ways that they can communicate in the real world. However, there are more ways that they can potentially communicate within an AR application. If real-world communication mechanisms are masked, then all communication is mediated through the AR application. Hence, if the software was good enough, the AR application could do real-time language translation between participants. Current translation software is not adequate to fully achieve this, but it is an example of the kind of mediation that can take place in an AR experience. Likewise, if participants are too far apart to hear each other, there could be an audio channel in the AR application to allow the participants to hear each other, but one could also do more "AR-ish" things such as display large font text over each of the participants so that everyone can see what they are saying. Bear in mind that though one might be able to see the other participants in a totally realistic way, with the magic of AR, each participant could potentially see an altered representation of the others in the AR experience (such as to see them wearing a costume or represented as an animal).

There can be other modes of communication between participants in an AR experience. For example, each person might see a map or be able to summon a map that shows the location of the other participants. Each person is tracked, thus making it possible to display their location on a map or otherwise. One could make a giant arrow that floats in the sky that points down toward where a participant is located. By simply moving an object that another participant will later find in its new location, one participant has "communicated" with the other participants in the experience. In the real world, people can track other people by looking for their footprints, noting which way sticks and brush have moved, and other indicators that someone has passed that way. All of these types of communication and more can be emulated in augmented reality.

Simply being able to see the same objects at the same time can foster communication. Often when there is a shared object of some sort, whether a gear, a whiteboard, a piece of pottery, or any other tangible thing, it provides a point of focus and common understanding that can aid in communication. AR is particularly good at this type of scenario. It is also possible for participants to join in from remote locations as though they are at the same place (telepresence) and engage in meaningful collaboration.

Augmented reality developer Robert E. McGrath suggests that AR is especially suitable for multimodal communication and provides provocative ideas that could exploit the affordances of augmented reality for the purposes of synchronous and/or asynchronous communication in an AR experience. One such suggestion is the idea of attaching a message (text, audio, or video) to a concrete object from either the real world or the virtual world, such as a rock or perhaps a can of Spam. The message originator could then hand that object to another participant or could leave the object in a certain place. When another participant encounters the object he or she can then read or listen to the message. In this sense, this idea is similar to the "message in a bottle" idea used in collaborative virtual reality applications. McGrath extends this idea, however, by requiring participants to engage in some other action in order to retrieve the message, such as bringing several physical objects (one might be a key) to the location to enable them to retrieve the message, or to engage physically by doing a specific dance in order to uncover the message. McGrath, with a grin, refers to this as "MailMailRevolution."[1] This is primarily an example of an asynchronous collaboration (not done at the same time). In synchronous collaboration, the participants are all engaged at the same time.

The possibilities are endless when it comes to how AR can support interaction between individuals within an AR experience.

There is also the issue of a participant communicating with the AR application itself. Beyond the typical interactions of a changing point of view and interacting with buttons and other interface elements, it is sometimes necessary to communicate with the application about something other than the typical virtual world interactions. For example, one might need to indicate to the application that you want to load a different virtual world or change the content in some other way. This type of communication can take place via a traditional computer system keyboard, via commands entered directly on a smart tablet or phone, or issued in other ways from within the application virtual world. For example, you might be able to summon a "system menu" from which you can choose to change the content of your experience or to enter the number of minutes you want the experience to last. Getting text and numeric input into an application without using a physical (or virtual on a device) keyboard can be challenging. Some techniques include enumerating all the possible values on a menu and then simply choosing a menu item using one of the techniques just described or one could use a speech interface to issue text and numeric information to the application. One could maneuver him- or herself to a virtual keyboard (typewriter) in the virtual world and type out the desired information (Figure 6.12).

Interaction in Projected Augmented Reality Environments

Because projection-based AR applications have different characteristics than other AR applications, some mention about interaction in them is prudent. With projection AR, interface elements can be projected directly onto the real world in registration with it. While it is also possible to create the appearance of interface elements in registration with the real world in other AR paradigms, there is a more immediate sensation that the interface element is actually a part of the real world in projected environments. It is typically the case that computer vision is used to interpret the participant's actions in such

---

[1]The term "MailMailRevolution" is a play on the name of the popular dance game "DanceDanceRevolution" by Konami.

FIGURE 6.12
It is relatively easy to provide input to an AR experience when using a device that provides either physical or virtual buttons. It is much trickier to input alphanumeric information if not using any kind of physical device. *Photo courtesy of Alan B. Craig.*

scenarios. Sometimes it is easy to help the computer vision algorithms interpret the participant's actions and desires by utilizing something that is very easy for the vision software to "see."

One thing that is easy for vision algorithms to see is a very bright spot of light. Hence, it can be useful to use a device like a laser pointer to indicate your intentions in a projected AR environment. The light (such as a laser pointer) can be much brighter than the rest of the projected light, and can also be a specific color that the vision algorithms can look for. It is also a relatively pin-point indicator to help remove ambiguity of where the pointer is being pointed (Figures 6.13 and 6.14).

Subjective vs Objective Point of View

There are two basic points of view that participants can take in augmented reality applications. The most commonly used point of view is the one in which participants see the real and augmented world as though they are seeing it from their own eyes. This is termed *subjective point of view*, or *subjective view augmented reality*. This can also be termed *first person augmented reality*. The other primary point of view used in augmented reality is termed *objective view augmented reality*. In objective view augmented reality, participants see themselves in the environment and interacting with the environment. This leads to a sort of "one step removed" form of interaction in that participants don't see whatever it is they are interacting with directly in front of them as they would see it from the first person, or *subjective*, point of view, but rather looking at a projected (or some other type of large monitor) display and seeing themselves interacting with the virtual world. In essence, they are watching themselves in the virtual world. As such, instead of looking

FIGURE 6.13
In projected AR environments, a laser pointer can be used to interact with interface elements. In this example, a participant is indicating her desire by shining the laser pointer on projected interface elements.

FIGURE 6.14
Menus can be used in projected AR environments. Here, the menu is projected onto the real world, in this case onto a sand table. Users choose their menu selection with a laser pointer. The computer vision algorithms can sense the spot of light from the laser pointer. Alternatively, computer vision could interpret if a hand touches a particular menu item to make the selection. *Photo courtesy of Simtable.*

directly at what they are interacting with, they look instead at some kind of a display and then interact while watching themselves on the display rather than watching directly what they are interacting with. Objective view AR has been referred to as *second person* AR in some other texts.

Generally, AR applications use one point of view or the other instead of using both within the same application, although there is no reason one couldn't use both within a single application to advantage. For example, it might be

FIGURE 6.15
Mall visitors are able to interact with miniature dinosaurs thanks to the magic of objective view augmented reality. The image shown here is actually of the display screen on which the participants see themselves in the augmented world. In order to see the dinosaurs, the participants must look at the screen. *From Appshaker Ltd. © All rights reserved.*

possible for a participant in a subjective view AR experience to temporarily choose to change to the objective view to see an overall "big picture" of his or her current circumstances. One case where this might be useful is in applications used to aid in navigation. The person might see the world with navigation aids in the first person but temporarily switch to an objective view to get a more traditional "map view" of his or her environment and where he or she is within that environment.

While there are exceptions, subjective view applications tend to be implemented with head-mounted or handheld displays, whereas objective view applications tend to be implemented with projection or some type of stationary display, such as a computer monitor or large screen.

National Geographic demonstrated objective view augmented reality with a spectacular display of National Geographic content on a large screen in a shopping mall. Participants stood near a fiducial marker and could see themselves along with the augmentations in their world. More detail about this application is available on this book's companion website and in Chapter 8 in this book (Figures 6.15 and 6.16).

FIGURE 6.16

The AR environment decribed in Figure 6.15 is displayed on the large screen seen here. Hence, the participants must look at the screen to see themselves interacting in the augmented world. *From Appshaker Ltd. © All rights reserved.*

SUMMARY

This chapter has shown that potential interaction mechanisms are endless and up to the creativity of the application designer. Likewise, because AR is a relatively new medium, it still has a lot of untapped potential in how people will interact with it in the future.

There are a number of different scenarios by which a participant can interact with a virtual world, an AR application, or other people in the experience. One can use physical buttons, keys, sliders, or other manipulators to interact in an AR experience, or those same types of elements can be "virtualized," allowing participants to have access to those same types of devices even though they don't have the physical counterpart available.

Because AR experiences take place in the real world, many real-world inter-actions are available (such as moving a physical object from one place to another by carrying it). Likewise, real-world elements can be used to affect changes in the virtual world.

Multiple people can interact with each other in an AR experience using real-world interactions such as speaking and waving, but in AR one can also use the application to mediate interactions between people such that one can do things in the AR experience that are not possible in the real world. Because other people are not as predictable as a computer program, multiple participants in an AR experience can lead to very interactive and richly different experiences.

Interactivity is a key ingredient to the medium of augmented reality. It is prudent for AR application designers to study interaction techniques in use in other AR applications (more to come on this in Chapter 8) as well as to use their creativity to invent new interaction capabilities. Later, as more applications are more widely available, it is likely that certain interaction schemes will become ubiquitous and somewhat standardized. However, the medium is very rich in the types of interaction that can be supported. It would be wise for AR developers to stretch their creativity to the max when it comes to creating interactions in their AR applications.

CHAPTER 7

Mobile Augmented Reality

INTRODUCTION

One trend is certain. People, more so than any other time in history, are on the go, and while they are on the go, they carry technology with them. The notion of having to "go to" a specific place to do something that could potentially be done via technology they carry is very unappealing to people today, especially young people. Augmented reality (AR) exists in the world, and people are in the world wherever they are. Consequently, there is a very strong trend toward mobile augmented reality applications that can be used anytime, and anyplace, with technology that is considered mobile enough that it is with a person all the time, no matter where (or when) he or she is.

WHAT IS MOBILE AUGMENTED REALITY?

Simply put, mobile augmented reality is AR that you can take with you wherever you go. Most specifically, this means that the hardware required to implement an AR application is something that you take with you wherever you go. There is an important distinction between *mobile* augmented reality and *portable* augmented reality.

Portable augmented reality uses technology that you can move from place to place. A desk-side computer with a monitor is somewhat portable in that it can be moved from one place to another relatively easily. A laptop computer is even more portable. If the batteries are charged you can carry it easily from place to place. You can even operate the laptop while you are walking, but it is awkward and not something you want to do on a regular basis.

A smartphone, however, is a truly mobile device. It fits in your pocket and is easy to operate wherever you are, even if you are walking or otherwise engaged. Likewise, most tablet devices are mobile devices in that you can carry them easily wherever you go. They are lightweight and you can operate them while walking. For the purpose of this chapter, I consider smartphones and smart tablets to be mobile technology, but anything larger and

209

more encumbering than that to be either portable or permanent technologies, where permanent technologies are those that are virtually impossible to move to a new location.

There is another class of devices that needs to be considered. Handheld gaming consoles and e-readers are easy to carry around. They may or may not provide the technological support for AR at the current time, but these and portable tablets seem to be encroaching on each others' territory in terms of the applications they run. That is, tablets are running e-reader applications and games, and game consoles are evolving toward doing more things than just games. E-readers are doing more things than just serving as e-readers and are becoming more "tablet like." The big distinction between these types of devices and smartphones and tablets comes down to whether people would likely be carrying the devices with them anyway or not. That is, many people would carry a smartphone whether or not it had anything to do with augmented reality. Some people might carry a gaming console on a day-to-day basis, and some would not. These are clearly portable devices, but the real win in mobile augmented reality comes when the participant is not required to carry anything more than he or she would have been carrying anyway (Figures 7.1 and 7.2).

Many head-mounted displays are mobile in nature but are still rather cumbersome, and most people do not wear them on a daily basis. Newer

FIGURE 7.1
Devices such as e-readers are becoming more like smart tablets, and smart tablets are able to run e-reader software on them, making the distinction between the two more blurry. This particular e-reader does not contain the sensors required for augmented reality applications, but some do. Hence, an e-reader might someday serve as a mobile AR device. *Photo courtesy of Alan B. Craig.*

glasses-oriented displays are more likely to be worn on a daily basis and thus make a mobile AR system that provides the capabilities of a head-mounted display a possibility. With contact lens displays or lightweight glasses displays, the mobile AR experience can become totally seamless with your everyday life. Applications that currently require you to "look through" a tablet or a smartphone become much more compelling when you are not required to "do something" to experience the AR and that "remind you" that you are doing something special in order to experience the augmented content.

Even though personal projectors are available for around $300, and some phones have built-in projectors, portable projected augmented reality systems are not commonplace. However, it will not be too long before mobile projection becomes a practical reality and, along with it, portable projected augmented reality applications. Projection systems are especially sensitive to ambient lighting conditions where they are deployed due to the possibility of bright light "washing out" the projected image. It is also possible for bright lights to wash out the display on smartphones and tablets, but it is an especially serious consideration with mobile projectors.

FIGURE 7.2

The difference between mobile augmented reality and portable augmented reality is treated somewhat differently from person to person. Camille Goudeseune of the Beckman Institute at the University of Illinois, shown here, was participating in an outdoor augmented reality environment that required a hefty amount of technology to experience. Most of the technology was built onto a bicycle helmet, and the computer portion of the hardware was carried in a backpack. Note that the shuttering stereoscopic glasses were not required for this particular application but are seen in the place where a stereoscopic head-mounted display would normally be. This application used both visual and audio components that were placed in the environment. *Photo courtesy of Beckman Institute for Advanced Science and Technology at the University of Illinois.*

ADVANTAGES AND DISADVANTAGES OF MOBILE AUGMENTED REALITY

As with most things, there are advantages and disadvantages to using mobile devices for mobile augmented reality applications. The advantages are related primarily to the fact that AR applications can be experienced anywhere and at any time. The disadvantages are related primarily to constraints that are imposed in exchange for mobility, although there are sometimes advantages to using a permanent or semipermanent installation at a particular location. There are also other special considerations for those planning to create mobile augmented reality applications.

Advantages of Mobile Augmented Reality Applications

There are many advantages to using mobile technology to support AR applications. Many of them are obvious, but some are less obvious. First and foremost is the fact that augmented reality, as seen in earlier chapters, exists in the real world, wherever that might be. That is, in general it does not make sense to house the AR application in a purpose-built "facility" much like a virtual reality CAVE, video teleconference facility, or other major infrastructure. By using mobile technology, the AR application can be experienced at the location where it makes the most sense. This is not to say that, for example, there is never an occasion for an AR application to be limited to a specific geographic place. Indeed, if one builds an AR application around the (real) Eiffel Tower, then the participant(s) would need to be *at* the Eiffel Tower. However, mobile augmented reality allows people to bring the required technology with them. In fact, in many cases of mobile augmented reality, they would already be carrying the required hardware with them whether or not they were planning to experience augmented reality at any given moment.

Mobile augmented reality is especially well suited to ideas such as "ubiquitous learning" in which the plan is that every person learns all the time, wherever they are, when they need to. One example might be that if someone is visiting Gettysburg and wants to learn more about the Battle of Gettysburg that (assuming the fields have been AR enhanced) he or she can use his or her mobile phone or tablet to gain additional information about the battle, perhaps to see the field as it was at a historic point in time, to see the battle taking place, and also to see overlays on the fields to show how the terrain was used in the battle strategy.

One advantage of mobile technologies that might not be obvious on first blush is that they are often very low cost compared to more permanent or special-purpose technologies. In this case, I am referring specifically to smartphones and tablets. These technologies are gaining power and features on a daily basis, while at the same time their costs are dropping.

FIGURE 7.3

Some things are just too big to bring to an AR laboratory. Consequently, if one needs to use AR in conjunction with such a large thing, it is necessary to have a portable or mobile AR system. In this case, one could conceive of a mobile augmented reality application that allows you to see wind flow over the wings of this airplane. *Photo courtesy of Clarita on morguefile.com.*

Some AR applications are only possible with mobile technology. For example, if one wants or needs to "see" simulated airflow over the wings of a (real) jet airplane, it is reasonable to take a tablet to a parked jet, but it is not possible to bring the airplane to an AR facility (Figure 7.3).

At the same time, however, as shown in an earlier chapter, it is sometimes advantageous to have a semipermanent "kiosk" at a point of sale in order to use the AR experience as an enticement to bring customers into a retail setting. In this case, it might be advantageous to have something that *can* be done with mobile AR but also something important that can only be done at the point of sale. Perhaps, there could be an AR application that could be used anywhere to see an example of a product in three dimensions, but only by coming to the point of sale could you see the interior of the product, and when you see the interior, you see an image of the prize you won.

Probably the *key* advantage of mobile AR is that in addition to being inexpensive, many people *already own* the necessary hardware. Current smartphones and tablets already contain the sensors, processing, and displays necessary for mobile AR applications. Having a large number of potential users already in possession of the required hardware is a very compelling attribute. As AR software improves, it is likely that there will be a handful of "master" AR client software programs (i.e., you only need to download one or two "apps" to your device to experience *many different* AR applications). In this case, it is likely that you would need to be connected to a network of one sort or

FIGURE 7.4

Augmented reality applications are shown on a smartphone the same as any other application. This photo shows the icons for the QCAR Dominoes application and the daqri AR application among the other (non-AR) applications loaded on this particular device. You invoke an application by touching its icon. *Photo courtesy of Alan B. Craig.*

another in order to retrieve the *content* for those different uses, but many smart devices like these are already connected to a network that would be suitable for this purpose (Figure 7.4).

Disadvantages of Mobile Augmented Reality Applications

Of course, along with advantages, there are a number of disadvantages with mobile augmented reality and using mobile technology to implement augmented reality applications. The most serious disadvantages are those related to constraints that must be placed on mobile AR applications due to the mobile technology itself, as well as the lack of control over the environment in which the mobile application will be experienced.

Constraints of Mobile Augmented Reality Applications

There are a number of constraints that limit what can be done with mobile AR applications and/or additional things that the application developer must address to overcome those constraints. The primary constraints fall into two broad categories: (1) technological and (2) environmental. These are clearly interrelated. The constraints are generally related to the limited capabilities of mobile devices, and that the application must be workable in a very wide variety of environmental conditions.

Technological Constraints

One of the key constraints on mobile augmented reality applications is that the resources on most devices are limited. These are manifested primarily as limited memory and limited computational capability, as well as limited graphics capability, limited input and output options, and, especially in

FIGURE 7.5

If a fiducial marker to be used by a typical AR system that uses computer vision in the visible spectrum looks like the one pictured here, it will not be useful if the AR application is deployed in the dark, on a moonless night, in a cave.

the case of nonprojection environments, limited screen real estate. Even if the mobile system includes some type of head-based, display such as glasses, they often have a limited field of view and limited resolution. Memory is a primary limitation on the amount of content that can be resident on a mobile device at any given moment. In real-world, practical terms, this means that there is an upper limit on the number and/or complexity of graphical and/or sound objects that can be kept on the device. There are two primary ways to overcome the limited memory available on a device. The first is to use clever schemes to limit the amount of memory that the content occupies. One way to do this is to limit the number of polygons and size of textures that are associated with visual objects and to limit the applications in the number of objects that are expected and/or required. The other way to overcome the issue of limited memory is to create a scheme by which content is loaded onto the device when needed and off-loaded when not needed. In this scenario, though, there is still a maximum amount of content that can be resident on the device at any given moment. There is more detail on this issue later in this chapter in the *Architectures for Mobile Augmented Reality Applications* section.

Environmental Constraints

Beyond the technological constraints imposed by the devices themselves, there are often environmental constraints that the mobile AR application developer must consider. It is often the case that there is no way a priori for the application developer to know what lighting, humidity, noise, and other environmental conditions might exist where the end user will experience the application.

In all cases of augmented reality applications and devices that use computer vision for tracking, it is essential that there is enough ambient light of the appropriate wavelength in the environment for the vision system to "see" the world (Figure 7.5).

Likewise, if an application is used outdoors, in particularly sunny areas, it is important to use screens that can be seen even in harsh glare if screens are used. Shadows in sunny spaces can also be problematic, especially when using vision-based tracking. Bright spaces are particularly difficult for projection AR environments.

For AR applications that rely on any kind of client server architecture or other means for downloading content or relying on a server system in any way, there must be an adequate network available in the area in which the system is planned to be deployed. If the system relies on the network, the end users must be made aware of this constraint, as otherwise they may take the application to an area with no network available and be disappointed when the application fails to perform as expected. One could question whether this is an environmental constraint (something essential is missing in the environment) or a technological constraint (no network available), but the presence or absence of a network can make or break the success of an AR application if a network is required.

Ambient sounds and noise are also a concern for the mobile AR application developer. If the application generates sounds, it is necessary that the participant is able to hear those sounds. Conversely, if the application is to be deployed in an area where extraneous sounds are not welcome (e.g., a church or funeral service), then it is important that the application not create unwanted sounds. Sound can be controlled more or less by a volume control and/or using headphones or earbuds, but it may be that neither of those tools can solve the sound problem in certain circumstances.

If an AR application requires sound (speech or other sounds) as an input to the system, then it is important that there not be extraneous sounds in the environment that might mask those signals.

In some circumstances, such as perhaps in medical applications that will be run in a hospital, electromagnetic interference can be problematic. Many hospitals insist that cellular phones not be used in certain areas because of the possibility of interference with medical testing and/or treatment systems. Hence, if an application requires use of a cellular telephone for communication, network, or other functions, then it is prudent to learn any appropriate restrictions or technical specifications that the system must adhere to.

Other locations might restrict the types of devices that you are allowed to carry/use. For example, many devices are restricted in some courthouses. Some industrial facilities limit the types of devices or emissions (such as radio frequency emissions) that are allowed. Computer rooms in data centers often have restrictions on the types of equipment that can be used in them. Virtually all devices are restricted on commercial air flights during takeoff and landing, and only certain devices are allowed while the plane is at altitude.

Many devices have a temperature below which they don't operate correctly. This can be an important consideration if the application might be deployed in very cold regions. This can be a concern if an application is for collecting science data on the North or South Pole, at great altitudes, or in other areas (walk-in freezers?) that are very cold. The converse is also the case; there are technologies that cannot be used effectively in very hot environments—your potential "Desert Cactus Identification" AR application might be affected adversely if you are in a particularly hot area of the planet.

All other environmental measures, such as humidity, pressure, and magnetic fields, can have an effect on mobile devices and consequently on mobile AR applications. If you are planning to deploy AR systems in any kind of extreme area, it is important to know the limits of the technology you are using. These concerns will primarily be important to military, science, and other similar application areas but can be important to other groups as well. For example, a mobile AR application to assist firefighters could potentially help save lives and property, but only if the technology doesn't fail under severe conditions.

User Understanding

In fixed location augmented reality, it can be made obvious that there is AR content at the location and what to do with it. There can be signs pointing this fact out, personnel who make it obvious to visitors what to do to make the AR work, etc. Mobile augmented reality presents the challenge that there could potentially be content *anywhere*. In one scenario we can imagine people walking through the world pointing their AR device at everything and everybody they see just to see if they happen to be "activated" for AR. It is likely that every person will have more than one AR application available to them at any time. How do they know which application they need for content that they may or may not know exists at any specific location? What about multiple, different competing sets of content at any given location? One could consider a scenario much like over-the-air radio and television in which one "tunes in" to different "channels" of information. Much like over-the-air broadcasts, such a scenario would require coordination and the ability of participants to make informed choices of what content they want to tune in to.

It is easy to imagine that spam could overwhelm the augmented world with unwanted advertising or unwanted information of any kind. Of course, one person's spam may be another person's treasure. How do we allow users to choose which content to participate with and which to filter out?

In the same way that all AR applications require intuitive, easy-to-use, perhaps standardized interaction schemes, it is especially important to have these schemes for mobile AR applications because of the potential for them to be so open ended in so many different environments. How is a participant supposed to know how to interact with new content at a new location unless it is reasonable to figure out what to do based on a history with other content at other locations? Embedded, contextual help systems in AR applications can provide one solution to this problem.

ARCHITECTURES FOR MOBILE AUGMENTED REALITY SYSTEMS

As shown in Chapter 3 (*Augmented Reality Hardware*), we learned that there are different architectures that an AR application can use. As a review, these included:

1. Application run on handheld system such as smartphone
2. Application run on handheld system connected to remote server(s)
3. Application run on desktop/laptop computer
4. Application run on desktop/laptop computer connected to remote server(s)
5. Application run as a web application
6. Application run on a cloud with a thin client
7. Other combinations of local and remote systems

The same can be said basically for mobile augmented reality applications [except for #3 (application run on a desktop/laptop computer) and #4 (application run on a desktop/laptop computer connected to remote server(s))]. However, there are (as seen earlier) certain constraints that a mobile AR application must consider. Except for architecture #1 (application run on handheld system such as smartphone), each of the other mobile architectures requires some type of network connectivity. Does this mean that there is no possibility for mobile AR applications that require more resources than are on your mobile device if the Internet is not available? Of course not. There are some applications that need to be connected to the Internet at large, and some that only need to be connected to a server system for the purpose of additional computational power and/or additional memory for content and content management.

In the event that you need to deploy a mobile AR application in an area that has no network coverage, and if you need to be connected to a server, but not the Internet at large, you can install a network [most likely wireless for maximum mobility of the participant(s)] for the express purpose of connecting the mobile devices with the server.

It is not a very significant hurdle to set up a wireless network that will communicate within an area you would like to allow the mobile AR application to communicate with a server. In order to do this you only need power, the server(s), and some basic networking equipment. If you need to extend the range of the network, there are commercial, off-the-shelf solutions for that purpose as well. If the area you are working in is outdoors and/or accessible by the public, you will need to take precautions to protect all of the equipment from weather and vandalism/thievery.

An example application that might make use of such a network and server is one where a public park (that is not covered by the Internet) might provide an AR application to show how the park looked in the past or to assist visitors in identifying flora and fauna in the park. The possibilities are endless.

This solution (building a network to allow the mobile AR application to communicate with a server) is very useful for mobile applications that take place in a specific area, but that area is not necessarily too mobile itself. That said, though, it is possible to install a network as described earlier on a bus or on a truck such that the bus or truck could travel from school to school to allow schoolchildren to experience that particular AR application. There would need to be provisions made to provide power to the server(s) and network hardware. As long as there is power available, there is no reason that such an application could not be made functional on a bus or on a train while it is in motion. Such an AR application might be considered a "mobile mobile augmented reality application."

SUMMARY

Mobile augmented reality is one of the most explosive growth areas for AR applications currently. Mobile AR takes advantage of the widely distributed base of hardware such as smartphones and tablets. Because AR exists in the world, it makes sense for AR applications to be mobile and that people can experience them wherever makes the most sense in the world, whether it is at a specific exhibit in a museum or in an open field in Africa. Mobile devices that can support AR are becoming more powerful and less expensive at a very rapid pace. Additionally, new hardware possibilities are emerging, such as mobile projection devices that will allow new types of mobile AR applications to function and make sense. There is a difference between "portable" and "mobile" augmented reality applications. Some people are more willing to accept the requirements of carrying additional technology for AR applications than others. Some mobile technology is very obvious to others in the environment, whereas some is "stealth" in the sense that others in the area might not even realize that someone is engaged in an AR experience. If necessary, a computer network can be deployed if there is not already suitable connectivity in the area that the mobile AR application is intended to be used in. As computer vision algorithms become better, there will be less need to "set up" an area to be AR enhanced ahead of time in any way by utilizing natural features of the area, such as skylines or famous landmarks, to aid the AR application to determine where the device is in the environment (Figure 7.6).

FIGURE 7.6
Landmarks such as the Eiffel Tower serve to help people find their way and know where they are in both the real world and in augmented environments. In this case, the real-world Eiffel Tower serves as a landmark for mobile AR experiences that take place specifically around the tower. *Photo courtesy of Greg Runyan.*

The next chapter addresses augmented reality applications in general, what makes a compelling AR application, how to evaluate AR applications, AR application styles, how to apply AR to a problem, and collaborative AR applications and illuminates several AR application "case studies" to show some ideas that are currently being used in AR applications as well as applications that were created for differing purposes and technologies.

CHAPTER 8

Augmented Reality Applications

INTRODUCTION

As discussed in Chapter 1, augmented reality (AR) is much more than a set of technologies. Augmented reality is, in fact, a medium. Viewing AR as a medium allows us much more leeway in considering different ways that AR might be applied in the world rather than what a certain set of technologies can support today. Indeed, until AR is applied to a problem of some sort, whether it is for utilitarian purposes, for education, for artistic expression, or just plain fun, the technology itself might be interesting as a novelty for a brief time, but will not sustain deep interest until it is made to do something of importance to the AR application developer and/or whoever experiences that usage of AR.

This chapter addresses many different aspects of augmented reality applications, including the following core ideas:

- What makes a good augmented reality application?
- Application areas
- Collaborative augmented reality
- Applying augmented reality to a problem
- Evaluating augmented reality applications
- Augmented reality application examples

By examining these ideas, as well as some example applications, I hope that you will get ideas for compelling ways that augmented reality can be used in your area of interest.

WHAT MAKES A GOOD AUGMENTED REALITY APPLICATION?

When thinking about what makes a good AR application, there are really two core questions that need to be addressed. These two questions include:

1. What makes a good candidate for an AR application?
2. What makes a good AR application?

There is a difference between those two questions in that the first addresses how well matched the candidate application is to the affordances offered by AR, whereas the second question addresses how well the AR application is executed and meets the needs of the user of the application.

Recall that some of the key affordances are that the AR experience takes place in the real world, at a specific place at a specific time. AR allows one to superimpose digital information onto the real world in a way that the user perceives the digital information as part of the real world. Keeping these affordances in mind, then, a good candidate for an AR application is one that exploits those affordances in a positive way to solve a problem of one sort or another. Note that even in this case, there are two broad categories of applications that fit this criterion. The first is any application area that can use AR in a way that is advantageous. The second is the set of application areas where there is no other way (or only significantly different ways) to experience the application.

FIGURE 8.1

This application from daqri allows you to see different floor coverings in place on your own floor. Here, a colorful rug is shown flush on a bare concrete floor via augmented reality. *Image courtesy of Gaia Dempsey, daqri.*

An example of the first is the example from Chapter 5 regarding the story of Pinocchio. Obviously the story of Pinocchio can be, and has been, experienced through many different media, including books, movies, puppets, and games. Clearly, the medium of AR allows the story to be experienced in new and different ways, but other media are also suitable for the expression of the story.

An example of the second type of application, one that AR is really the only medium that is directly suitable, allows a person to experience his or her own home with a variety of different floor coverings to allow him or her to previsualize, *in his or her own home*, what his or her living room or kitchen will look

like if he or she replaces his or her current floor with hardwood, red carpet, brown carpet, or Astroturf. Sure—one could do this (sort of!) by taking a photo of the room in question and using Photoshop to alter the image to show what the room would look like with different floor coverings, but no other medium allows the participant to see what his or her room will look like, in place, at full scale, in real time, from every possible angle with different floor coverings (Figure 8.1).

Granted, the technology doesn't currently address the different *feeling* of the different floor coverings under your bare feet, but the *medium* supports that idea. It is just a matter of time for the technology to address the tactile sensations of the various floor coverings. Note, too, that this application of AR (previsualization of floor coverings in your own home) can be implemented with a variety of different technologies. One could use projection technology as the display, use a head-based display such as glasses or a see-through head-mounted display, or use a handheld display such as a tablet to serve as a magic lens through which to see one's room in the altered states. Likewise, on the computer vision side, one could place fiducial symbols around the room or could use natural features of the room to assist the application in presenting the correct view of the room. As noted, currently it is not realistically feasible to allow one to walk around barefoot in the room to experience the different feeling of hardwood vs shag carpeting vs vinyl. It is possible now, however, to simulate room acoustics such that one could potentially "hear" the difference in sounds of conversation in the room as different materials are placed on the floor or to hear the click clack of high heels on a laminate floor vs a hardwood floor. Indeed, one could conceive of an AR application that allows one to visualize the reflections of sound waves in a room to aid in determining the optimal placement of acoustical panels such as broadband absorbers to help make a room more suitable as a home theater (Figure 8.2).

The example of an AR application being used to visualize floor coverings in a home is, of course, generalizable to a much larger class of applications that are meant to allow homeowners to visualize different materials in their home. For example, one could use AR to visualize what new colors of interior paint will look like or it could assist people in envisioning what a new sofa will look like in their living room, even offering numerous different choices and allowing the participant to press "Buy It Now" on their tablet to have the desired sofa purchased and delivered.

Indeed, this same class of application could extend to the exterior of a home to allow one to choose different colors of siding, shutters, or garage door styles. There is a tremendous advantage to being able to see different choices for your home *in context, at your home,* as opposed to from a catalog photo or a collection of carpet samples.

In fact, augmented reality could also be used to help visualize your entire home, from the exterior, on your vacant lot. This could help you make decisions about how to place your home on the lot and potentially make design changes early in the process of designing and constructing your home before it becomes too costly to make changes.

It is not a large leap at all to imagine how this same class of application could be used for commercial buildings and facilities. In fact, AR is a very appropriate medium to use to visualize how a new skyscraper might impact the skyline of a major city. With AR, developers, zoning planners, and concerned public can see the visual impact of a new building from as many perspectives as they care to view to see

FIGURE 8.2
An AR application can be used as a "magic lens" to let you see the unseen. In this case, the lens is being used to see (normally) unseen sound waves emanating from a speaker. *Diagram courtesy of Beverly Carver.*

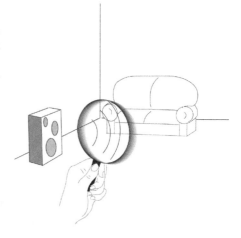

how a new building will look amid the other buildings. By embedding additional information in the application, one could also determine and visualize different sight lines to know what can be seen from various parts of the building and what can be seen from the windows of the new building. Likewise, the building could be visualized to show how it will appear in the daytime, at night, and in different seasons of the year.

The same building model could then be displayed via AR in a book about the architecture of the city, allowing readers to gain a more complete three-dimensional (3D) appreciation of the building. The building model could also be viewed on a pamphlet about the building. As you can see, this application can be considered to be an example of a large class of AR applications that all make up a group of applications that could be grouped together and labeled as *architectural visualization* applications. In fact, these applications could all fall under an even larger umbrella of *architecture* applications and/or *visualization* applications. Note that the application that allows you to purchase a new sofa based on how it looks in your home could be considered a *shopping* application, or a *commerce* application. Additionally, each of the applications described earlier could be implemented with different technologies. Consequently, if they were implemented with projection technologies, they could be considered *projection AR* applications or could be considered (if implemented as such) *smartphone AR* applications.

Coming back to the original question of what makes a good AR application, it can be seen that some of the essential elements are whether it exploits the affordances provided by AR such as that it is situated in the real world at a particular place and time and that it adds digital information to the real world that is registered with the real world. It solves a problem or otherwise makes life better in some way that takes advantage of augmented reality to do it in a different way than other media or does something that can't be done in other media. It allows the participants to experience some sensory phenomena that they couldn't otherwise. Today that is implemented primarily through vision and hearing, but in the future it will potentially use other senses as well. Another criterion for good applications is that they are implemented well and in a way that works to solve the problem at hand. This aspect of AR applications is covered more fully later in this chapter in the section on evaluating AR applications.

As can be seen from the examples given previously, classifying AR applications is a nontrivial task and is tackled in the next section of this chapter. This section was meant to set the stage of what is involved in classifying AR applications.

APPLICATION AREAS

As can be seen earlier in this chapter, there are numerous different ways to classify AR applications. One of the most obvious ways to classify AR applications is by the content area that they address. For example, some applications might cover content that is primarily for entertainment purposes, whereas other applications might cover content that is related to some specific content area such as art. The following list is of some categories of AR applications that might be useful to you as you think about your own potential development and use of augmented reality.

Education
Science
Business and manufacturing
Medicine
Public safety and military
Art
Advertising
Entertainment

Clearly this is not a comprehensive list, but rather this list addresses some broad categories that cover many of the AR applications currently available (Figure 8.3).

There are a few styles of augmented reality applications that are emerging that are worth considering for a while. These styles might sound very constrained, but consider them to represent a very broad coverage of many different styles of applications. After the list of styles, I address what each style represents.

- Magic books
- Magic mirrors
- Magic windows and doors
- Magic lens
- Navigation assistance
- Nonreferential augmentation
- Objective view augmented reality

There is clearly overlap between many of these styles, and the same application could conceivably be categorized in more than one style, but it is hoped that by thinking about these classifications it might help one to envision the different possibilities of AR. The point here is *not* to suggest that these are the extent of different application styles or that it is a clean categorization, but to spur creativity on the part of the reader to think about how any of these styles (or any others that the reader can imagine) could be used in his or her area of interest.

Note that several of the styles allude to *magic*. AR and magic are similar in many ways. Both of these ideas rely on the idea that the world that we perceive is based on information provided to our senses and they both rely on fooling the participant in some way. Magicians are adept at redirecting attention and sleight of hand (and other techniques) in order to cause a person to believe something occurred that is different than what actually occurred. AR developers do a similar thing in that they create imagery (for any senses, not just sight) that causes a person to believe something other than what is actually

FIGURE 8.3

This AR artwork, created by artist Margaret Dolinsky, is particularly interesting in that it escaped from a virtual reality (VR) application to become part of an augmented reality experience that took place in the streets of San Francisco as part of an exhibition called "Out of the Box." This exhibition featured a number of virtual reality experiences created between 1997 and 2011 that were reinterpreted as mobile augmented reality applications. The Straight Character (first image) is a character from the VR application "Straight Dope" and is seen here in the real world at the Chinese Gates in San Francisco. Dolinsky explains: "I create imagery (from the unconscious) by using a technique called active imagination. My artworks situate emotional and subversive confrontations between the real and the virtual." The second image shows the virtual reality (CAVE) application from which the AR application was derived. "Out of the Box" is launched by reading a QR code or at http://www.layar.com/layers/hellofor/. "Out of the Box" is curated by Tracy Cornish and Todd Margolis of the Future of Reality artist collective and features artwork by Applied Interactives, Atlas in silico, Bino and Cool, Sheldon Brown, Ben Chang, Margaret Dolinsky, Diana Domingues, John Craig Freeman, Paul Hertz, Will Pappenheimer, and Silvia Ruzanka. Visit futureofreality.org for more information. *Images courtesy of Margaret Dolinsky.*

occurring. Sometimes when thinking about ideas for AR applications it is helpful to think about "If I had a magic wand and could make something occur in the world that would be beneficial to me, what would I do?" For example, if I could wave a magic wand and have a tour guide show up to take me to my destination, it could provide an idea for a navigation application. Of course, it

FIGURE 8.4
Kirsten Uszkalo, project lead for the Witches in Early Modern England Project, used augmented reality to demonstrate that the idea of a witch's medium, a frog, exists not only in spiritual and magical space, but in physical space and digital space. In the first image, the medium is freed from the flat woodcut by augmented reality and exists in digital space. In the second image, the medium is brought back into physical space through the use of 3D printing. *Photos courtesy of Kirsten C. Uszkalo.*

is not currently feasible to implement every magic idea you can think of, but thinking this way can lead to creative ideas for applications (Figure 8.4).

Magic Books

Magic books were one of the first styles of augmented reality to emerge and certainly one of the first to be seen by the public. It is widely acknowledged that Dr. Mark Billinghurst was the inventor of the augmented reality "magic book" in that he first created a children's book that was animated when viewed using a see-through head-mounted display.

One of the more interesting aspects of the original magic book "MagicBook" project begins with the fact that the book was totally standalone in physical space. That is, even without any of the augmented reality aspects of the book, it served as a children's book in its own right. It was a useful, tangible object. Beyond that, it offered the augmented reality overlays that we think of when we think of magic books. Finally, the book served as a gateway into a full virtual reality environment. That is, you could immerse yourself into the virtual world of the book and interact in a fully digital environment. Hence, the original magic book served in the purely physical space, the augmented reality space, and the fully digital space.

Books have served the population for thousands of years. Books offer many very useful affordances. They are portable, they convey a lot of information via text and potentially images, they have weight, readers can easily gauge how far they are in the book, they can be printed in any language, they can be annotated (by writing in the margins, etc.), and they can be indexed to make it easy to find the information you are looking for.

FIGURE 8.5

Pop-up books have existed for a very long time. This is an old-fashioned way to include three-dimensional content in a traditional two-dimensional book. *Photo courtesy of Michael Simeone.*

Books, however, have some limitations that are difficult to overcome using traditional book technology. Books are not good at portraying three-dimensional information and are not good at conveying time-varying information (animation). Some books have addressed the issue of three-dimensional information by including "pop ups" that allow the reader to unfold something on the pages into a 3D object. However, that pop up is static in time. One could rotate the book that it is in, and hence the object, thus allowing the point of view to be varied over time, but the object is otherwise (almost always) static and does not vary its shape, color, or other properties over time (Figure 8.5).

In general, it is very difficult to convey time-varying information in a traditional book. Of course, typically, a book proceeds in time from front to back, but any visual information, such as pictures or even pop ups, do not vary in time. One way this could be overcome in a traditional book is to use the technique of flipbook animation. With flipbook animation, images are drawn on successive pages that each represent a step in time. Then, readers can flip through the pages very quickly to see the apparent motion of animation as the images flip before their eyes (Figure 8.6).

Another way that motion is conveyed in traditional books is via a picture that exposes different time steps as a filter is moved across the page. This can give the impression of motion/animation.

The medium of augmented reality, and the technology associated with it, offers very compelling ways to overcome these limitations of traditional

FIGURE 8.6

Flip books are an old-fashioned way of showing time-varying information in a traditional book. In this series of pictures, there are a series of different images on each page. When the reader flips the pages, as seen in the second picture, the reader can see an animation that looks as though the images are in motion. *Photos courtesy of Michael Simeone.*

books. Enhancing the book as an augmented reality magic book does not lose the good affordances of traditional books. The best part is that a traditional book can still function as a traditional book even by those who lack the technology to experience it as a magic book. That is, transforming a traditional book into a magic book loses nothing, but potentially much is gained.

A chemistry book, for example, can exist as a traditional book that is every bit as good as any other book. But if the book is made as a magic book, students can *also* view molecules as three-dimensional time-varying entities and can interact with simulations and other exercises with the magic chemistry book (Figure 8.7).

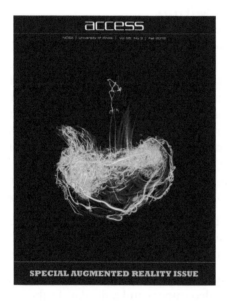

FIGURE 8.7

The National Center for Supercomputing Applications (NCSA) at the University of Illinois publishes a (physical and digital) magazine that covers a variety of topics related to science and high-performance computing. As an experiment, NCSA, in collaboration with daqri, created a magic book version of the magazine. Each of the major stories in the magazine was enhanced by augmented reality. Readers could obtain an app for their iOS or Android device and use their tablet or smartphone as a magic lens through which they could experience the extra digital augmentations via augmented reality. The experiences included some videos that played in registration with the physical magazine and some interactive 3D experiences. Among the experiences were three-dimensional molecules that were discussed in the stories. By pointing the camera of their device at the two-dimensional image of the molecule(s), the participant could see a 3D rendering "pop up" from the page and they could then explore the molecule by changing their point of view by moving their device around the 3D molecule. Even the magazine's cover image, featuring the work of a research team led by Stan Woosley, was active and played a movie (in place) of the cover image, rotating to provide different viewpoints. If you would like to try the magazine with AR enhancements, see the companion website of this book for directions on how to download the magazine to print out and how to obtain the application for your tablet or smartphone. *Image courtesy of the National Center for Supercomputing Applications (NCSA) and the Board of Trustees of the University of Illinois.*

FIGURE 8.8

This image shows an artist's conception of what a history book of the future might be like. Note that there is a real-world (physical) book overlaid with an animated simulation of a battle scene. In this image, there is no electronic technology shown to indicate that in the future, the technology to support augmented reality will be totally nonencumbering.
Photo composite courtesy of Dave Bock.

A book about the civil war can act just like any other civil war text, but a magic book can show how the terrain on a battlefield impacted military strategy as students watch the battle play out in front of them (Figure 8.8).

Clearly, augmented reality can be used to make a magic book with any type of content. One could consider a book about tropical fish that comes alive with beautiful tanks of fish, 3D models of individual specimens, and visualizations of water chemistry and even allows you to "feed the fish."

Magic Mirrors

The basic idea of a magic mirror-style application is that there is a "mirror" in which what is reflected includes the real world, but also enhancements to the real world. Note that most instantiations of objective view augmented reality fall into the realm of magic mirrors. Recall that in objective view augmented reality you see yourself in the real and augmented world from an external point of view. However, with a magic mirror it is not essential that you always see yourself in the scene. In a real-world mirror, when you stand off axis to the mirror it is possible to see a reflection of the real world, but not see yourself. For example, if you use a mirror to look around the corner, you can see the world around the corner, but not see yourself in the mirror (Figure 8.9).

A magic mirror has been used in children's books for decades. In this particular situation, a physical mirror is used alongside a physical book to allow the child to see the missing part of an image in the book (Figure 8.10).

In augmented reality, the "mirror" part of the magic mirror is typically implemented by using a video camera and a display. In the most direct implementation of an application that is a magic mirror, one would likely have a video display with a camera mounted at the top of it or in the center of it that faces the same direction as the display. Imagine a television screen with a camera sitting on top of it with the video signal feeding the images the camera captures directly to the screen. When you walk up to the screen you see yourself facing the screen as well as other elements of the real world that the camera captures. In AR, there can also be additional digital information integrated with the video signal.

One very obvious application of AR in a magic mirror style is to look in a mirror and see yourself in a way that is altered. For example, you could look in the mirror and see yourself dressed in a costume or perhaps different clothing. You could allow AR to adorn you with jewelry, a new style of glasses, a new hat, etc. The application could be interactive (beyond the interactivity of the changing point of view as you move around in front of the camera)

FIGURE 8.9

In the real world, a real (physical) mirror can be used to do things such as look around corners and be able to see things that are normally out of our view. In this picture, one can look out the window without being seen by placing a mirror judiciously. This technique can also be used by bedridden individuals to see things they normally can't see. *Photo courtesy of Michael Simeone.*

FIGURE 8.10

Magic mirror books have existed for a long time. In these books, a child uses a mirror to complete a picture that is drawn only partially. By looking at the page and in a mirror simultaneously, the child can see the complete picture. *Photo courtesy of Michael Simeone.*

to allow you to try new clothes, then change the color of those clothes, and choose from a variety of jewelry, etc. For a commercial application, there could even be a "Buy it now" button to allow you to order the virtual clothes that you are "wearing" at the moment.

The same technique could be used in a museum by implementing a kiosk that includes a magic mirror. One could then potentially see oneself in clothes from a different time period, in a suit of armor, with a hairstyle of a historical figure, and so on.

The mirror can, of course, add enhancements to the person or persons looking in the mirror and/or to the rest of the environment reflected in the mirror. A wonderful example of an objective view AR magic mirror is the National Geographic augmented reality application. In the primary implementation of that application, a giant screen displays everything that is "reflected" in it, but adds much additional content that any people in the vicinity can interact with, ranging from dinosaurs to thunderstorms to dolphins to wild animals (Figure 8.11).

Magic Windows and Doors

A magic window or magic door is just what one would expect it to be. It can be a window or door through which you can see the real world as it is seen through that door or window, only augmented by digital information; you can see the real world at some other real-world location through that door or window that is enhanced by digital information; or you can see a fully digital rendering that is situated as though it is part of the real world at the location of the door or window.

The third case, where what is on the other side of the door or window is purely digital, could arguably be called virtual reality. However, because it is presented registered in place in a real-world location, and the digital world behaves as would be expected in the real-world location (i.e., if you move your head around or walk around the door, the scene updates appropriately), this scenario also qualifies as an augmented reality application.

These three scenarios can all make compelling augmented reality applications. For example, one could look through a window and see the world that exists outside that window, enhanced by wind velocity vectors, weightless tracer particles, and other tools to visualize the current weather at that location if there were real-time data available to use to create them.

Magic windows and doors offer an interesting way to visualize something in a place that you don't have room to show the real object. For example, imagine a car dealership that is in a very small location. One could enable magic windows or magic doors to allow you to see various makes and models of cars. Additionally, because this is augmented reality, one could also choose what color car one would like to see through the window or door. One could also provide a magic door or window that is a glimpse into a fantastic space that one couldn't experience otherwise. For example, you could look out a magic

FIGURE 8.11

This collection of pictures shows the National Geographic augmented experience by Appshaker. In this experience, mall visitors have the opportunity to interact with content from National Geographic. The experience is an objective view, "magic mirror" application in which the participants see themselves interacting with the content on a large screen [as opposed to a subjective view where they see the content as though they are seeing it directly (without seeing themselves in the scene)]. The final two photos in this set show some of the "behind-the-scenes" aspects of the technology behind the project. Appshaker has a very nice video that shows people interacting with the content. See the companion website of this book for a pointer to the video as well as other video demonstrations of compelling applications. *Picture credit: Appshaker Ltd. © All rights reserved.*

FIGURE 8.12

In a creative application of AR, daqri's movie poster concept allows the viewer to play a minigame using marketing materials for the film as a target image. Based on their performance (or random luck), players could have the opportunity to win perks such as free popcorn at the theater. Once the game is over, no matter the outcome, the app enables the viewer to purchase movie tickets at the nearest theater, thanks to global positioning system awareness. In the example here, the participant peers into a primordial jungle scene in "negative space" (using the movie poster as a "magic window"), inhabited by a fierce predator. Players must shut the lever of a metallic cage before the T. rex gets too close or suffer the consequences. *Images courtesy of Gaia Dempsey, daqri.*

window and see the surface of the moon or a scene from a period of time in history (Figure 8.12).

Likewise, you could visualize the interior visual impact of a new addition for your home using a magic door. You could place the "door" in different locations and visualize the different sight lines of what can be seen in different locations in the proposed part of the building from different locations in the real part of the building to see where you would like to place the door and how to lay out the new addition.

Magic Lens

The magic lens can take (at least) two different forms. The first form is when the participants in the AR experience perceive they are using a "lens" of some sort to look at the world to see the additional information that the augmented reality application provides. That is, there is something in the world, either a physical object or a virtual object, that serves the purpose of a lens through which the participant looks or listens. For example, there could be an object that resembles a magnifying glass that the participant picks up and then looks through to see digital enhancements to the real world. Some technologies for AR imply the sense of a lens by their form factor. For example, with many mobile AR applications, the participant views the world through a lens in the form of a smartphone or a tablet computer. In the case where the AR application relies on computer vision, the participant *is* literally looking through a lens (the camera lens). This does not mean that there cannot be a separate lens that the participants use even if the technology that they use to experience the application (tablet or smartphone) uses a physical lens.

The other major form that the magic lens can take is that of an invisible lens. In this sense, *all* AR applications fall under the umbrella of the magic lens. That is, no matter what the technology used to implement the experience and no matter what the form of interaction is, in all cases, AR applications are in a sense a lens over the real world that allows the participant to see or hear information that is not otherwise perceptible. Indeed, in the future when AR applications make use of displays in eyeglasses, contact lenses, or hearing aid-style transducers (for audio), the participants will be constantly encountering the real world through a conceptual lens that allows them to see or hear things that aren't physically present in the real world (Figure 8.13).

An example of an explicit magic lens would be an AR application where the participants use their tablet or smartphone to look at the real world and see fingerprints that are not visible otherwise. The fingerprints could be either fully virtual or the application could use image processing to enhance fingerprints that are actually on what the participants are looking at. Another application of an explicit magic lens is to allow people to look at their own body, such as their forearm, and see their bones in place, thus providing an X-ray view of their arm. Of course, the AR application would need appropriate data, perhaps from a real-time magnetic resonance image or ultrasound, in order to create the appropriate displays. This same concept can be carried out to allow builders to see what is behind walls in a building. In this case, builders can use their magic lens to see where pipes for plumbing, conduit for electrical wiring, and other hidden items are behind the drywall of the wall they are viewing through their lens. Data for this application can be provided by a database containing the computer-aided drafting information for the building.

For X-ray-style applications, special thought must be given to the graphical display to avoid the appearance that the unseen elements made visible do not appear to be sitting *on* or floating *above* the surface that normally hides them.

FIGURE 8.13

These two photos from String show a magic lens application. When you look at something through your magic lens (such as a smartphone or tablet), you see the augmented reality content and can view and interact with it from any perspective. String is a software development kit (SDK) for augmented reality applications. It integrates with Unity and provides a robust development environment. *Photos courtesy of String (www.poweredbystring.com).*

This requires displaying additional graphical elements that cause the appearance of a cutout or pit in the surface of the object (Figure 8.14).

There is a case where the digital enhancements seen through a magic lens are two dimensional in nature. That is, an image or a video is placed in the scene that is only visible when seen through the magic lens. For example, a room with blank walls could be seen as a room with artwork on the walls through a magic lens. Or, a video could play in a certain location on the surface of a table or a magazine. But is it augmented reality? Some people don't consider two-dimensional overlays such as text, pictures, or videos to be true augmented reality. However, according to the definitions given in Chapter 1 of this book, such an enhancement would be considered augmented reality *as long as the information is registered with a specific location*. Thus, if there is a video (appearing to be) playing on the page of a physical magazine, but the video stays tied to the specific part of the page that the video is on, then it

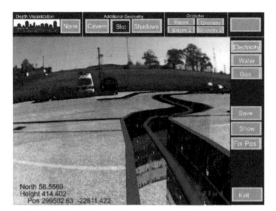

FIGURE 8.14

This application is an example of an X-ray view of an underground object. Note that the cavern walls were drawn in by the application to cause the participant to perceive that the object is below the surface of the parking lot rather than sitting on top of it. *Courtesy of Dieter Schmalstieg, Graz University of Technology.*

FIGURE 8.15

By pointing her smartphone at University of Illinois baseball player Davis Hendrickson's trading card, a user triggers a video bio of Hendrickson by way of the "Virtual Dugout" app created by Illinois students in Assistant Professor Charles "Stretch" Ledford's spring 2012 independent study. Virtual Dugout uses Automony's augmented reality engine "Aurasma" for this functionality. *Image courtesy of Charles "Stretch" Ledford.*

fulfills the requirements of the definition in this book. However, some applications do not portray the video "in place" and simply start the video playing when it sees a certain image or icon. Then the video takes over, and even if you direct the physical device away from the trigger, the video continues to play on the AR device (smartphone, etc.), and the video travels with the device rather than being pegged to where the marker was in the real world. Though interesting, this is not AR by the definition given in this book.

Triggering a video in AR can be particularly compelling when the fiducial symbol that denotes the location for the video is made of the first frame of the video that is played. Hence, when someone sees the picture of the first frame of the video as a physical image in the real world, but it is then overlaid by the (digital) video, the effect is quite chilling as the person sees the picture come to life and animate. This effect has been utilized to great advantage by using the images on sports cards to provide a trigger and a location for a video of a "talking head." That is, normal baseball, football, or basketball cards that show a picture of a player and provide their statistics when viewed through a magic lens appear to "come to life" and the picture of the sports star begins to speak and move, etc. (Figure 8.15).

Note that all of the techniques listed previously (magic books, magic mirrors, magic windows and doors) can also be considered magic lens. Those designators are more specific labels saying something further about how the AR lens is manifested in those applications (Figures 8.16 and 8.17).

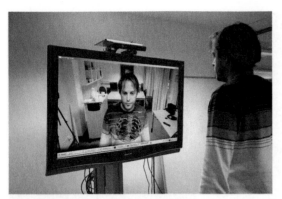

FIGURE 8.16

This magic mirror AR application called Mirracle from Technical University of Munich allows participants to see a virtual X-ray in place on their body. Mirracle uses a Kinect device to track the participant and software from OpenNI and PrimeSense NITE. *Photo courtesy of Tobias Blum.*

FIGURE 8.17

This is a screenshot from a system, also from Technical University of Munich, that uses a head-mounted display to view an overlay of magnetic resonance data on a person. *Photo courtesy of Tobias Blum.*

Navigation Assistance

There is a class of AR applications that are specifically meant to help people find their way through the real world by providing artificial cues that aid them in knowing which direction to go to get to their desired destination. Examples of these applications were discussed earlier in this book. The AR system might provide arrows for the participants to follow, a humanoid guide, a trail of breadcrumbs, or any number of ways to indicate what direction the participant(s) should go. Note that audio information can also be used to implement navigation assistance.

Nonreferential Augmentation

Nonreferential augmentation of the real world is a case of augmented reality in which the images that the participant receives are not additions or radical changes to the real world, but rather are enhancements of existing objects or persons. For example, in a nonreferential augmentation of a real-world application, colors might be brighter, sounds louder or clearer in some way, and so forth. The term "nonreferential" is not a commonly used term in the field of AR, but rather was borrowed from semiotics to denote the ideas being portrayed here. There doesn't seem to be a commonly accepted term in the field of AR for what is being described here. Nonreferential augmentation of the real world allows one to encounter a fantastic, more sensorial environment like one might encounter in a dream or fantasy. Nonreferential augmentation of the real world could also include applications such as automatically transforming the real world into a caricature world, or even a fully cartoon

FIGURE 8.18

Nonreferential augmented reality doesn't add new objects to the world or eliminate objects, but rather changes the world in different ways. This series of images shows a few different ways of seeing the real world with computer intervention. The first image shows the world as we typically see it. The second image shows the real world as it would be seen through rose-colored glasses. The third image shows the world in a more impressionistic sense, and the final image shows a more radical extrusion of the real world. As can be seen, the world is not specifically altered, but the way we see it is. These particular examples are driven more from an image processing perspective, but any number of techniques could be used. As you might surmise, even the image processing approach can alter the real world in an infinite number of ways, ranging from turning it to (appear to be) a cartoon world to a pencil-drawn world to a world where humans glow with colorful auras. *Photos courtesy of Beverly Carver.*

world, as though one was stepping into a cartoon version of the real world. Likewise, any number of other transformations to the real world could be done, such as stepping into what appears to be a child's crayon drawing of the real world. It can also be subtler than the vivid cases described earlier. For example, one could use AR simply as a "touch up" (as is done on the cover of a beauty magazine) where the intent is to be subtle rather than overt. The idea of nonreferential AR is a furtherance of the idea of nonreferential utopia as described by Richard Dyer. The technicolor musicals that Dyer uses in his description of nonreferential utopia are an example of nonreferential enhancement in a different medium (film) (Figure 8.18).

Objective View Augmented Reality

Recall from Chapter 6 that objective view augmented reality is a scenario in which the participants see a representation of themselves in the augmented scene. That is, rather than seeing the world as they normally do, through their own eyes, the participants see the real world, including digital enhancements, as well as see themselves in the view, as though the scene was seen by someone else. The magic mirror paradigm is somewhat an example of objective view augmented reality, but there are other scenarios that also qualify as objective view AR.

The National Geographic application from Appshaker described in Chapter 6 is a classic example of objective view AR. Yes, one could consider the display screens in that example as being a giant magic mirror, but a magic mirror more typically applies the augmentations to the participant, whereas objective view AR focuses more on adding enhancements to the environment. Consequently, the dinosaurs added to the scene in the National Geographic application represent an addition to the environment, whereas an application in which the participants see themselves wearing a pair of sunglasses (that they are not actually wearing) represents an augmentation to the participants and thus is considered a magic mirror.

COLLABORATIVE AUGMENTED REALITY

People tend to think of augmented reality as a solitary experience. However, as a medium, AR is very well suited to providing an experience for multiple concurrent or asynchronous participants. By concurrent, I mean that the participants participate at the same time, whereas by asynchronous I mean that the joint participation takes place at different times for different people.

In much the same way that the real world supports multiple participants, augmented reality also can support multiple participants. An example of a concurrent collaborative AR application is a game in which multiple participants, at the same time, work together to defeat a common enemy. The participants might be at the same location (such as a field in a park) as each other or might be in different physical locations (someone in Europe, someone in a park in the United States, etc.). The different participants may or may not experience the same augmentations as each other. In the case where the augmentations are different, one person might not see the same augmentations as another or might see a different version of the augmentation. In this fictitious game, it might require multiple participants to gather different (real or virtual) objects and bring them together to a specific real-world place for something magical to happen.

An example of an asynchronous collaborative AR game might be a scavenger hunt in which one participant hides virtual objects that a different participant needs to find. The time between the hiding and the finding can range from

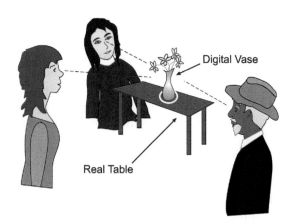

FIGURE 8.19

With collaborative augmented reality, multiple people can view and interact with the same digital object(s), each from their own point of view. In this example, the participants are viewing a digital vase, but they could also potentially make changes to the vase (color, pattern, size, etc.) or any individual could potentially move the vase, etc. *Diagram courtesy of Beverly Carver.*

minutes to months or years, or the "game" might be the ability to annotate and/or create objects at a location that another participant might find later.

Beyond the realm of gaming, collaborative AR can be used for more utilitarian purposes. For example, multiperson collaborative AR can be used to allow multiple people to see a virtual prototype of a new product, each from their own viewpoint, so they can examine, discuss, and alter the (not yet existent) prototype in a collaborative way (Figure 8.19).

Many of today's technologies and media foster a "getting away" from other people. We see people texting on their smartphones to the person sitting next to them. We see people watching movies privately on their smartphones. Seemingly, people are becoming more isolated from each other with new media and new technologies. Collaborative AR offers the potential to encourage people to come together, in the real world, for real world as well as virtual interaction. In fact, a collaborative AR application can "force" people to come together in the real world if that is necessary to fulfill the goals of the AR application. For example, in a collaborative AR game, it could be that in order to win the "prize," different participants must bring physical artifacts to the same physical location at the same time, with each touching the collection simultaneously in order for the collaborative task to be completed.

APPLYING AUGMENTED REALITY TO A PROBLEM

Augmented reality remains a technological novelty until it is applied to assist in solving a problem of one sort or another. That problem could be anything from "I need to find my way" to "I need to be entertained" to "I need something to help me understand the three dimensionality of this molecule." Often, the "problem" that AR is called on to solve is not stated as a problem, but more as something that just needs to be done. Other media, as well, are called on to solve a problem that is not always stated explicitly as a problem. For example, a piece of modern artwork is actually created to cause people to think. A movie is often used to convey a message as well as to entertain.

The first step in applying AR to a problem is to determine whether AR might be a good medium to use for the problem at hand. This may not be totally obvious right out the gate, but it is worth some thought beforehand to consider whether the affordances of the medium would be appropriate to the problem at hand. It may be that it is worth making a rapid prototype of an application that you have an idea for to see if AR provides a promising solution. After determining that AR is a viable medium for the problem, the next question to answer is "What is it that I want the AR application to do?" This question deserves considerable thought and should be answered at a deeper level than just a superficial response. From that point on, the methodology for applying AR to a problem is very similar to developing any other technological solution, while simultaneously creating work in a medium with the caveat that the designer needs to consider those aspects of developing for AR that are different from other media. For example, with AR, it is not purely a matter of thinking about the virtual content that will be created, but also about the aspects of the real world (physical objects, etc.) that will be part of the application and how they interact with the virtual aspects of the content.

As such, the methodologies for creating media works, as well as systems engineering, apply. The steps to applying AR to a problem can be boiled down to an iterative process that consists of a series of steps.

Ten steps for applying AR to a problem:

1. Identify the problem
2. Determine if there are other solutions to the problem
3. Determine the affordances of AR that will aid with the problem
4. Design AR application
5. Implement AR application
6. Test AR application
7. Evaluate results of AR application with respect to the problem
8. Modify design and application
9. Test modified application
10. Loop iteratively to appropriate step

One should not underestimate the importance of studying other works, whether or not they are directly applicable to the problem at hand. By studying different AR applications, it is possible to get a feel for, and even to predict to a certain degree, what types of hardware, software, interaction mechanisms, and so on will be most suitable for a new application. The caveat to this, though, is that because AR is a relatively new medium, there may be mechanisms and methods that have not been invented or published yet that may be beneficial to your application. Hence, it is wise to not only look at what has come before, but to also maintain an inventive spirit and be willing to try things that have not been tried before.

EVALUATING AUGMENTED REALITY APPLICATIONS

"The unexamined life is not worth living."

Socrates

In much the same way that Socrates claims that an unexamined life is not worth living, it is important that we examine AR applications to evaluate them if we are ever to improve our understanding of AR and our ability to create useful, compelling, and enjoyable AR applications.

Why Evaluate Augmented Reality Applications?

The easy thing to do would be to simply create AR applications, make them available to the world, and kick back and wait for people to use them, as is, for whatever purpose they deem fit. In the real world, however, it seldom works that way. It is unlikely that a first attempt at creating an AR app results in the perfect application for your purposes. In light of this reality, it is important to carefully evaluate what aspects of an application are working, what are not, why that is, and how to remedy or improve on the aspects that are less than stellar.

Evaluation Questions

There are three primary questions to ask when evaluating an AR application:

1. Does the application fulfill the goal that drove the creation of the application?
2. Is the target audience actually using the application and using it in an effective way?
3. Is AR the right medium to use for the application?

At first blush it would seem that answering only one of the questions would suffice, but they are actually getting after different thoughts and each question may help answer the other ones. For example, if one designs an outdoor, AR-enhanced game that fulfills all of the stated design criteria, yet no one plays the game, it is important to learn why. It could be that though the application fulfills all of the stated design criteria, it requires the participant to carry 50 pounds' worth of gear. If the weight of the gear was not specified in the design of the application, it could be that it fulfills the design criteria, yet is impossible to use in the real world. That is, the second question can sometimes help tease out additional criteria that should have been included in the design specifications, but for some reason or another (often just not thought about) were omitted from the original design criteria.

Another reason that people might not use our example AR game application is that it is just plain *not fun*. Fun is not always something that can clearly be specified through a design document. One could include the criterion that an application be fun, but actually ensuring that is a very difficult thing. A mistake AR application designers often make is that they are very careful to ensure that the design fulfills many specific technical criteria, such as a maximum amount of latency allowed and the ability to work with the hardware and network available, but fail to adequately specify and ensure the usability of the design. People like to use things that are easy and inviting to use, but are less likely to use things that are cumbersome, difficult, or tedious to use. People like to use things that are *cool*.

The best way to evaluate AR applications is to follow the methodology used for *user studies* and *usability testing*. That said, there are plenty of less formal methods that can be used to evaluate AR applications. The basic idea is to see if the application fulfills the goals it was intended to fulfill regardless of whether those goals were stated explicitly in any formal way.

Some of the things one should consider include the following:

1. Is the application pleasing to use (i.e., is it fun)? Aesthetically pleasing? Is response time adequate (i.e., does the application work in a suitably real-time way)?
2. Does the application do what it is supposed to do? (not all do)
3. Is the application either self-explanatory or does it contain adequate instructions for someone to be able to use it?
4. Is the hardware form factor suitable for the application (i.e., if intended to be portable or mobile, is it)?
5. Does the application work well in the environment it is intended to be used in (e.g., if intended to be used outdoors, can the display be seen without problems of glare)?
6. Is the application providing something of real value beyond being a technological novelty?
7. Is the application robust or does it throw errors during the normal course of use?
8. Is the application extensible if needed?

9. Does the application carry any unintended cultural biases?
10. Is there a mechanism by which the intended user community can provide feedback to the developers?

These same questions are also useful when evaluating a third-party application for your own use.

The only way to really evaluate any AR application is to use it, with the target user population, at the location it is intended to serve, on the hardware it is intended to run on, and to do the activity that it is intended to support. Sometimes, it is only after answering all of these questions and extensive use of the application that it becomes apparent whether or not AR was the ideal medium for the application.

EXAMPLE AUGMENTED REALITY APPLICATIONS

One of the best ways to get ideas for AR applications, or how to do different tasks in an AR application, is to examine extant examples of augmented reality applications. Even if the example isn't a superb application, there still is much that we can learn from looking at it, whether it is an idea that is a good idea within the application, or bad ideas that we wish to avoid. After all, even bad ideas must have seemed like good ideas before they were actually implemented and tested. Consequently, it is wise to take advantage of the lessons learned by other developers rather than make the same mistakes ourselves.

Throughout this book there have been examples of applications that demonstrated ideas that were being covered at that point. This section covers a few example applications in order to give a somewhat more expansive close-up view of the applications. These applications were chosen not necessarily because they are considered superb (although some are) in some way, but rather because they are either somewhat generic or iconic of a class of applications or they are representative of something unusual in AR applications.

The *Ethnobotany Workbook*

The *Ethnobotany Workbook* is an example of the magic book class of AR applications. To date, the magic books category is one of the most prevalent categories of AR applications.

The *Ethnobotany Workbook* began its life as a pure, physical book. AR was added later to retrofit the physical book with 3D computer graphics enhancements.

The original *Ethnobotany Workbook* was created by the University of Nebraska Medical Center SEPA (Science Education Partnership Award) staff using

Black Walnut (eastern black walnut, American walnut)
Juglans nigra
Walnut family: Juglandaceae

Dakota: Hma   **Ho Chunk:** Chak   **Omaha:** Táge

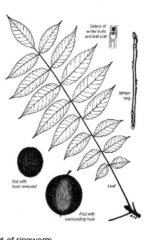

Flowering Period
Mid April to mid June

Description
Medium sized tree. Height: 70-150 feet tall. Usually matures in about 150 years. The branches are widely spread and form a massive crown. The bark is thick and brown to grayish-black in color with deep furrows and narrow forking ridges forming a diamond pattern. The large fruit ripens between September and October. It's seed is sweet and edible.

Habitat
Found in fields and rich woodlands. Thrives in deeper, well-drained, neutral soils. Must have direct sunlight to grow optimally.

Propagation
By seed is recommended. Should be planted in the fall in moist, well-drained deep soil that is rich in organic matter.

Plains Indian/Settler Uses
The bark was used by many native groups in tea as a laxative, chewed for toothaches, and ground to make brown and black dyes. Black walnut was also used to treat athlete's foot, hemorrhoids, and as an insecticide. A paste was also created from the leaves and husk of the fruit for treatment of ringworm.

Additional Information
The bark should be used cautiously in medicine, because it is poisonous. Black walnut creates a toxin knows as "juglone," which inhibits the growth of other plants around it, thereby reducing competition.

FIGURE 8.20

A page from the *Ethnobotany Workbook* before it was enhanced by augmented reality. *Image courtesy of Maurice Godfrey.*

information provided by the Pioneer Park Nature Center in order to provide information about the native plants in the Nebraska area to a wide audience, but primarily to young Native Americans in that region. The workbook functioned as a sort of field guide to help the middle school reader identify the native plants, as well as learn the name of the plant in their native tongue (Dakota, Lakota, Ho Chunk, and Omaha) and how the plants have been used historically. The book had a simple, two-dimensional line drawing of each plant and each plant was allocated a double page in the workbook (Figure 8.20).

The augmented reality magic book version of the workbook was created as a collaboration between The University of Nebraska Medical Center, the Institute for Computing in Humanities, Arts, and Social Science, and the National Center for Supercomputing Applications. The project came to be when Maurice Godfrey saw some AR work that Robert E. McGrath and Alan B. Craig were doing on a magic book version of a chemistry textbook in which molecules were represented using AR as 3D graphical objects above the pages of the book.

Of particular interest to Godfrey was the ability to change the visual perspective by turning the physical book to the appropriate point of view.

Consequently, a collaboration ensued to create an AR-enhanced version of the *Ethnobotany Workbook*. Because the application would be deployed in the field, the original version was made to work on a laptop equipped with a web camera that could be deployed as a kiosk in the field. Because all models were resident on the laptop, there was no need for a network connection. Later the application was deployed on smart tablets (including the iPad 2) to make a truly mobile version of the application.

McGrath and Craig created the application in consultation with Godfrey using the ARToolKit v.4.5 AR tracking library from ARToolWorks. The application was to activate 15 plant species in the workbook. Ryan Rocha, a 3D graphics designer, created the plant models based on photos and descriptions provided by Kim Soper, educational consultant for the SEPA project. He created the plant models using the Maya modeling software package and saved as .obj files that were then read by the OpenSceneGraph library that was called by the ARToolKit. He created the plants as polygonal surfaces that he subsequently textured with images of the plants. Later, he found he was able to create the plants using simple colors and materials to save on memory and processing by avoiding the need for textures. Because natural feature tracking wasn't yet mature, the team chose to use abstract fiducial markers, one per plant, to aid the computer vision algorithms in the application. The fiducial markers were simple black-and-white bar codes. The idea was that the markers would be printed on sticky labels that the student could peel from the page of markers and place in their workbook on the proper page (Figures 8.21 and 8.22).

Once the student has used the overall sheet of fiducial markers, he or she can peel the proper sticker from the sheet and place it on the page that represents that plant. Thus, the workbook becomes enhanced for AR on that page.

The software was made available via a distribution package for Windows and Mac. The package also included instructions for use and documentation. The software also runs on the iPad, and plans are being made for broad distribution (Figure 8.23).

The AR application was well received, and the students found the experience enjoyable and educational. The capability of students to see the plants in 3D is very helpful before going out into the field for plant identification. Also, this medium allows for use of the study at a time when these plants may not be growing and available to students. It also enhances the study because students love technology and they make a connection with the material.

Note that this magic book is very similar to other magic books and that the software used can be used with different content than the plant models.

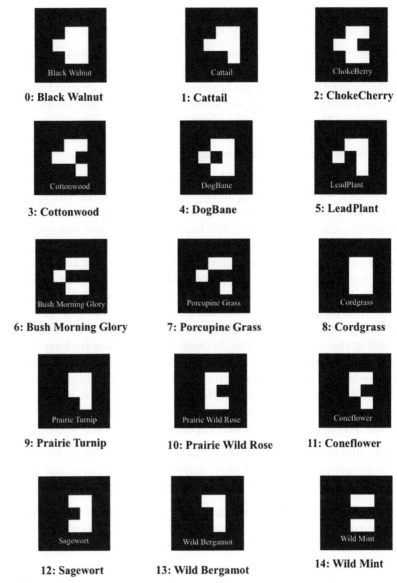

0: Black Walnut   **1: Cattail**   **2: ChokeCherry**

3: Cottonwood   **4: DogBane**   **5: LeadPlant**

6: Bush Morning Glory   **7: Porcupine Grass**   **8: Cordgrass**

9: Prairie Turnip   **10: Prairie Wild Rose**   **11: Coneflower**

12: Sagewort   **13: Wild Bergamot**   **14: Wild Mint**

FIGURE 8.21
Each plant has its own fiducial marker. By printing them on stickers, the students can peel the sticker from the sheet and place it on the proper page. *Image courtesy of Robert E. McGrath.*

Consequently, the same software system can be used to convert other books into magic books the same way by changing the content. There is a configuration file in the software to inform the software of what graphical models correspond to which fiducial marker. Hence, if you have different graphical

FIGURE 8.22
Students can see the choices of plants as 3D representations when viewed via augmented reality. *Photo courtesy of Michael Simeone.*

FIGURE 8.23
When the student attaches the sticker to a page in the workbook, that page is then made into a magic book page through the use of augmented reality. When the page is viewed through the AR kiosk or a smart tablet, the student sees the page enhanced with a 3D graphical representation of the plant. *Image courtesy of Robert E. McGrath.*

models, this same application could be used to convert other books into magic books.

colAR—*Amazing Animals of New Zealand*

An example of another magic book with an interesting twist comes from Dr. Adrian Clark and Dr. Andreas Dünser of the University of Canterbury's

FIGURE 8.24
The colAR application from the University of Canterbury allows children to color on a page and see their drawing pop to life on the AR display (see http://www.idealog.co.nz/blog/2012/08/childrens-drawings-brought-life-through-ar). *Photo courtesy of Adrian Clark.*

Human Interface Technology Laboratory New Zealand (HIT Lab NZ). This application is particularly interesting in that the AR representation displayed is created from a child's own crayon drawing (Figure 8.24).

The colAR application provides pictures of two of New Zealand's native birds described in the book *Amazing Animals of New Zealand*. Children can color the pictures and then point a web camera at the pages and see their own coloring pop up off the page. Of course, they can manipulate the picture and the camera to see the images from any perspective, as is the case with most AR applications.

This type of application can encourage kids in their endeavor to read and also in content creation. The fact that the child actually colored the picture provides a personal tie to the AR content. As the application developers point out, usually when a child finishes coloring a coloring book page the activity is over, but with the colAR application the fun has just begun (Figure 8.25).

This application can theoretically be applied to any coloring book pages to allow youngsters to have a direct hand in the creation of AR content.

T. rex

The T. rex application from daqri represents a great example of using an image as the fiducial symbol (Figure 8.26). In this application, when you point your device toward the image of the dinosaur, the dinosaur becomes visible as an animated 3D entity. As such, you can change your visual perspective on the dinosaur by repositioning yourself with respect to the image

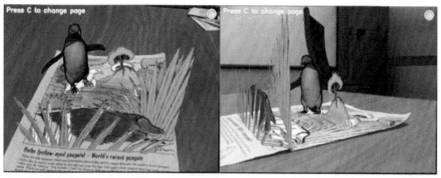

FIGURE 8.25

This pair of images shows the coloring book page from the colAR application in AR from two different perspectives (see http://www.idealog.co.nz/blog/2012/08/childrens-drawings-brought-life-through-ar). *Images courtesy of Adrian Clark.*

 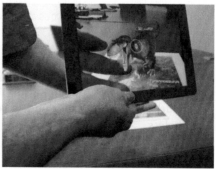

FIGURE 8.26

This pair of photos shows the T. rex from daqri. This is an excellent example of using a picture as a fiducial symbol. *Fiducial symbol and application courtesy of daqri; photos courtesy of Michael Simeone.*

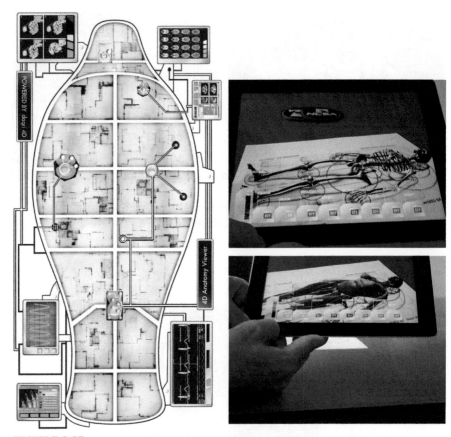

FIGURE 8.27

This interactive anatomy application from daqri allows you to view a human body via an augmented reality experience. The participants can turn various systems on and off from view by using virtual buttons on the device. They can also make the skin more and less transparent by using a virtual slider on the device. Of course, the user can change his or her perspective on the body by moving the device with respect to the fiducial. *Fiducial marker and application courtesy of daqri; photos courtesy of Michael Simeone.*

or, conversely, by reorienting the image with respect to your device. Another noteworthy aspect of this application is the use of sound. The sound is not particularly interactive, but it adds a very compelling aspect to the experience nonetheless.

Anatomy

The interactive augmented anatomy application from daqri provides a very compelling early example of an application that is created and is useful as an educational experience (Figure 8.27). With the application, the participant can choose whether to display a male or female (virtual) body. Via controls (virtual buttons) on the device, the participant can choose to display or hide different physical systems (skeletal, muscular, circulatory, etc.) in addition to changing the visual perspective and level of zoom on the model. Additionally, a virtual slider allows the participant to make the integumentary system (skin) fully opaque, fully transparent, or any level of transparency between. The virtual body is scaled to the size of the fiducial marker and, as such, the experience can be made to be fully life size, larger than life size, or smaller than life size. Indeed, the marker could be printed in an anatomy textbook to allow students to experiment with the body in their book. In addition, via a foldout or a separately printed marker, students could have a life-size "virtual cadaver" that they could explore on a laboratory table or even on any table of suitable size, such as a dining room table.

In the future, this and other applications will improve in their verisimilitude with the real world and/or in ways that support more compelling pedagogy. It is not too much of a leap to imagine being able to do virtual "operations" on the body and to remove and examine different organs. Indeed, such a tool, coupled with a pair of AR glasses so that the student has both hands free, could reduce the amount of need for real-life cadavers and animals for dissection. Hence, such "real" cadavers and animals could be saved for cases (such as training for surgery) where it is essential to have the real subject. However, for more routine education, virtual animals could be utilized wherever possible.

SUMMARY

This chapter has shown that AR is only really important when it is applied to some problem or goal. There are a number of factors to consider when determining whether AR is an appropriate medium for a given application. One of the most critical factors is how well the application is able to make use of the unique affordances of AR, as well as the logistic concerns of the application under consideration.

There are a number of application areas for AR, including education, science, business and manufacturing, medicine, public safety and military, art, advertising, and entertainment. The application areas that are currently being most widely deployed include advertising, education, entertainment, and art. Other application areas are closing in rapidly.

Many different styles of AR applications can be classified into one or more of the following categories: magic books, magic mirrors, magic windows and doors, magic lens, navigation assistance, nonreferential augmentation, and objective view augmented reality. These categories aren't hard edged, but basically describe some different genres of AR applications. Almost all of these categories are actually subsets of the "magic lens" category.

Augmented reality applications can be created for single users or can be made for multiple users, either at the same time or at different times, and at the same location or at different locations. Collaborative AR applications allow multiple participants to work together in a digitally enhanced world where they can manipulate the same or different real and virtual objects together or alone. Sometimes, to achieve a goal in AR, the participants must bring different virtual objects to the same place in the real world.

It is important to evaluate augmented reality applications in order to determine an application's suitability for a given purpose and to make meaningful improvements to an application. A number of questions can serve as guides in evaluating AR applications.

Finally, it can be beneficial to study existing AR applications to learn what does and doesn't work in different circumstances. The best way to learn about building AR applications is not only to do it, but also to be informed by what others have done. You can learn from the lessons of others, but the field is still young enough that there is room to develop your own, never tried before, ideas and techniques.

CHAPTER 9

The Future of Augmented Reality

INTRODUCTION

Imagine a world in which you can go about your life, as you normally do, with no apparent technology, where the world itself helps you through your day. You can summon digital information at will and interact with it as though it is part of the physical world. You can summon different environments as you wish, whether it be for the purpose of aiding yourself or others or just for the fun of it. The digital information can be portrayed as though it is a fantastic addition to the world or it can be so photorealistic and behave so much like what it represents that it is indistinguishable from the real world. You reach out to touch digital information and you can feel its texture, weight, and temperature. You hear sounds that would otherwise be unhearable. On entering your home you smell fresh bread baking in the oven, and you can taste it as well, even though the bread came from the grocery store. Then, when you have interacted with digital information in the real world, you can summon it to be manufactured on demand such that you have a physical copy of what you have been interacting with and manipulating. These things will be possible in the future. Some of them are possible right now. Augmented reality (AR) is on the cusp of turning the corner into becoming a mainstream part of life. As technology to support AR becomes more refined and less intrusive, as digital content becomes easier to create, as newer, better interaction mechanisms and representations become prevalent, and as personal fabrication moves to the mainstream, we will see AR become a part of everyday life, impacting our sense of the world, our education, our medical analysis and treatment, our entertainment, and much more.

THE CURRENT STATE OF AUGMENTED REALITY

Although the field of AR is changing rapidly, it is good to take stock of where we are in the development of AR. This section takes a look at where things stand from several points of view. This section assesses the current state of affairs in the following three areas:

1. Augmented reality applications
2. Augmented reality technology
3. Augmented reality content development

The State of Augmented Reality Applications

At the time of the writing of this book, augmented reality has not become an everyday thing for the mass public. However, AR is quickly being adopted in a variety of application areas that are bringing it to the attention of the public. Advertising campaigns are already under way that utilize augmented reality as a key part of the advertising campaign. However, many advertisers are still banking on the novelty of the AR experience to draw attention to their advertisements. Consumers will only find the image of a shoe floating above a magazine interesting for a brief period of time, and attention is being paid to building more interactive, customer-centered advertisements.

Augmented reality is currently being tested in medical and surgical applications, but most of the mass public will never see those applications unless they are in the medical community or read medical or technical journals. However, like most advances in medical technology, AR promises improvements that are likely to benefit the population whether they realize that AR is involved or not.

One of the key areas that AR is currently being tested in is the area of education. In addition to magic books, AR is being used in education in conjunction with games and to allow students to participate in virtual "lab" experiences.

Another area in which AR has seen numerous applications built is in art. Artists are often first adopters of technology as they view it as a new medium in which they can express their ideas. Numerous experimental AR applications have been built.

Augmented reality has already become popular for games and other entertainment. There are quite a few games that utilize AR that run on gaming consoles, and even more that run on mobile devices.

The State of Augmented Reality Technology

The good news is that AR hardware and software are improving at a tremendous rate. Even as this book goes to publication, the capabilities of smartphones and tablets are making astonishing strides in computational, graphical, and sensory power, with clearer, more high-resolution displays, and improvements in battery life and other specifications. The limiting factor at this point in time is the amount of memory available on portable devices to store digital objects on the portable devices. Network latency requires careful thought about system architecture of whether content should be stored on the device or on a remote content server.

Great strides have been made in the use of natural feature detection such that the need for artificial fiducial markers is less critical. However, there is still room for improvement in the computer vision algorithms used for analyzing scenes and determining the users' pose.

The State of Augmented Reality Content Development

Content development is currently the biggest bottleneck in creating AR applications. Although there are some content development environments available that simplify the content development process, on the whole, it requires time and skill to create AR content.

In order for AR to become pervasive, it must be democratized so that it doesn't require specialized engineering and artistic skills to create content and applications. Of course, there will always be a difference in content and applications developed by experts vs mere mortals, but putting the proper tools into the hands of the masses will enable many more to participate in the creation and consumption of AR content and applications.

WHY CONSIDER THE FUTURE?

The technology of AR is changing very rapidly. As application developers it is critical that we create applications not for the technology of today, but for the technology that will be in place at the time of the application release. It is completely apparent that computing devices, especially mobile devices, are in a period of rapid change in capability. Hence, it behooves the AR developer to track hardware and software developments and any emerging standards that might impact AR developers. To the greatest extent possible, AR developers should develop open standards to allow maximum sharing and interchangeability among applications, content, and components.

As of the publication of this book, there are no overarching standards for AR content and applications. There are, however, standards related to many aspects of AR applications and content, as were seen in earlier chapters. There are some grassroots efforts at establishing standards for AR applications and content, and it would be a wise endeavor indeed for the AR application developer to pay attention to and provide input into any groups seeking to develop standards.

The summary for why to consider the future is twofold. First, it is a given that if you develop applications for today's technology, before your application is developed, there will be new technology that you will likely wish your application took advantage of. The other main reason to consider the future is that as standards emerge, you will want to develop your applications with those standards in mind. Also, you will want to participate in any standards groups to ensure that as standards are developed for the future they will support the needs that you, as an AR developer, require.

TRENDS IN AUGMENTED REALITY

In almost all cases in AR, the mantra "faster, better, cheaper" applies. Indeed, the marketplace is driving computing, sensing, and display devices to be faster, better, and cheaper.

Trends Toward Mobile Augmented Reality Applications

The prevalence of an installed base of mobile devices and the expectation that information is available on an "on-demand" basis where you are, and when you are, indicates a likelihood of the continued emphasis on mobile AR applications. Indeed, one of the key criteria of AR applications is that they take place in the real world, in real-world locations. Hence, it is apparent that the trend toward mobile AR applications will likely continue for the indefinite future.

The improvements in mobile technology will support the needs of AR applications. Some of the more important are that we can expect mobile devices to have more onboard memory, as well as higher bandwidth and lower latency network connections to make it possible for more content to be available for mobile AR applications, whether that content is carried onboard the device or retrieved from a remote server.

Another key development with mobile devices is that they will have higher resolution displays that can be seen under a wider range of lighting conditions. Additionally, mobile devices are trending toward less power consumption and increased battery life, enabling applications to be run for a longer time without the need to recharge the device. Wireless service will be available more ubiquitously, enabling networked mobile applications to be run in more geographic locations than are possible today. The processors will be faster, and the graphics will be better with higher resolution, faster rendering, and faster display.

On the flipside, not all applications will necessarily go mobile. There is ample room for sophisticated educational applications that can run in schools, museum applications, medical applications, point-of-sale applications, and so on that have the luxury of not requiring small mobile devices to carry out the desires of the application developer. It is highly likely that in all of these scenarios there will be a combination of both nonmobile and mobile

AR systems in any given location. For example, a museum might have several semipermanent AR installations, but patrons may also use their mobile device to interact with museum content in additional ways.

A Trend Away from Specialized Fiducial Markers

We have already seen a rapid shift away from the quick response code-type abstract fiducial markers. They will always have their place, but improvements in computer vision have allowed developers to use more natural features and more "normal" imagery as fiducial markers. This trend will continue and also move toward using truly natural features, such as city skylines and common landmarks in conjunction with global positioning system (GPS) information, to allow the developer to rely on enough real-world information to be useful in AR applications that it is less important to create special markers.

A Trend Toward Improved Tracking and Hybrid Tracking Technologies

Faster, less expensive, more accurate, and less encumbering tracking is necessary for the future of augmented reality applications. In order to truly achieve a ubiquitous, fully realized, augmented reality-enhanced world, tracking technology needs to improve, and it will, probably via a trend toward hybrid tracking technologies. Current tracking methods work well for specific purposes, but for widespread, ubiquitous AR, there need to be tracking methods that work regardless of geographic location and distance from specific devices, that don't require carrying complex technology, and so on. The most likely scenario for tracking in the future is a combination of technologies that are used in tandem with each other to provide an overall tracking capability that is greater than the sum of the parts that comprise it. For example, combinations of GPS (to get the general area), accelerometers (to get rapid motions), and optical tracking (to determine precise pose) can provide a more compelling experience than any of those can in isolation. Other combinations will be explored and improved.

A Trend Toward Less Encumbrance with Augmented Reality Systems

Eyeglass displays, contact lens displays, better sensors, and smaller, lighter computing power will allow participants in AR applications to work hands free, without even perceiving that they are using an AR system.

Other sensors in smartphones and tablets can provide a means to provide interaction outside of the view of the camera and/or buttons and screen. For example, a Kinect-like depth-sensing device in a phone could provide multiple other channels of information to the phone based on what the participant and/or the environment is doing.

Projection AR systems promise potentially completely unencumbered AR experiences. Of course, this relies on appropriate lighting conditions and other environmental conditions. Portable, personal projection also offers the likelihood of experiencing AR applications without explicitly holding something in your hands.

A Trend Toward Display to More Senses with Augmented Reality Systems

At the present, the vast bulk of AR systems focus on primarily visual displays with some offering some information via sound. Over time, we will see a trend toward more sonic information in AR experiences and trending toward other senses as well, including olfaction (smell), gustation (taste), and haptic (touch) displays. In the beginning we will likely see simple uses of other senses, such as vibration or temperature in haptic displays, but ultimately we will see extensive use of multisensory AR systems.

Another area that is being explored is the use of AR with "emotional senses." That is, AR applications conducive to building empathy, self-realization, and other less tangible sensory experiences.

A Trend Toward Higher Fidelity Representations and Displays

The regular march of technology will lead to higher quality, higher fidelity displays and sensors for all senses. Along with an increase in fidelity comes the possibility of an increase toward realism if desired. Beyond just the displays, computational simulations will create higher fidelity signals to be displayed, with the ultimate (if so desired) system making it indiscernible where the real world leaves off and the augmented world begins.

A Slow Trend Toward Projection Augmented Reality Systems

The vast bulk of AR applications today (with exceptions) are created with either computer monitor style or handheld displays. Projection AR will be utilized more widely in wide area applications that support multiple participants simultaneously. Portable personal projection devices already exist. Very small projectors (such as could be mounted in a shirt button) offer the possibility of *projection on the go*, meaning that wherever you are, you can display information on the environment. Low-cost projectors the size of a smartphone are available, and even smaller ones are coming very quickly. Need to do something? Walk to any wall and your shirt button projector will display there and a camera in another button in your shirt will watch what your hands are doing and interpret your gestures appropriately.

A Trend Toward More Control Being Done in the Real World

Along with the trend toward lightweight displays, such as glasses or contact lenses, as well as projected environments, we will see more control being done in the world, as opposed to buttons (either real or virtual) on devices. Today, many applications require that you hold some type of device such as a smartphone or tablet in order to experience an application. Hence, it is reasonable to use physical or virtual buttons or sliders on that device since you are holding it already. With projected environments, as well as with glasses and contact lens displays, you will no longer be required to hold a device while experiencing the application. But there will still be the need to interact with buttons, sliders, etc. Consequently, I believe there will be a trend toward using the real world as an interface to AR applications in much the same way (and extended to new ways) as in the simtable example and the teapot example shown earlier in this book.

A Trend Toward Multiperson Applications and Private Applications

The bulk of AR applications today are for a single participant at any one time. Some AR games support multiple participants. Some objective view AR systems (such as the National Geographic AR experience in malls) allow for multiple participants and multiple observers. I believe we will see a trend toward more multiperson AR experiences. At the same time, I believe we will see a trend toward very private AR experiences personalized for the particular participant and no one else. An example of this might include an application that allows a person to track his or her own preferences in food, environmental conditions, and so on.

A Trend Toward Applications with Readily Swappable Content

Certain application types make sense for the application to remain the same, but to load with different content. One example of this is a magic book. There really need not be a totally different application to augment a history book vs a chemistry book. The difference is in the content that is displayed. Of course, there may need to be specialized interactions created for special circumstances (such as simulating a chemical reaction or choosing a battle strategy for a simulated historical battle), but there is no reason there can't be a single application that loads different content if the idea is simply to see augmented content with a book. This trend is already being fulfilled. A number of generic "AR browsers" allow you to see different content using the same core application and allow developers to add new content that can be viewed using such a browser after the fact. That is, the developer can add new content that can be seen by an AR browser that was installed even before the content was created.

In general, this is done in a scenario where the content is housed on a server and viewed using a client application in much the same way that web pages are housed on a server and viewed using a web browser client.

A Trend Toward Repositories of Augmented Reality Content and Applications

There is no need to continuously reinvent AR applications. If a teacher is teaching a lesson on "DNA," he or she should be able to easily find applications that have been created for that type of lesson that he or she could then use or modify. If he or she creates his or her own application or the students create their own applications, they should be able to be made available for others to try.

There will be a YouTube-like repository for AR applications and content where people can publish or consume AR content and applications. The major difference between something such as YouTube and "ARTube" is that the content on YouTube runs in a standardized video display. AR content is more diverse than movies. Hence there will need to be a way to deposit and retrieve AR applications and tie content to appropriate applications to ensure that you have the correct "viewer" for the content. There will likely be a push toward a common "AR browser" to circumvent this problem, but as powerful as an AR browser might seem, it would be unwise to limit the functionality of AR applications to a certain subset of capabilities or "least common denominator."

A Trend Toward More Application Areas

It remains to be seen what the AR applications are that percolate up as "killer applications." As of now, the preponderance of applications fall into the arena of advertising, medicine, games, or education. This will expand as developers find niche audiences for their applications. For example, there might be an application for chefs, an application for model railroad hobbyists, or an application for stamp collectors.

Along with new content areas, there will be a trend toward tying AR with personal fabrication to make it easier to turn virtual augmentations into material objects.

A Trend Toward Ubiquitous Content and Channels of Augmentations

As alluded to in Chapter 7 (*Mobile Augmented Reality*), there is the potential for AR content to be applied everywhere. This is likely to lead to a need for some kind of organization of that content so that individual users can *tune in* or *tune out* to any given content. In much the same way that radio and television broadcast content of many different types, so will the AR augmentation of the world. In the same way that users are able to use a tuning device to choose between content on the radio or television, it is possible that AR content will likewise be able to be *tuned in* via different *channels* or some other type of filtering scheme. Layar and other mobile applications have already demonstrated this idea. This idea will evolve and improve and also allow for considerable user customization. Customization may include a variety of different factors that are combined to determine what content to present to specific individuals based on where they are, their mood, their expressed preferences, and many other pieces of information. Spam could become a potential problem in the augmented world. Hence, the trend toward ubiquitous content is simultaneously very exciting, but it also poses the challenge of how to manage that content and allow people to choose appropriately exactly what content they want to interact with. In the very distant future, there could be a problem with people knowing what is the *real world* vs what is *augmentation* of the real world. It may become necessary to have some type of indicator to let participants know what they are interacting with. This sounds far-fetched, but even today people are often unaware of whether they are listening to a "real" clarinet vs a simulated clarinet. In many cases it is unimportant to know the difference. In some cases it is critical to know the difference.

A Trend Toward New Mechanisms for Augmentation Discovery

Currently, people need to be told actively that augmentations are available at certain places, or at least they need to see some sort of obvious marker that indicates that something magical can happen at that place. With the trend toward natural feature detection and other "markerless" technologies, there needs to be a way for people to know that they can invoke augmented reality at that place and time. Another trend that goes along with this is that currently, in general, one needs to have a different AR application for every experience. This can become quite tedious if someone discovers that AR is available somewhere, but they need to download an AR application to experience it. Currently, the model for AR discovery and deployment is a "pull" model in which the participant has to look for AR-enabled spaces and then download an application. There are discussions of a more "push" model in which people are actively signaled that there is AR available where they are and the required application is pushed to their device automatically and/or uses an application that they already have. In this scenario, the application is not only loaded but can be started as well.

A Trend Toward Easy-to-Use Authoring Tools for Augmented Reality Experiences

As seen throughout this book, content is a critical element to all AR experiences. Tools are already emerging that make it easier to author AR experiences. This trend will (must) continue to make authoring AR applications as easy as choosing some items from a menu or dragging and dropping content elements, etc. It is quite likely that at some point AR applications will be authored from within an AR application.

A Trend Toward Attention to Disabilities and Challenges

Augmented reality offers much potential for improving our lives in many different ways. However, it is essential that we, as AR developers, do not ignore that not every person can use every application equally. For example, in this book we have seen that the most attention in AR currently is involved with visual experiences. We as AR developers need to ask ourselves how the applications we are developing will be experienced by people with visual impairments or disabilities. Also, some people are more visually oriented than others, whereas some are more attuned to sound or touch. As we develop AR applications we need to consider multimodal presentation (to many senses) and also provide alternate presentation and interaction methods to enable people who might be visually impaired, not able to hear, and so on to use applications.

A Trend Toward Better, More Formal Evaluation of Augmented Reality Experiences

As augmented reality becomes more pervasive, people will be interested in learning how effective the applications are for different purposes. Consequently, new methods and instrumentation for measuring the effectiveness of AR applications will be developed. I believe that the field of education will lead the way in the improved evaluation of AR experiences. (Is AR an effective learning tool? Is this particular application effective for teaching X, Y, and Z? Does AR enable diverse populations with different talents, skills, learning abilities, and disabilities?) Likewise, companies that invest in AR development, deployment, or use will want to know if they are getting a solid return on their investment. In much the same way that there are critics who study other media (film, literature, etc.), so, too, will a community of scholars begin to study, in a critical way, AR applications and their impact on individuals and society.

Intellectual Property in Augmented Reality Applications

In much the same way that virtual content has questions surrounding it in all media, augmented reality shares those same dilemmas and problems. If you purchase a book and have it on your bookshelf at home, you would be quite upset if the publisher came and removed that book from your bookshelf. However, if that content was available on a website and the publisher removed or altered the information, it feels much less invasive. Likewise, if one procures an augmented reality application, does the model for the content follow the model of a physical book or is it more like material available on a website? These kinds of questions need to be considered and made clear. If one creates his or her own content for an AR application procured from someone else, who does that content belong to? In this scenario, one can consider that it is a similar model to YouTube in that the application (YouTube) is not owned by the user, but the content is. What then about the scenario where someone is using your (virtual) content but prints it out as a physical artifact using personal fabrication technology? All of these questions require clarification and understanding. Largely, they are the same considerations as maintained in all other media, but their application to the medium of AR does not have as long of a history as in other media.

SUMMARY

The outlook for augmented reality is good. Although AR hasn't become a part of everyone's daily life, it is on the cusp of potentially doing exactly that. The technological pieces are in place and are improving daily. Content development is the current bottleneck, but developers are creating powerful content development and publishing platforms as this text is being written. AR will extend its reach from its current place in education, advertising, and a few other key areas to virtually all aspects of everyday life. Applications will become multiperson, but also personal. In some cases, applications will be tied to personal fabrication. In the not so distant future, more of our sensory experiences will be augmented, including touch, taste, and smell.

It is an exciting time to be part of the developing medium of augmented reality. The biggest limitation right now is our imagination for the possibilities, combined with a lack of widely available, easy-to-use development tools. Very shortly, the biggest limitation will be our imagination. Let's get to work, dream big, and show the world the possibilities that can be achieved through augmented reality.

Index

Note: Page numbers followed by "*f*" and "*t*" refers to figures and tables, respectively.